Management ⟶ ⟶ ⟶ Local Government

Edited by

Ian Sanderson

Series editors: John Benington and Mike Geddes

LONGMAN

Published by Longman Industry and Public Service
Management, Longman Group UK Ltd, 6th Floor, Westgate
House, The High, Harlow, Essex CM20 1YR
Telephone: Harlow (0279) 442601; Fax: Harlow (0279) 444501;
Telex: 81491 Padlog

A catalogue record for this book is available from the British Library

ISBN 0-582-09104-7

Printed and bound in Great Britain by
Dotesios Ltd, Trowbridge, Wiltshire.

Longman Local Government Library

The Warwick Series on Local Economic and Social Strategies

This series is designed to contribute to the ability of policy makers and managers in local government to meet the challenges of the 1990s. The focus is on strategic questions of local economic and social change. The series deals with issues which confront local government (and local public services more widely) at the level of corporate or inter agency strategy (for example, industrial restructuring, Europeanisation, ageing, poverty, transport, the environment). These issues are challenging local government to move beyond its traditional and primary role as a distributor and deliverer of services and to explore the potential for influence in new economic roles (as a major employer, investor and purchaser within the local economy) and in its political and ideological roles (as a democratically elected body, with a mandate to represent the interests of the whole community).

The series will present the results of applied research and innovative policy initiatives in key areas of local government strategy, policy making, organisation and management. Its primary aim is to contribute to the development of good practice in local government policy making and corporate management, but it will also contribute to a better conceptual understanding of the role and functioning of the local state.

We hope this series will stimulate a lively and critical exchange of ideas and experience about policy making in the public sector. The editors welcome contributions to the debate from local policy makers, managers and academics.

John Benington and Mike Geddes

Contents

Notes on contributors

John Benington is Director of the Local Government Centre in the Business School at the University of Warwick. Previously, he was Chief Officer and Head of the Department of Employment and Economic Development with Sheffield City Council, and Director of the Community Project (CDP) in Coventry.

Tim Blackman is Research Manager in the Chief Executive's Department of Newcastle City Council. He has lectured in social policy at the Universities of Newcastle and Ulster, and was also a Research Associate in the Policy Research Institute in Belfast.

Bill Cooke is a Senior Lecturer in Organisation Development and Behaviour at Teesside University. Previously he was a partner in the Cooke Burton Consultancy and has also worked with British Telecom and in local government.

Lucy Gaster is a Research Fellow in the Decentralisation Research and Information Centre at the School for Advanced Urban Studies, University of Bristol. Previously, she worked in local government with the London Boroughs of Hackney and Islington after many years of social research in the UK and Africa.

Mick Paddon is Professional Group Leader for Public Policy and Administration in the Business School at Leeds Metropolitan University. He was previously Head of the Association of Direct Labour Organisations having also taught and researched at Manchester Polytechnic and at Essex and Durham Universities.

Ian Sanderson is a Senior Policy Analyst in the Policy Research Unit at Leeds Metropolitan University. He was previously Head of the Policy Planning Unit at Fife Regional Council following many years of applied research and also previous local government experience.

Matthew Taylor is a Research Fellow in the Local Government Centre at the University of Warwick. He was previously Director of the West Midlands Health Service Monitoring Unit after a period in politics as a member of the ruling group on Warwickshire County Council.

Wendy Thomson is Assistant Chief Executive in the London Borough of Islington with responsibility for the development of quality programmes. She has extensive previous public management experience in Canada, notably in social services with the City of Montreal.

1 Introduction: The context of quality in local government

Ian Sanderson

Concern with the quality of local government services is not new but concern with 'Quality', as a distinct concept, is a relatively recent phenomenon. Indeed, it has become something of a 'buzz-word' in the public sector, dominating discussion of improvements to services. It seems that nearly every initiative to improve public services is now launched under the banner of 'quality' and the main political parties vie with each other to achieve the high ground in terms of policies to improve the quality of public services.

Quality now tops the agenda for private sector companies operating in increasingly competitive markets. Its origin lies in the post-War Japanese drive for Western markets founded upon the rigorous development of 'Statistical Quality Control', subsequently refined into 'Quality Assurance' (QA) and 'Total Quality Management' (TQM) with an emphasis on ensuring that quality is 'built in' through appropriate systems and working practices and attitudes. Companies in the West are increasingly recognising that quality is the route to competitive advantage and, indeed to survival, in the international market place (Atkinson, 1990).

But what is meant by 'quality'? Conventionally, at this point, we turn to the Oxford English Dictionary which defines quality as 'degree of excellence'. However, this does not get us very far. What constitutes excellence? Whose opinion is to count? Nevertheless, if we start to think about how we would judge a product or service to be 'excellent', we would highlight two considerations. First, we would consider certain 'technical' attributes like specification, reliability and standard of workmanship. Second, we would consider the extent to which it satisfied our requirements. This gives us two basic dimensions of quality: a *technical* dimension capable of 'objective' measurement; and a *subjective* dimension referring to the attitudes and opinions of customers.

Definitions of quality in the private sector context emphasise the technical and subjective dimensions in varying degrees. For example, amongst the 'quality gurus' Crosby emphasises 'conformance to requirements', while for Juran quality is 'fitness for purpose'. Deming defines quality as a 'predictable degree of uniformity and dependability, at low cost and suited to the market'; for Oakland it is 'meeting the requirements of the customer' (Oakland, 1989). The gurus spread an almost evangelical message; Oakland (op cit, p. 305), for example, argues that ' . . . TQM is a new operational philosophy which is vital to pursue the continuation of most organisations in the world.'

This enthusiasm for quality has been 'imported' to the public sector in recent years and has established a firm hold in the local government community. The Government's 'Citizen's Charter' placed the improvement of quality in local authorities' services high on the political agenda (HMSO, 1991). The Labour Party's 'Quality Programme' aims '. . . to ensure that quality is the hallmark of all local services' (Labour Party, 1991, p. 1). A recent publication by the local authorities associations argues as follows:

> Quality has a role to play in helping local authorities to provide the right services at the right time, in the right place to the right people (and for the right price). It has a role in not only ensuring local government's survival but also in strengthening it. Quality has a role to play in improving local democracy.
>
> (ACC, 1992, p. 10)

Given such enthusiasm for quality, is there any room for scepticism? There are doubtless many in local government who remain unconvinced, even cynical, about the 'quality bandwagon'. If the 'Quality Revolution' is to have a significant and lasting impact on local government it must be based on the conviction that there is real substance to the concept of quality and that it produces improvements in the service which people receive from their local authorities. The purpose of this book is to explore the basis for such a conviction and to discuss critically various aspects of quality and what is involved in seeking to achieve it. In this chapter we examine the context in which the concern for quality has arisen and give a brief introduction to the arguments presented by various authors in subsequent chapters. Therefore, in the next section we examine briefly the social, economic and political context in which the concern for quality has developed; in our view this is fundamental to an understanding of the meaning and significance of quality.

The social context of quality

The fundamental nature of recent changes in the economy, in technology, and in the social and political context in which local government operates is widely appreciated. However, the way in which these changes have impacted upon local government is the subject of debate. Several commentators have suggested that recent developments in the public sector, and in local government in particular, are part of a process of re-structuring of the state in the context of a broader transformation from a 'Fordist' to a 'post-Fordist' society (Hoggett, 1987, Stoker, 1989).

From this perspective, 'traditional' forms of organisation of local government arose in a society dominated by economic and technological systems of mass production and consumption, standardised products, and low technical innovation. The labour process associated with such systems was characterised by fragmented and routinised work undertaken by unskilled or semi-skilled workers organised by mass unions. On the other hand, decision making was the sole prerogative of management organised in vertical hierarchies through which central control could be exercised.

Under Fordism, it is argued, the Welfare State developed both to support and underpin the economic infrastructure and to provide for collective consumption of welfare services. Hoggett (1987, p. 223) argues that:

> The Keynesian welfare state has traditionally been concerned with the mass production of a few standardised products. Economies of scale have been constantly emphasised. Flexibility of production has been minimal.

Fordist local government is seen as epitomised by these characteristics of large scale, standardisation and inflexibility. Hambleton (1987) uses the term 'bureaucratic paternalism'. Stewart (1986, 1989) argues that local authorities have traditionally been dominated by the bureaucratic mode of organisation founded on the principles of hierarchy to enforce control, uniformity to enforce equality of treatment, and functionalism to enforce division of work according to the expertise required. In addition, professionalism reinforced departmentalism and continuity of service provision in accordance with officer perceptions.

The characteristics of this traditional model have been summarised by Walsh (1989, pp. 3–4) as follows:

- *Bureaucratic:* organisation dominated by detailed rules and procedures to produce uniformity, equity and predictability in dealing with people.
- *Large and centralised:* size seen as necessary to achieve economies

of scale but created a gap between those who delivered services and those at the centre with whom power lay.

- *Self-sufficient:* assumed that local authorities should employ all the staff required to deliver services directly with little reliance on other agencies.
- *Professionally-dominated:* officer structures dominated by professionals who had the main influence on decisions.
- *Concern for structure:* management conceived in terms of organisational structure to the neglect of processes and 'culture'.

These traditional assumptions and principles of organisations have come under severe challenge during the past decade or so and widespread changes are occurring in local government. The context for these changes is provided by the transition to 'post-Fordist' society, founded upon the development of new information technologies (Rustin, 1989; Hoggett, 1987; Stoker 1989). Such technologies permit accelerated technical innovation, more flexible small-batch production and niche marketing for a more diversified market. This encourages the formation of small and medium-sized enterprises and the break-up or decentralisation of large organisations. Vertical control hierarchies are replaced by lateral structures with devolved control and a new emphasis on 'organisational culture'. Flexibility is introduced into the labour process by supplementing a 'core' workforce of skilled labour with a 'peripheral' workforce of low-skilled, part-time or sub-contract labour. Employer/employee relations are increasingly individualised and trade unions play a diminishing role (Thompson and McHugh, 1990).

There is considerable debate about the extent to which Western capitalism has become 'post-Fordist' (Thompson and McHugh, 1990), and about the implications for the nature and role of the public sector (Cochrane, 1991). However, these developments can be seen as providing the context of recent changes in local government. Certain social and economic developments have placed increasing pressure on local authorities. Thus, the economic transition in Britain has been characterised by a process of de-industrialisation creating mass unemployment, deprivation and inner city dereliction which has presented serious challenges to local authorities (Lawless, 1989). In addition, local authorities are facing increasing demands on their services due to demographic changes, in particular the rising number of elderly people. Thus, the population aged over 85 is projected to rise from 0.7mn in 1986 to 1.15mn in 2001 placing increased demands on health and social services (HMSO, 1989).

A further important development has been an increasing awareness by people of their rights as consumers, reflected in the increasing influence of consumer organisations such as the National Consumer

Council. This trend has been strengthened by the growth of awareness in the private sector of the imperative of meeting the requirements and expectations of the customer in increasingly competitive markets. This has required local authorities to become more responsive to the expectations of their 'customers'.

While the pressures and demands on local authorities have increased, the resources available to meet these demands have been severely constrained as public spending has been restrained by central government. The process of expenditure restraint commenced in the mid-1970s under the Labour Government and was strengthened during the 1980s by the Thatcher Governments (Newton and Karran, 1985). In such a context of increased demands and constrained resources, local authorities have been faced with difficult choices between competing demands and interests and this has strengthened the political dimension of local authority decision making.

The increasing politicisation of local government over the past 15 years is widely recognised (Gyford, 1985; Hambleton and Hoggett, 1987; Stewart, 1988). Stewart argues that:

> . . . economic pressures, societal change, and ending of the certainty of expenditure growth and growing disillusion with previously accepted professional solutions led to a new assertive style in local politics. Local politicians became more determined to assert political control and to pursue distinctive policies.
>
> (op cit, p. 13)

Local interest groups have also become more assertive, notably women, ethnic minorities and environmentalists. The new assertive style of local politics is manifested in a growth of party control, growing differences between parties, particularly of the 'radical' right and left, and greater influence of elected councillors on policies and decisions (ibid, pp. 13–15).

In response to these pressures and challenges, local authorities have introduced major reforms and innovations arising from an 'internal' commitment to change. This commitment can be seen as involving both a political and a professional dimension as certain members and officers have sought innovative policy and organisational solutions. Examples include policies to promote local economic development in response to the economic crisis and moves to decentralise service delivery in order to improve responsiveness to users (Lawless, 1989; Hambleton, 1988). However, in addition to this internal commitment to change, there has been a requirement to change due to an extensive programme of legislation introduced by central government since 1979 which has sought to transform the nature and role of local government.

The implications of the Thatcher Governments' policies for local

government have been examined extensively elsewhere (e.g. Stoker, 1989; Stewart and Stoker, 1989; Flynn, 1990), and we will not discuss these in detail here. The rationale of Thatcherite policies is the subject of some controversy. Thus, Stoker (1989, p.155) argues that the Thatcherite strategy 'involves an attempt to create new institutions, rules and social relations to support its vision of a post-Fordist society . . .' and, more specifically (op cit, p. 159), 'to create a local government compatible with flexible economic structures, two-tier welfare system and enterprise culture which in the Thatcher vision constitutes the key to a successful future'. However, this view is disputed by Cochrane (1991) who sees the changes in local government as part of the wider break up the welfare state as it becomes restructured around business interests. Moreover, Murray (1991) argues that Thatcherite polices have actually contradicted the elements of the post-Fordist model by strengthening centralised control, deskilling front-line workers and introducing competitive tendering.

Notwithstanding this dispute about the rationale of Thatcherism, it is possible to identify certain key themes of the government's legislative programme (Stewart and Stoker, 1989; Flynn 1990). The first theme is a commitment to competition with a range of services subject to competitive tendering from the private sector, schools competing for students, housing landlords competing for tenants, etc. Competition is seen as a spur to efficiency and customer orientation and as promoting individual choice.

The second theme is a reduced role for local authorities in service delivery which should be shared with other agencies. Authorities should increasingly adopt an 'enabling' role, retaining responsibility for provision but contracting with other agencies for service delivery. A related theme is a challenge to producer interests through this reduced role in direct provision and through contracting out which should reduce the power and influence of public sector trade unions and professionals and achieve a shift of power to the consumer.

A key theme, then, is the focus on the 'customer', free to choose in a market place of public and private sector providers, and exercising choice rather than being administered to by a monopolistic public provider. Local authorities must become more responsive to the expectations of customers and more accountable to them directly and through mechanisms for paying for local services.

Therefore, due to pressures from a changing economic and social context and imperatives deriving from government legislation, local authorities must focus increasingly on achieving 'responsiveness to the customer' and address the organisational and management implications. As indicated earlier, there has been an 'internal commitment' to reform in local government but this has now been reinforced by an 'external imperative'. As a result, local authorities are grasping the nettle of organisational and managerial reform and examining new approaches to the delivery of services. Walsh (1989, pp. 4–5) argues that a 'new management' of local government is emerging with the following characteristics:

- *Responsive:* continually adapting services to meet the varied and changing needs of local people.
- *Smaller and decentralised:* involving a devolution of power from the centre to place authority and responsibility with those who deliver services, and to create smaller units within large organisations.
- *Co-operative:* working with other organisations, public, private, and voluntary, creating and maintaining service networks for the management of the authority.
- *Consumer-controlled:* seeking the views of consumers/clients/citizens and giving them an influence over the services that are provided.
- *Concerned with process:* focusing on the culture and systems of the organisation and on process as much as structure.

The characteristics of this 'new management' can be compared with those of the traditional model outlined above. In essence, this change can be characterised as a shift from a 'bureaucratic production orientation' to a 'post-bureaucratic service orientation'. The new thinking is clearly embodied in the notion of the 'public service orientation' (PSO) propounded by John Stewart and the Local Government Training Board in the mid-1980s. According to Stewart and Stoker (1988, p. 16), the public service orientation:

> . . . recognises that services are provided for the public, and they must be judged by the quality of service and that those for whom the service is provided should have a key role in assessing them.

Therefore, the notion of 'quality' was seen as central to the PSO although there was no extended discussion of the meaning of quality in this context beyond a recognition that it is defined in relation to the value of a service to the customer (Stewart and Clarke, 1987). More recently, Walsh (1989, pp. 6–9) has defined the four main dimensions of the public service orientation as follows:

- *Quality:* a quality service is defined as one which is fit for its purpose, provided by skilled and understanding staff, and which satisfies those who experience it.
- *Access:* services should be fully accessible to those who need or want them; efforts should be made to identify and overcome barriers to access deriving from cultural, social, linguistic and psychological factors or from lack of information.

- *Choice:* within a framework of collective provision individual choice should be accommodated where possible.
- *Participation:* those who need or have an interest in a service should be encouraged to play a more active role in its provision and management.

The ideas embodied in the public service orientation are now well-established in the local government community but discussion of these ideas has recently been subsumed within the notion of 'quality'. Therefore, from being one dimension of the PSO, quality has essentially replaced it as the over-arching concern for local government. However, the definition and meaning of quality in the local government context is by no means a matter of consensus. The debates around quality issues are reflected in the contributions to this book and the next section provides a brief summary of these contributions.

Outline of the book

In the next chapter, I attempt to map out the 'conceptual territory' and identify issues which arise in the pursuit of quality. First, I discuss the meaning of quality in the local government context, emphasising the limits to a 'technical' definition in terms of 'conformance to specification' and the need to address the more subjective issue of whether a service achieves its intended purpose. Problems arise in defining purpose due to the existence of multiple stakeholders but 'satisfying the requirements of the customer' has become the watchword of quality. I present a critique of the 'consumerist' perspective which takes issue with the individualisation of relations between local authorities and their publics, epitomised in the 'government by contract' model of the enabling authority.

In discussing how quality is to be assessed and measured, I identify three dimensions: 'service effectiveness' (the extent to which a service achieves its intended purpose); the 'service relationship' (the nature of the interaction between the authority/provider and public/recipient on an individual and collective level); and 'service organisation' (organisation parameters of quality). Because of the complexity of service contexts and the multiplicity of interests, I argue that there is need for a pluralistic framework to achieve a balanced assessment of quality, incorporating all aspects and interests.

The final question which I consider is: how is quality achieved in local government? I argue that approaches must be tailored to the specific circumstances of local government: the variety of service types; the importance of the political process; the need to work with other agencies. Quality cannot be achieved through 'technical fixes'; it requires a process of organisational change, involving structures, systems, processes and culture, which must involve the renegotiation of power relations. Quality can be built in through the development of sound quality systems appropriate to particular service contexts, consolidated with culture changes within a politically-defined value framework. Training and development of professional competence are of particular significance given the importance of the 'service relationship' and the 'people-intensive' nature of many services.

Lucy Gaster, in chapter three, considers the proposition that in at least some areas of local government activity, a decentralised, devolved service is more likely to improve quality for the consumer and community. Discussing decentralisation first, she argues that changes must go beyond structures to address broader cultural issues. She considers various forms of decentralisation, emphasising their common feature: an emphasis on the role of 'front-line' staff as the visible boundary of the authority and the consequent significance of their formal and informal relations with local consumers and residents. She discusses the implications of decentralisation in terms of various attributes of quality: accessibility, responsiveness and choice, local accountability and equal opportunities, indicating the need to achieve a balance in trade offs between these attributes. Decentralisation, she argues, promotes an integrated, holistic approach to service provision, and flexible working, better teamwork and joint working across divisions and departments, and through coordination between agencies (statutory, voluntary, community) at the local level.

In the second part of her chapter, Gaster argues that effective decentralisation requires the devolution of responsibility and accountability to empower those close to the public and able to respond to local needs. The devolution of political and managerial power must go together and must overcome the traditional dominance of the centre in order to give local committees and groups the power to influence decisions, and local managers real control over resources at the point of delivery. However, a crucial question arises in relation to the potential 'tension' between local responsiveness and central, corporate values and priorities: 'how can consistency of standards and equity of provision be maintained while at the same time enabling local and possibly quite strongly variable needs to met?' Gaster again argues for balance in this trade off to achieve local responsiveness within a framework of centrally-defined priorities. She emphasises the need for involvement of front-line staff and the public in quality systems, promoting more of a 'bottom-up' approach to policy development and decision making 'bringing the realities of experience and local knowledge nearer to the levels of strategic policy.'

In chapter four, Mick Paddon discusses issues around the achievement of quality in an enabling context with services provided increasingly through contractual arrangements. At the outset, he highlights two key questions. First, how are appropriate outputs to be determined and their achievement ensured? Second, how is the 'quality of interaction' between provider and recipient to be achieved through training and other employment considerations? Following a discussion of the different conceptions of 'enabling' propounded from the political left and right, Paddon evaluates critically the evidence on the impact of CCT on quality, arguing that research casts doubt on the claims that CCT reduces costs with no adverse effects on quality. He identifies a number of areas for concern including problems in specifying meaningful standards, ensuring conformance to specification and poor employment conditions for front-line staff. He discusses the applicability of BS 5750 certification, arguing that it neglects various factors relevant to quality assurance including financial standing, health and safety considerations and how specifications are determined. He considers the extension of CCT to 'white collar' services under the 1992 Local Government Act and the limitations of the 'quality threshold' approach which separates quality from cost considerations.

Paddon then goes on to examine the role of contracting in the 'mixed economy of care' which is being introduced in the context of the implementation of Community Care. Following a discussion of problems which arise due to the purchaser/provider split, he outlines an approach based upon developments in Birmingham where less formal Service Level Agreements provide the basis for provision of services by voluntary sector agencies. Finally, he discusses issues raised by EC directives concerning the incorporation of quality considerations into contractual arrangements.

In chapter five, I examine the role of strategic planning and performance review in the achievement of quality. I argue that the concern with developing sound quality systems for quality assurance has resulted in a resurgence of enthusiasm for rationality in the form of planning, monitoring and evaluation. Strategic planning plays an important role in defining purpose, identifying needs and objectives and developing action plans to address them. It becomes particularly important in the context of devolved, 'post-bureaucratic' forms of control, where there is a need for central strategic direction to provide a steering framework for devolved decision making. I argue that strategic planning must be fully integrated into broader management processes including resource planning and budgeting, must accommodate the role of elected members and the views of all stakeholders, and should incorporate a performance review process.

Moving on to consider performance review systems, I discuss their role in promoting effective management and accountability, emphasising the importance of the question: whose view of performance is to count? In discussing the concepts and principles of performance review, I highlight the importance of measures relating to 'service effectiveness' and the 'service relationship' but argue that there is a need to incorporate measures relating to 'service organisation' due to the problems of measuring quality in outcome terms. I argue that performance review systems must be developed as an integral part of the broader process of planning and management and that a commitment to evaluation, learning and improvement should be central to the 'culture' of the authority.

Effective performance review requires a clear expression of objectives and priorities, relevant measures of performance which express key elements of value, and clear targets and standards which show the public what they can expect and staff what is expected of them. The views of users and those affected by services must be of central importance in determining performance indicators and standards and in judging performance against them, but a balance is required between all interests. Finally, I discuss some organisational implications, relating to structures, the involvement of elected members and staff and the potential value of the Quality Audit approach.

In chapter six, Tim Blackman considers the role of research and intelligence activity in local government in improving quality. He argues that concern with quality in a devolved, post-bureaucratic context enhances the importance of information on needs and performance. Research plays a key role in turning information into intelligence for quality management. First, he discusses the role of research in assessing needs and evaluating services, arguing that the focus on the consumer is helping to focus research more on tangible questions relevant to the development of user-led services. He examines the role of consumer surveys, emphasising the need for targeted surveys and for qualitative research to add meaning to quantitative findings. He also discusses potential uses of GISs.

Blackman then goes on to consider the role of research in assisting in the process of user consultation, emphasising the need to ensure that it supports the democratic political process, and contributes to the empowerment of citizens rather than alienating and marginalising people. He also emphasises the importance of involving front-line employees in research. He examines issues in the interpretation of research findings criticising, for example, the use of league tables of performance indicators. Finally, he argues the need for a strong commitment to research, maximising the use of data which is collected already.

Blackman concludes by proposing a three-stage research design involving the development of social indicators from secondary data, sample questionnaire surveys to obtain reliable quantitative results, and in-depth interviews to obtain supplementary qualitative information. He advocates a partnership approach with other agencies but highlights potential obstacles to an enhanced role for research deriving from limits on resources and an 'unsympathetic' organisational culture.

In chapter seven Bill Cooke addresses the problem of changing the organisational culture in local government to promote the achievement of quality. First, he discusses the problem of defining culture, adopting Edgar Schein's approach which distinguishes between 'surface level' artifacts and deeper values and basic assumptions. He argues that this approach focuses on the need to go beyond superficial changes and to understand the bases for resistance to change.

Cooke goes to on examine the culture of local government, identifying the bases for cultural variation in professionalism, history, size, leadership and political control. With regard to the latter, he considers the relationship between culture and political control and the implications of changes in such control. He argues that the existence of considerable cultural diversity means that those seeking to achieve culture change must adopt an approach grounded in an understanding of the idiosyncracies of their organisation's culture and must be seen to do so in order to gain the commitment of the organisation's members.

Cooke then discusses the specific characteristics of services which lead to a definition of quality grounded in customer perceptions and the distinctive nature of local government services. He considers the relevance of different approaches to quality management in terms of achieving culture change, focusing on quality assurance (QA) and total quality management (TQM). He discusses the characteristics of TQM which make it particularly appropriate in a service context.

Finally, in considering approaches to achieving culture change, Cooke compares TQM with Organisational Development, arguing that the latter allows for the development of culture change processes more sensitive to the unique character of local government.

The starting point for the argument developed by Matthew Taylor and John Benington in chapter eight is the neglect in the literature on quality of the issue of democratic representation. They see the 'renewal of politics' as a crucial component of the search for excellence in local government. They argue that the post-war welfare state has been more concerned with issues of quantity than quality and the main role of local government came to be seen as the mass production and efficient delivery of standardised services. The local political process became 'bureaucratised' with elected members diverted into operational and management issues.

Taylor and Benington go on to consider the perspectives on quality of the 'New Right', the 'New Left' and the 'New Managerialism', arguing that — notwithstanding their differential focus on the market place and consumer, on the development of citizenship and on managerial processes — they all neglect the role of the elected member and representative democracy. They contextualise the de-politicisation of quality in relation to broader changes in political economy, and examine the emergence of 'total quality' ideas in the context of post-Fordism. They argue that the emphasis in 'total quality' on strategic planning, on targets, on measuring impacts and on devolution of decision making to the 'front line', provides a context for the renewed importance of the political process. A broad conception of the role of local government is required, committed to strengthening local democracy with a more active role for elected members.

In the final chapter, Wendy Thomson presents a 'practitioner's' perspective on quality, based on local experience in Islington. Her starting point is a critique of the 'managerialist' approach which echoes the arguments of Taylor and Benington — the importance of broader 'democratic relations'. Thomson sees quality as 'a way of communicating a commitment to improved public services' to local residents and users, and it must be defined and assessed on the basis of their views. In Islington the strategy to make services more relevant and popular to local people has involved programmes of decentralisation, democratisation and equality of opportunity which are seen as providing the basis for involving people in changing the way services are organised.

Thomson addressed various questions which might arise in developing quality initiatives: What's new? Is there any scope for local discretion? Is it all hype? In developing quality strategies she emphasises the importance of the involvement and empowerment of residents and service users. She discusses the role of consumer research to find out what residents and users think, reinforcing many of the points made by Tim Blackman in chapter six. She considers 'consumer care', emphasising the need to focus on the front-line, but also to regard people as citizens with rights, echoing Lucy Gaster's arguments in chapter three. She discusses the role of complaints policies and procedures and considers in some detail the process of implementing consumer contracts, emphasising the importance of involving residents and users in this process.

Thomson then presents a critique of the national league tables of performance arising from the Citizen's Charter, arguing that performance should be assessed in relation to local needs and locally-defined objectives. She advocates the use of Quality Audits to accommodate a range of perspectives on performance — consumers, various interest groups, staff and elected members. This echoes my own arguments on the need for a pluralistic approach to defining and assessing quality in chapter two. Finally, Thomson considers the appropriate organisational setting for a Quality Unit which can integrate quality into broader management processes, into the 'political process and ensure appropriate links with outside organisations'.

The contributions to this book present a variety of perspectives on quality and its implications for local government. There has been no attempt to develop an integrative view. If there is a common theme it derives from a belief in the role of local government in our society and a recognition of the significance of the debate about quality. For, in an importance sense, it encompasses debate about the very purpose and role of local government; about the role that authorities play in providing local services; about the importance of elected local authorities within the political system and the relative power of different interests within the local political system.

The 'quality revolution' is in its early stages in local government and it is important to recognise diversity and to foster debate and argument. It is hoped that this book contributes to that process.

References

ACC (1992) *Signposts to Quality: Local Authority Case Studies*, Associations of County, District and Metropolitan Councils, Association of Metropolitan Authorities, London.

Atkinson, P. E. (1990) *Creating Cultural Change: The Key to Successful Total Quality Management*, IFS, Bedford.

Cochrane, A. (1991) The changing state of local government — restructuring for the 1990s, *Public Administration*, Vol. 69, No. 3, pp. 281–302.

Flynn, N. (1990) *Public Sector Management*, Harvester Wheatsheaf, Hemel Hempstead.

Gyford, J. (1985) *The Politics of Local Socialism*, George Allen and Unwin, London.

Hambleton, R. (1987) Developments, objectives and criteria, in Willmot, P. (ed.) *Local Government, Decentralisation and Community*, Policy Studies Institute, London, pp. 8–24.

Hambleton, R. (1988) Consumerism, decentralization and local democracy, *Public Administration*, Vol. 66, No. 2, pp. 125–47.

Hambleton, R. and Hoggett, P. (1987) Beyond bureaucratic paternalism, in Hoggett P. and Hambleton R. (eds) *Decentralisation and Democracy — Localising Public Services*, Occasional Paper No. 28, SAUS, University of Bristol.

HMSO (1989) *Caring for People — Community Care in the Next Decade and Beyond*, Cm 849, HMSO, London.

HMSO (1991) *The Citizen's Charter — Raising the Standard*, Cm 1599, HMSO, London.

Hoggett, P. (1987) A Farewell to Mass Production? Decentralisation as an Emergent Private and Public Sector Paradigm, in Hoggett, P. and Hambleton, R. (eds) *Decentralisation and Democracy — Localising Public Services*, Occasional Paper No. 28, SAUS, University of Bristol, pp. 215–32.

Labour Party, (1991) *The Quality Commission — A Consultation Paper*, Labour Party Policy Directorate, London.

Lawless, P. (1989) *Britain's Inner Cities*, Paul Chapman, London.

Murray, R. (1991) The state after Henry, *Marxism Today*, May, pp. 22–27.

Newton, K. and Karran, T. (1985) *The Politics of Local Expenditure*, Macmillan, London.

Oakland, J. S. (1989) *Total Quality Management*, Butterworth Heinemann, Oxford.

Rustin, M. (1989) The politics of post-Fordism — or, the trouble with 'new times', *New Left Review*, No. 175, pp. 57–78.

Stewart, J. (1986) *The New Management of Local Government*, Allen and Unwin, London.

Stewart, J. (1988) *Understanding the Management of Local Government*, Longman, Harlow.

Stewart, J. (1989) The changing organisation and management of local government in Stewart, J. and Stoker, G. (eds) *The Future of Local Government*, Macmillan, London.

Stewart, J. and Clarke, M. (1987) The public service orientation — issues and dilemmas, *Public Administration*, Vol. 65, No. 2, pp. 161–77.

Stewart, J. and Stoker, G. (1988) *From Local Administration to Community Government*, Fabian Research Series 351, Fabian Society, London.

Stewart, J. and Stoker, G. (eds) (1989) *The Future of Local Government*, Macmillan, London.

Stoker, G. (1989) Creating a local government for a post-Fordist society: the Thatcherite project? in Stewart, J. and Stoker, G. (eds) *The Future of Local Government*, Macmillan, London.

Thompson, P. and McHugh, D. (1990) *Work Organisations — A Critical Introduction*, Macmillan, London.

Walsh, K. (1989) *Marketing in Local Government*, Longman, Harlow.

2 Defining quality in local government

Ian Sanderson

Introduction

In this chapter, we attempt to 'set the scene' for the detailed discussion in subsequent chapters of issues relating to the achievement of quality in local government. In doing so, we shall address the basic questions: Why? What? and How? First, what is the rationale for pursuing quality in local government? Second, how do we define quality in this context? Third, how can we assess quality so that we know when we are achieving it? Finally, how do we achieve quality? It is certainly not the intention to claim to provide definitive answers; quality is a relatively new concern for local government and a very healthy debate is underway in relation to these questions. There is, as yet, little evidence from the evaluation of quality developments in local government to help in answering them. Consequently, the discussion is concerned mainly to attempt to map out the 'conceptual territory' and to identify issues which arise in the pursuit of quality.

We begin, in the next section, with a discussion of the meaning of quality in the local government context. We examine, in particular, the development of 'consumerist' thinking, deriving from the private sector, and consider criticisms of the relevance of such thinking to local government. We then outline a framework for the consideration of factors relevant to the assessment of quality in local government and this leads on to a discussion of issues which arise in the development of approaches to achieving quality. Finally, a brief concluding section highlights some of the main themes and issues.

The meaning of quality for local government

Quality and consumerism

As indicated in the previous chapter, we can identify two basic dimensions to quality. First, there is a 'technical' dimension: the extent to which a product or service conforms to its specification (cf.'quality of conformance'). Second, there is a more 'subjective' dimension: the extent to which the product or service as specified satisfies our requirements or achieves its intended purpose (cf. 'quality of design') (Walsh, 1991, 1992; Oakland, 1989; Pfeffer and Coote, 1991). What is the relevance of these different aspects of quality to the local government context?

'Conformance to specification' is important in situations where specifications can be drawn up in advance in terms of discrete, measurable attributes of a product or service. In fact, it is most appropriate as a criterion of quality for physical products which can be assessed against technical standards relating, for example, to manufacturing tolerances, reliability and safety. However, the fact that local government is concerned with services which meet a variety of needs in the community presents some problems for this technical criterion of quality. First, it neglects whether the service as specified meets these needs. Moreover, there are certain distinctive characteristics of services which are important to the achievement of quality, and these are summarised as follows by Jessome (1988, p. 176):

> Service industries, by their nature, have less control over factors which affect quality: because services cannot be stored for later use, and because of participation by the customer in the process, there is a much higher level of external uncertainty than in manufacturing industries. The intangibility of services makes it difficult to set standards, to conform to them and to measure them. Good service is an expectation of individual customers, which may vary from customer to customer. The customer himself (sic) participates in the process, to a greater or lesser extent, and therefore has impact on the quality of services. Finally, service quality is difficult to measure because of its subjective nature.

Consequently, service quality cannot be reduced to the internal management of technical conformance but must address '*the experience of the interchange* between provider and recipient' (AMA, 1992, p. 12). This can be a highly subjective and intangible attribute not easily expressed in a measurable standard (Walsh, 1991). However, local authority services vary considerably in terms of the nature of the service provided and its 'conditions of production'. Thus they can be seen to range from the more 'technical' services like refuse collection, cleansing, highway design and information technology, through the more 'people-oriented' services like education, social services and housing, to what might be termed 'social improvement activities' such as information provision, advocacy and persuasion relating to factors which can improve the broader quality of life of local people (e.g. pollution, poverty, health). In the more 'technical' services, standards specifying measurable attributes of quality subject to internal management control are more readily derived (e.g. reliability of service, standards of outcome). In situations where the interaction between provider and recipient (or user, client or customer) is a major element of the service, measurable standards are more problematical and subjective perceptions and judgements become more important (Stewart and Walsh, 1989; Bone, 1992).

Consequently, quality in local authority services cannot be reduced to a matter of 'conformance to specification'. In addition to the problem of defining standards, important questions arise as to whose views are to count in judgements about quality. This introduces the more subjective dimension of quality: the extent to which the service achieves its intended purpose. What is the purpose of local government services and activities? Clearly, given the range of different services there will be a multitude of specific objectives which will be relevant to defining quality in particular service contexts. However, consideration of a broader perspective on purpose, related to the notion that local government services should 'meet the needs of the local public', raises a number of questions about what this means. Thus, should the purpose of services be:

- *to satisfy the wants and expectations of customers?*
- *to meet the needs of actual and potential customers?*
- *to meet the collective needs of local communities?*
- *to achieve the broader development of active citizenship?*

Different 'stakeholders' in local authorities will have different views on the relative importance of these aspects of purpose: individuals as actual or potential customers, as voters, as local taxpayers; groups with an interest in specific services or localities or in broader social policy outcomes; local businesses, both individually and collectively through business organisations; trade unions; professional groups within authorities; elected members. Moreover, as indicated in the previous section, central government has an important influence by setting the bounds of freedom of action and choice for local authorities. The crucial question is: Whose views are to count in determining the relative balance of these different aspects of purpose in particular service contexts? Clearly, there will be an important element of discretion for individual local authorities to derive solutions appropriate to local circumstances.

However, there are a number of factors promoting a much greater emphasis than hitherto on satisfying the requirements of customers of local authority services. In the previous chapter we referred to the rise of consumerism and the development of the 'public service orienta- tion', which emphasises 'getting close to the customer'. The latter arose partly from the literature on 'excellence' and quality in the pri- vate sector. We discussed above the importance of the relationship with the customer for many services and hence the importance of the customer's views about the 'quality' of this relationship. Finally the Government's perspective on quality, reflected in a number of legisla- tive provisions, emphasises the 'empowerment' of the users of public services (HMSO, 1991a, 1991b).

Consequently, discussions of quality in local government place con- siderable emphasis on 'meeting the requirements of the customer'. From this perspective, improvements in the effectiveness of local authorities and the quality of services are seen primarily in terms of 'getting close to the customer' and becoming more *responsive* to their expectations and needs. This perspective can be seen as embodied in the Audit Commission's view of the 'well-managed' authority which emphasises the following attributes (Audit Commission, 1988):

- *understand customers*
- *respond to the electorate*
- *set and pursue consistent and achievable objectives*
- *assign clear management responsibilities*
- *train and motivate people*
- *communicate effectively*
- *monitor results*
- *adapt to change.*

Clearly, this model implies a substantial degree of common ground between the public and private sectors, the only element not in com- mon being the need to 'respond to the electorate'. It is a model of a 'responsive organisation' which can meet the wants and needs of cus- tomers economically, efficiently and effectively — the three 'Es'. As such it embodies two important assumptions about the nature and pur- pose of local government. First, it assumes that local government is primarily about delivering specific services to satisfy the needs and expectations of local people. Second, it assumes that local authorities should become more responsive to the demands and expectations of people conceived of as 'customers'. In this sense, it embodies what has been termed a *consumerist* perspective.

'Consumerists seek to redress the balance of power between those who provide goods and services, and those for whom they are provid- ed' (Hambleton, 1991, p. 19). Consumerism emphasises five key principles: first, all people must have *access* to the benefits offered by a product or service; second, people should be able to exercise *choice*; third, consumers should have access to full and accurate *information*; fourth, people should have the right and means of *redress*; finally, consumers have a right to the *representation* of their views in decision making by organisations (ibid).

The Conservative's view on quality in public services, as set out in the 'Citizen's Charter' (HMSO, 1991a), embodies the consumerist perspective. The main themes of the Government's programme are: first, improving the quality of public services; second, increasing choice for consumers; third, setting standards for services; and fourth, ensuring value for money. They key principle is seen as choice:

> Choice, wherever possible between competing providers, is the best spur to quality improvement.
>
> (op cit, p. 4)

The main routes to increased choice in the local government context involve a reduction in the role of elected local authorities in providing services. This is achieved firstly through compulsory competitive tendering (CCT) whereby services are contracted to the private sector and, secondly, through giving 'consumers' the right to 'opt out' of local authority provision into alternative forms of provision (in relation to education and housing).

Implicit in this perspective on quality is a model of local government in which elected local authorities play a diminishing role as 'enabling authorities':

> The task of local authorities lies in identifying requirements, setting priorities, determining standards of service and finding the best way to meet those standards and ensuring they are met. This implies a move away from the traditional model of local authorities providing virtually all services directly and a greater separation of the service delivery from strategic responsibilities. Local authorities will then be able to concentrate more fully on their core responsibilities.
>
> (HMSO, 1991b, p. 22)

However, these 'core responsibilities' will be progressively diminished to the extent that rights to opt out of local authority control are exercised by tenants and school governors. Moreover, the ability of authorities to exercise local discretion is limited by central financial controls and could be further undermined by the proposed system of standard performance indicators which are to be developed by the Audit Commission (undated) and will be used to compare authorities in national league tables.

The Labour Party also emphasises quality in its programme for local government but claims a different perspective from that propounded by the Conservatives who, it is argued, 'equate cheapness with success' (Labour Party, 1991a, p. 10). In Labour's view, quality local government should provide 'value for people' as well as 'value for money', meeting 'the all round needs of local people, whether as an enabler or as a direct provider of services' (ibid). The key to quality is seen as 'changing the culture of local government' with 'better management, more training, sharing best practice and welcoming participation and innovation' (ibid).

It is argued that the people who use council services should have a right to know the level and standard of service they can expect and this should be set out in customer contracts. Customer and employee participation should be encouraged and authorities would be given broader powers to act on issues of concern to their community. A Quality Commission would have a statutory duty to promote 'good practice' in local government in terms of customer contracts, complaint procedures, management practice, training, innovation and undertaking 'quality audits' (Labour Party, 1991a, 1991b).

There are certain similarities between the Government's and Labour Party's perspectives on quality, particularly the focus on specifying standards in customer contracts and on providing choice for *consumers*. Nevertheless, Labour's approach does give greater recognition to the role of local government in addressing the collective needs of communities, in promoting the participation of local people as citizens in the process of government, and in taking more positive action with wider powers in relation to the full range of issues which affect the quality of life and well-being of their communities. The Conservatives' perspective implies an increasingly restricted role for elected local authorities with, on the one hand, increased control from central government in relation to financial 'inputs' and performance 'outputs' and, on the other hand, increased power for 'consumers' in terms of choice, information and redress and, ultimately, the ability to choose to opt out of local authority control. Following their re-election to a fourth term of government, the Conservatives are committed to implementing the 'Citizen's Charter' with its 'consumerist' perspective on quality. To what extent will this promote the 'reduction' of purpose to a matter of 'customer satisfaction' at the expense of elements of a broader conception of purpose relating to collective needs and the promotion of 'citizenship'? We address this question in a brief critique of consumerism.

The critique of consumerism

The critique of consumerism is based upon the premise that there is a fundamental distinction to be made between the conditions for effectiveness and the purpose of the activities of local government on the one hand and private sector organisations on the other. In the private market the power of consumers derives from access to resources and ability to choose, and efficiency derives from competition between firms in responding to the choices exercised by consumers. It is a world of individualised exchange relations in which consumers are 'sovereign'.

However, there are a number of reasons why people's choice is limited in relation to local government services. For example, people may lack information about available services and there may be educational, cultural or linguistic factors which hinder people's ability to express their needs in the market. This matters when the services in question are for the benefit of the community as a whole, meeting needs which individuals are not always able to articulate fully. As Stewart and Clarke (1987, p. 170) argue:

> The customer of a public service is not the same as a customer of a service in the market. The customer does not necessarily buy the service; the customer may have a right to receive the service; the customer may be compelled to receive the service; customers may be refused a service because their needs may not meet the criteria laid down.

Moreover, local authorities are monopolistic providers of many services; people cannot go elsewhere. Therefore, effective accountability cannot be secured through consumer choice in the market place but rather must involve giving people power through representation in political structures and processes (Hambleton, 1988, 1991).

Limitations on individual choice arise fundamentally from 'market failure' due to factors which inhibit market mechanisms from achieving socially efficient and equitable allocations of resources (Levacic, 1987, LeGrand and Robinson, 1984). The existence of 'external' costs and benefits has traditionally provided a strong rationale for government 'intervention', on the one hand to seek to reduce the impact of social costs such as pollution and traffic congestion and, on the other hand, to seek to promote the incidence of external benefits deriving from, for example, education, heath care, policing and the preservation of green spaces. Much of the activity of local government can be understood as the 'mediation' of externalities and the attempt to secure, in the broader public interest, a degree of equity in the incidence of the costs and benefits involved. Since, by definition, this can only be achieved 'outside' the market, it is contradictory to discuss the quality of local government activities in purely consumerist terms. If quality is defined solely in terms of customer wants and expectations, it will fail adequately to address the extent to which the wider *needs* of communities are being met. Thus, the 'customer' for local authority services may be individuals, groups, communities, or even the 'public' as a whole, depending on the service, or even element of service, in question. The concept of 'need' therefore extends beyond individuals' perceptions to address collective concerns and provide a basis for the achievement of the conditions for social efficiency and equity which the market manifestly fails to do.

The assessment of needs and determination of how they might be satisfied require processes which involve 'customers' (individually and collectively), professionals and elected members in the 'negotiation' of a set of priorities, rights, compulsions and refusals in relation to the services and activities of local authorities. Such negotiated priorities, mediated through the local political process, are required to achieve effectiveness in outcomes and a degree of equity in access and outcome terms. Traditionally, professionals have played a predominant role in this process; according to Walsh (1991, p. 508) '. . . for many years professionals have jealously guarded their claimed special right to make judgements about the proper character of service'.

As we have seen, it is widely accepted that the pursuit of quality involves the redress of this imbalance of power in favour of those who use and experience local government services. However, it is important to recognise that the 'empowerment' of some can imply the disempowerment of others and, therefore, to ensure that a consumerist strategy does not merely empower those best able to articulate their requirements at the expense of those who rely on professionals and elected members to represent their interests.

There is a danger, then, that consumerism devalues the role of elected members and the democratic process, embodying an individualistic, 'transactional' view of relations between local authorities and their populations (Mulgan, 1991; Edgar, 1991). From this point of view, local authorities are seen essentially as agencies for the delivery of specific services to individual customers, a view which devalues the potential broader role of local government in promoting the collective well-being of communities and in supporting and promoting political pluralism and the processes and structures of local democracy.

The emphasis on an individualised 'service relationship' between the service provider and customer can lead to a focus on the 'customer care' approach to quality. The risk here is that such an approach can be restricted to the 'charm-school-and-better-wallpaper' type which achieves public visibility but requires little real change in power relationships (Pollitt, 1987, p. 44). An impoverished conception of the local political process can result, both in terms of the involvement of people on a collective basis, and in terms of the role of that process in promoting participative and democratic habits and expectations over and above the delivery of specific services — in promoting *'citizenship'*.

The notion of citizenship is an old one but has recently enjoyed a revival in the context of debate about the role and purpose of local government which has been generated by the Thatcherite programme. The concept of citizenship provides, in Rhodes' (1987) words, the 'noble aspiration' for local government as a political institution which promotes political pluralism and education and helps to build the habits and processes of democracy. In this broader role local government plays, at the least, an important role in encouraging participation by people in local political processes. However, participation can take many forms ranging from consultation (which may or may not be genuine), through partnership arrangements, to attempts to empower communities to be fully involved in the processes of local government thereby promoting emancipation of the individual and the creation of a free society. It is the 'empowering' conception of participation which is embodied in the notion of citizenship. Rhodes (1987, p. 68) argues that the role and purpose of local government must encompass such a broad conception of citizenship:

> ... because local government is the pre-eminent location for the integrative political experience outside of parliament and the absence of this experience is a cardinal defect of advanced industrial societies.

Those who advocate a broader, positive political role for local government see the rejuvenation of active citizenship through the 'integrative political experience' as fundamental to the contemporary purpose of local government. From this perspective, the consumerist model only serves further to devalue this role and purpose through its de-politicised, 'transactional' view of relations between local authorities and their 'customers'. The process of local government is reduced to the administration of service transactions with customers which erodes further the prospects for the strengthening of local democracy on the basis of active participation in the context of positive community development initiatives (Berry, 1988).

The erosion of the power of elected local authorities is seen by Cochrane (1991) as part of the process of restructuring of the local state from 'provider of collective consumption' to 'defender of enterprise'. In this context, the role of elected local authorities is restricted as a wider range of non-elected organisations becomes involved in the process of 'local governance'. The role of local authorities then focuses on mediating between the different interests represented in a network of organisations. This new role for local authorities, replacing their traditional 'monopolistic' role in service provision, is embodied in the notion of 'enabling' which forms a key element in the Government's vision for local government as discussed above.

In this enabling model of local government, relations between the network of organisations are primarily of a *contractual* nature. The contract becomes the prime means by which local authorities can seek to achieve desired outcomes (Hoggett, 1991; Mather, 1991). It becomes the main vehicle for control, influence and empowerment. Legislation on compulsory competitive tendering increasingly forces authorities to 'contract out' service provision to the private and voluntary sectors. The Government's 'Citizen's Charter' conceives of relations between public sector organisations and their customers in terms of contracts for specific levels and standards of service (HMSO, 1991a). With the extension of such contractual relations the role and purpose of local authorities becomes progressively reduced to merely ensuring the provision of specific services whose nature can be specified in a contract. The more that 'performance' is assessed in terms of the measurable outputs which necessarily define the contractual requirement, the less scope local authorities will have to include activities with less tangible outcomes within their legitimate roles.

Clearly, quality is a contested concept (Pollitt, 1990). It is apparent that the Government has a particular view of the purpose and role of local government in our society and that its consumerist perspective on quality is consistent with that view. Nevertheless, there is still scope for considerable variation between authorities in their interpretation of the meaning of quality and how it should be assessed and achieved. Notwithstanding the limitations of 'consumerism' there is agreement in local government on the importance of judging quality from the point of view of those who use and need local authority services, although many would argue that such judgement must be placed in a context of consideration of wider collective community welfare.

The assessment of quality

We discussed earlier the difficulties which arise for the measurement of quality due to the characteristics of local government services, especially those with a strong provider/customer interaction and those with an indirect 'social policy' impact. There are two aspects to this problem. The first is the difficulty of specifying measurable attributes of quality which leads to a necessary reliance on subjective measures and judgements. The second, deriving from this, is the problem of whose views are to count in this process of subjective assessment. Of particular importance is the relative power and influence of providers and consumers in the process; they will have different perspectives and interests; and there will also be differences between various groups of consumers (individually and collectively) and providers (e.g. frontline, senior management, elected members).

In the previous section we argued that the ability of consumers to make informed judgements about quality will vary between different local government service contexts due to the role of local government in addressing 'market failures'. The assessment of quality will always require an appropriate *balance* to be achieved between provider and consumer perspectives, but the relative influence of different interests will vary according to the nature of the service or activity concerned. In service contexts where the personal interaction of provider and user is important, the views of the latter will be particularly important (Walsh, 1991, p. 511).

If we examine the criteria by which the quality of local government service and activities might be assessed, it is helpful to consider the distinction drawn by Donabedian (1980), in his seminal study of quality in health services, between attributes relating to 'outcome', 'process' and 'structure'. Donabedian sees 'process' as the central measure of quality, referring to the interaction between provider and recipient and defined as 'interpersonal' quality. 'Outcome' is seen as an indirect measure to the extent that it is influenced by factors other than the service in question. Finally, 'structure' refers to the resources needed to provide services and the ways in which they are organised 'both formally and informally'; this is also seen as an indirect measure since it influences performance but, in itself, is merely indicative of quality (op cit, p. 81).

If the quality of a service is defined primarily in terms of the extent to which it achieves the purpose for which it is intended, then Donabedian's view of 'outcome' as an indirect measure can be criticised since the outcomes of public services must be seen as central to the definition of their purpose. Consequently, in the assessment of quality we would emphasise the primacy of two dimensions of service performance based on Donabedian's analysis and consistent with the framework proposed by Stewart and Walsh (1989). The first dimension is *'service effectiveness'*, the extent to which a service achieves the purpose for which it is intended; the second is the *'service relationship'*, which refers to aspects of the interaction between provider and recipient. A third dimension, which provides an indirect measure of quality, is *'service organisation'*, the way in which the service is produced and delivered, referring to both formal and informal aspects of organisation. Clearly, these three dimensions are inter-related in ways which will vary according to the nature of the service concerned. However, the distinction is useful as an aid to analysis of quality and how it might be assessed.

As regards 'service effectiveness' then, the basic question is: does the service do what it is intended to do? There are various aspects to this. First, there are certain *technical* attributes. Is the service reliable? Is it provided promptly, consistently and accurately? Second, is the service *accessible* to all those who need it in both physical and economic terms? Does everyone have the necessary information to make use of a service? Third, are adequate levels of *choice* available to all those who need services or who want to make use of them? Fourth, does the service produce the intended *outcomes* in relation to its defined objectives? This involves maximising intended consequences and minimising unintended consequences in terms of impact on the expectations and needs of local people defined at both individual and collective levels. Finally, it is necessary to consider the degree of *equity* achieved between individuals, groups, communities and areas. Is there fairness of treatment in terms of access to service and choice? Is an acceptable degree of equity achieved in terms of the service provided and its outcomes?

The specification of consistent *standards* of attainment for services can be seen as fundamental to the achievement of quality — they state explicitly what people have a right to expect, and provide specific grounds for complaint and redress. They provide a clear basis for assessing achievement of quality and promote equity of provision. They can help to empower users, as Pollitt (1990, p. 437) argues: 'An explicit standard is de-mystifying: it can be used as the basis for a more intelligible system of public accountability'. However, as we have argued, the appropriateness of standards is likely to vary between different types of service. The more 'technical' and 'product orientated' services such as refuse collection, street sweeping, grounds maintenance, housing repair, etc. are more susceptible to the definition of uniform standards of achievement which can be specified in 'charters' and provide 'customers' with an entitlement and a basis for complaint and redress. Many local authorities have made substantial progress in this respect. On the other hand, in the more 'social' and 'people oriented' services, such as, social services, education and environmental health, it is much more difficult to specify meaningful standards because these services are more oriented to specific, identified, personal and social needs. In addition, because their outcomes are more difficult to identify and measure, there is more scope for conflicts of opinion about the effectiveness of such services.

This difference in service type is also relevant to the importance of the 'service relationship' relative to service effectiveness. Indeed, the problem of specifying meaningful standards of achievement can be seen to derive from the greater importance of the service relationship to those services which address personal and social needs. For these services, the nature of the interaction between provider and recipient is a key component of the service; indeed, it can become all-important in certain social service contexts, for example. There are various aspects of this interaction which are relevant to quality. First, we can draw the distinction between individual and collective dimensions of interaction. As regards the individual dimension, the *personal relationship* refers to the 'personality characteristics' of both the provider and recipient; the *organisational context* influences the attitudes, skills and behaviour of the provider, and the *service setting* defines the constraints and conditions for the interaction.

The importance of the service relationship is emphasised by Gaster (1991a, 1991b) and leads to a focus on practices and conditions 'at the front line'. The implication is that, particularly for those personal and social services in which the provider/user interaction is a key component of the service, the achievement of quality is likely to be much more about 'staff development' than about standards and charters. Thus, the selection and training of front-line staff becomes a key issue but, more fundamentally, there is a need to examine the broader organisational culture in terms of the extent to which it supports the values, commitments and motivation of employees required to sustain 'quality service relationships'. Finally, attention must be given to the settings in which front-line staff interact with the public, particularly the location of 'points of access' to the authority and the environment which they provide for people in terms, for example, of cleanliness, safety, security and facilities. Standards can be set for various aspects of the service relationship primarily in terms of levels of satisfaction of service users and the extent to which procedures are adhered to.

Consideration of the nature of the interaction between an authority and the local population should extend beyond the provision of specific services to individual customers. As Gaster (1991a) emphasises, and as discussed in the previous section, an important element of the potential role of local authorities relates to activities and services which address needs defined on a collective level. This dimension of the interaction between the authority and local people is neglected in the consumerist model which focuses on individualised service transactions with customers. If it is accepted that local authorities have a legitimate role in attempting to build 'citizenship' through active participation in the processes of local government, then the interaction between the authority and its 'citizens' should embody ways in which local people as individuals, groups and communities are involved and *participate* in these processes (cf. Hambleton and Hoggett, 1990). This perspective focuses attention on processes of representative democracy and the role of elected members in the relationship between the authority and local citizens.

Consideration of the factors which are important in the service relationship therefore raises issues relating to the *organisational* parameters of quality. At both the individual and collective levels, organisational structures, processes and systems underpin the factors which define the service relationship. We have referred to Donabedian's (op cit) argument to the effect that 'structural' factors can be seen as indirect, 'proxy' measures of quality. These have value because of various problems which arise in the measurement of quality in terms of service effectiveness and relationship. As regards effectiveness, we can identify four types of problem. First, for many services, especially those addressing personal and social needs, outcomes are difficult to measure directly. Second, outcomes are often not totally under the control of authorities through their available courses of action but are subject to a wide range of influences. Third, the impact of services may manifest themselves only in the long term. Finally, problems arise due to different interpretations as to what constitutes an acceptable and legitimate outcome.

This brings us back to the central issue of: whose view is to count in the assessment of quality? The above difficulties suggest that both provider and customer assessment of quality is problematical (Walsh 1991, p. 512). Where the service relationship is an important aspect of quality, assessment is particularly difficult but the views of users become especially important; according to Donabedian (op cit, p. 118) 'clients are the more authoritative sources of criteria, standards, and information' concerning this aspect of quality. In general, an emphasis on the outcome and interaction dimensions of quality implies greater power for users in the definition and assessment of quality; to quote Donabedian (ibid) again:

> The use of outcomes gives greater influence to the client's perspective in defining quality and facilitates the participation of clients in the effort to monitor and enhance the quality of care.

Of course, it is necessary to recognise certain limitations in the views of customers in relation to quality. Some people may lack the information and 'resources' to make choices and judgements in their own best interest. The views of individuals must be qualified in relation to services and activities which address externalities and public interest considerations (e.g. traffic management, planning and some aspects of social services) precisely because such services in effect control and over-rule the wishes of some individuals in the wider public interest. Finally, local authorities must ration services to match constrained resources and must decide priorities between competing claims and needs. Consequently, many people will be dissatisfied because outcomes do not meet their expectations.

Nevertheless, it is widely accepted that professionals in local government should not have a monopoly in judgements about the desirable character of services and priorities, although it is recognised that greater weight should be given to the views of those working 'at the front line', in close contact with service users in the service relationship. What is needed is a balance of perspectives, a *pluralistic* approach to assessing quality which seeks to combine attempts at measurement on various dimensions and the views of all the various stakeholders involved (cf. Pfeffer and Coote, 1991). Thus, a range of different forms of measurement will be needed: quantitative measures against standards; indirect, 'proxy' measures'; qualitative assessments. The views of all the relevant stakeholders should be accommodated, recognising collective as well as individual interests: actual and potential customers, interest and community groups, managers, front-line professionals, elected members. Measures will be required on all the aspects of quality: measures of service effectiveness, of the service relationship, and of service organisation. This pluralistic approach is embodied in the 'Quality Audit' which is being developed by several local authorities as a means for assessing performance in terms of quality (see chapter 5).

Consideration of the contribution of procedural and organisational aspects of quality brings us to the question: how do we achieve quality? We now consider this question briefly in the next section.

The achievement of quality

The concern here is to determine the forms of organisational structure, systems, processes and culture which will enable the achievement of required standards in terms of service effectiveness and relationships. This is the focus of much of the quality literature. The traditional approaches of quality control (QC) and quality assurance (QA) emphasise techniques and processes for ensuring that products or services meet defined standards. Accreditation under the British Standard for quality assurance (BS 5750) requires detailed conformance with specific procedures and processes. Total Quality Management (TQM) combines an emphasis on the 'soft' aspects of culture and management style with the hard technical processes of QC and QA (Atkinson, 1990).

In the local government context the procedural implications of the achievement of quality are complicated by three characteristics of the nature and role of elected local authorities. First, as we discussed above, local authorities are responsible for a wide range of services with different characteristics of relevance to the achievement of quality. For example, the processes appropriate to achieving quality in, say, refuse collection may be somewhat different from those required in the case of social work services.

Second, local authorities are political organisations elected by local people and therefore accountable to them as well as to central government. Authorities therefore face the issue of how to promote the legitimacy and accountability of their activities and this has procedural implications. Moreover, decisions on priorities are outputs from the political process and the achievement of quality can be seen to incorporate the perceived legitimacy of this political process.

Third, elected local authorities must work jointly with other organisations to promote the broader economic and social well-being of their areas; many outcomes which authorities will seek to achieve are influenced by a range of agents. The requirement for joint working and co-ordination is increasing due to certain developments: the 'hiving off' of certain local authority services, for example in housing and education; the adoption by local authorities of the responsibility for implementing care in the community; and the growth in importance of agencies such as TECs and of the voluntary sector. As local authorities take on more of an enabling role it will be necessary to consider increasingly the part played by inter-agency coordination and joint working in the achievement of quality.

However, there is clearly no one simple answer in terms of 'service organisation' which is appropriate to the achievement of quality. There is a lack of hard evidence on the contribution of procedural and organisational reform in the public sector to improved performance. Moreover, such reform must be tailored to the specific circumstances of individual authorities; there can be no 'organisational blueprint' for quality. Barrett and MacMahon (1990) argue that achieving organisational change involves re-negotiating patterns of interests and power within the organisation rather than simply reforming structures and systems. Their findings underline the limits of 'technical fixes' for quality, that is, initiatives, procedures and systems which are 'grafted onto' the organisation without changing fundamentally ways of thinking and working — the organisational 'culture'. Thus, it is easy for an authority to produce a 'mission statement' and a customers' or citizens' charter containing vague expressions of intent with no more than propaganda value. Performance review systems may provide merely an 'ex post' check on the impact of policies and programmes and be seen as an annoying imposition by service managers. 'Customer care' initiatives may do no more than provide a smiling face and a complaints box which, although valuable in themselves, are limited as means of achieving quality.

Of course, it is much easier to introduce such 'technical fixes' than to attempt to achieve real organisational change on the basis of a fundamental re-examination of structures, processes and values because the latter affect existing power relations within the organisation. The re-negotiation of these power relations requires the accommodation of the various interests involved and the resolution of conflicts between them. The management skills involved in achieving such change are very different from those required for the task of securing control within established structures, processes and values. Therefore, it is important that the implications of quality for organisational change are not underestimated by perceiving this process in purely 'technical' terms.

Indeed, traditional QC approaches reflect such a technical perspective, emphasising 'conformance to specification'. QC still represents the most widely-used approach to ensuring quality (Bone, 1992). It requires standards to be specified and relies on 'post-production' monitoring and inspection to assess conformance to those standards. It is possible to see the QC philosophy reflected in the traditional approach to performance review, as Walsh (1991, p. 505) argues:

> Most approaches to performance measurement in the public sector take a quality control approach, focusing on conformance, and emphasising the extent to which behaviour conforms with organisational procedures and controls.

QC relies on a capacity to 'learn' from assessments of actual performance against standards. However, even where standards can be specified precisely, QC is a relatively inefficient method, relying on the feedback of results to 'rectify mistakes'. There may be factors which restrict the capacity of the organisation to learn from these results; for example, a feeling of resentment and resistance may be engendered among those providing the service due to the perception of an 'imposed' system (Bone, 1992). The importance of the subjective perceptions of the public serves to magnify the limitations of QC due to the problems and relatively long timescale of feeding back customers' views into the service planning and delivery system.

A more effective approach to ensuring quality is to 'build it in' to the process of production; to develop systems and processes, an 'organisational capacity', which will ensure that quality is achieved continuously. This is the purpose of QA which therefore goes beyond QC (but nevertheless incorporates it where the circumstances are appropriate). QA transfers 'ownership' of quality to those who produce and deliver the service:

> QA will be successfully applied where there is commitment to quality by members, management and workforce. Documented procedures, written specifications, adequate training, and performance appraisal — in other words commitment to a quality policy — is what a quality assurance system is all about.
>
> (AMA, 1992)

There is a growing interest in developing QA systems in local government, primarily as a result of CCT legislation. Thus, authorities are increasingly insisting that contractors who tender for services covered by legislation must seek QA certification under the British Standard (BS 5750) or its international equivalent ISO 9000 (Bone, 1992). The main focus of QA certification efforts, therefore, has been the more 'technical' services subject to CCT legislation such as building works, catering supplies, cleansing, highways maintenance, etc. (AMA, 1992). However, attention is being given to the application of BS 5750 in the context of social care (British Quality Association, 1992); for example, certification has been achieved for a residential home for the elderly owned by Newcastle City Council (Casson and Humphrey, 1992). Moreover, attention is also being given to 'support services' in the light of the Government's intention to extend CCT to these services. Leeds City Council's Project Management Group, an internal consultancy service, is the first service of its kind to achieve certification.

Although full certification may not be feasible or appropriate for many services, the discipline of QA can be beneficial in 'providing a systematic and coherent framework for stimulating change' and in devolving power and responsibility such that 'front-line' staff 'who take ownership of the system that sustains their service will have much greater control over what they do.' (Bone, 1992, p. 6.6). For example, in Wolverhampton the principles of QA have been applied to leisure management services based on BS 5750 but do not proceed to certification, and it has been concluded that:

> The major advantage of a QA system is that it aids the process of decentralising control to leisure centre managers. In this way, they themselves control and review standards at their centres. This assists the 'teamwork' management approach and breaks down divisions.
>
> (AMA 1992, p. 52)

The focus in QA is on the internal systems and processes of the organisation in ensuring that specified requirements are met. Although formally QA is defined in terms of BS 5750/ISO 9000 certification, a broader view can be taken which sees the principles of QA as representing a 'model' of effective management — identify needs, set objectives and targets, organise services to achieve targets, monitor and evaluate performance. Such a perspective places the focus on the broader structures and systems of the authority. Indeed, the 'Quality Assurance bandwagon' (Centre for Public Services, 1992) is producing something of a revival of interest in 'rational' approaches to service planning and management. Increasingly, authorities are developing strategic planning processes and linking performance review to defined objectives and targets. Correspondingly, research and information activities become more important particularly in relation to needs assessment and service evaluation which require a new focus on obtaining the views of the public.

Organisational structures and management processes also come under scrutiny in a broader QA approach beyond the consideration of BS 5750 certification. A number of questions arise concerning *all* aspects of service organisation: managerial, political and inter-organisational. To what extent can quality be assured through contracts with external service providers? What arrangements are required to 'enable' other agents to provide and promote quality services and for joint working with such agents? What are the implications of establishing an 'internal market' for the achievement of quality? To what extent is the devolution of power and responsibility necessary to assure quality services? Are decentralised structures a pre-requisite for the achievement of quality? What are the requirements for quality in the 'service relationship', at the interface between the authority and its 'customers'? What changes to political structures and processes are required? These issues relating to service planning and management and political processes are considered in subsequent chapters of this book.

Criticisms of QA tend to focus on BS 5750, its 'bureaucratic' nature and the expense of certification. Moreover, its relevance is seen as largely restricted to the more 'technical' services (or components of services) where quantifiable standards can be specified. It is seen as largely inappropriate to circumstances where quality 'depends upon people and their commitment.' (Walsh, 1992, p. 4). However, a broader QA perspective would advocate the pursuit of formal certification *where appropriate* within the context of less formal approaches. For example, in a social services context, BS 5750 might be appropriate to specific service delivery systems (e.g. residential homes, 'meals on wheels') but many aspects of the service which embody personal interaction (e.g. social work, child welfare) will require a different approach to setting standards and assuring their achievement (e.g. Codes of Practice).

A QA approach can be seen as advantageous in promoting the devolution of responsibility to, and involvement of, front-line staff, thereby enhancing the potential for 'keeping the customers happy'. (AMA, 1992, p. 52). The focus on explicit standards can also be seen as enhancing 'consumer power' (Pollitt, 1990); standards do not have to be simple quantifiable measures so long as performance can be meaningfully assessed against them. Nevertheless, even when broadly conceived, QA can be seen as having limitations as a means to achieve quality. These limitations are addressed by 'Total Quality Management' (TQM).

TQM represents a development of QA to incorporate three requirements. First, that the achievement of quality requires a commitment throughout the *whole organisation* to certain ways of thinking and working. Second, that the commitment to ensuring 'customer satisfaction' must incorporate *internal as well as external customers*; the production of a service is seen to involve a chain of activities each with a 'provider/customer' interface at which customer satisfaction must be achieved. Third, the commitment to continuous quality improvement must be embedded in the *culture* of the organisation which should be shared by all members.

It should be recognised that there is no 'hard and fast' distinction between QA and TQM. Approaches to achieving quality can be seen as representing a continuum from QC systems, through a BS 5750-based QA system, to more comprehensive QA approaches, which 'shade' into TQM. This point is made by Bone (1992, p. 9.3):

> The cultural and managerial changes implicit in the comprehensive introduction of modern QA into a public authority would be no less than for a bona-fide TQM strategy. But for a TQM strategy such changes would be explicit, and perhaps the differences lie more in the philosophy that is driving the changes.

Consequently, the distinctiveness of TQM derives from its emphasis on the 'informal' aspects of service organisation — the 'soft Ss' of staff, shared values and style. The crucial issue to TQM is the achievement of explicit change throughout the organisation (Foster and Whittle, 1989). A true TQM strategy would involve the whole authority, with strong leadership 'from the top', within a framework of politically-defined objectives and priorities, explicitly-defined 'mission' and 'core values', training programmes to develop the required value commitments among all staff, measures to achieve the participation of all staff in the development of better services (e.g. Quality Circles) and measures to involve the public in processes of service planning and delivery (e.g. Quality Audits).

In a sense, TQM can be seen as extending the scope for analysis from the more visible systems and techniques to the underlying 'social relations' of the organisation: the distribution of power and the way control over employees and their work is exercised. This provides a basis for potential concern about the implications of TQM approaches in local government. We have seen how the devolution of responsibility and the attendant development of 'control by results' through contracts and performance appraisal implies the individualisation of relations between employer and employee. Hoggett (1991, p. 251) refers to this trend as the 'liberalisation of organisational authority' and argues that it produces a heavy reliance on 'the power of socialisation processes to regulate behaviour.' This trend is strengthened by TQM's focus on internal customers, which implies an extension of internal markets and contractual relations. According to the Centre for Public Services (1992, p. 29) 'TQM is becoming for the public sector a method for linking strategies aimed at achieving quality to a broader industrial relations approach' and has been criticised as representing a means for introducing changes to such relations 'through the back door'.

Pollitt (1990, p. 449) questions the validity of the assumption of 'cultural consensus' to public service contexts. The question arises: to what extent does this new emphasis on the 'quality culture' genuinely presage empowerment and participation for employees and a new consensual organisational politics? Alternatively, to what extent does it represent a new form of control over the labour process, a new regime for the exercise of organisational power, of a kind that 'insinuate themselves upon our better nature' (Hoggett, op cit). It is necessary to recognise the dual motivation for the pursuit of quality: better services for the public and reduced costs (cf. Feigenbaum, 1988). Pollitt (op cit, p. 444) argues that there is some evidence of priority being given to cost saving; those concerned for the interests of employees may, therefore, legitimately ask 'if quality is another cover for increased productivity.' (Bewsher, 1990).

Conclusion

I have argued for a *pluralistic* approach to quality in local government. Pluralism is appropriate because of the range of different service contexts — from repairing roads to providing social care to promoting better 'Health for All', services to 'external' customers and support services to 'internal' customers. It is appropriate because of the range of interests, or stakeholders, in services — customers, interest groups, front-line professionals and managers, trade unions, and elected members. Pluralism is required in the definition of quality — conformance to specification, satisfying the customer, achieving a broader purpose are all relevant to varying degrees in different circumstances. Pluralism is required in the assessment of quality, with measures relating to service effectiveness, relationship and organisation; involving measurable standards where possible in terms of both impacts and procedures, but also subjective, qualitative assessment; and incorporating the views of all interests — 'customers', interest groups, professionals, elected members.

What is required is real commitment and concrete measures to give people more power, both as individuals and on a collective basis, to influence the nature of local government services and activities. What are also required are concrete measures to give the 'front-line' workers, who have such an important influence on service quality, a greater say in decisions which affect their services, and greater responsibility and *capability* to provide a service which they and their 'customers' value. Moreover, the role of elected members should be recognised in representing the plurality of interests in their localities.

The achievement of quality must be based on the development of sound quality systems which are appropriate to the particular service in question. Consequently, a strategy to build in quality is founded upon a 'bottom-up' approach, starting with specific elements of a service, assessing them in terms of effectiveness, relationship and organisation elements, defining the criteria which can be used to measure quality, and identifying what needs to be done to achieve success on these criteria. However, such an approach should be developed within a framework of strategic direction based upon politically-defined purpose, role and values. There is indeed a need for leadership from the top to generate commitment to 'core values' — defining what the authority is seeking to achieve, providing the best possible service to those who use and need them (internally as well as externally), 'listening to' the views of the customer/public, getting things right first time, every time, etc. Such core values will be accommodated within rather different cultures in different service departments, or even units within departments, and it is important to recognise cultural diversity around these core values and commitments.

Local authorities have discretion to choose approaches to quality which are consistent with local political circumstances and their perceived mission and role. However, they face pressures from central government policies and legislation, within the framework of the Citizen's Charter, which induce them to take the 'consumerist/enabling' road — 'government by contract', to use Hoggett's (1991) term. Thus, Isaac-Henry and Painter (1991, p. 73) refer to:

> a manipulative process, inducing local authorities to define their role in one way rather than another and to move in a specified direction, that of customer focus. Here is a covert ideological bias, allegedly acting to the detriment of the local *governmental* role.

Is the Government's commitment to quality simply part of a broader political programme for elected local government, the real agenda of which is conveniently obscured by the apparently 'neutral' facade of the quality imperative — to reduce the cost of local services, to increase productivity and undermine the power of the public sector trade unions, to reduce the power and role of elected local authorities by 'opt out' provisions, to undermine the scope for authorities to provide a power base for interests structured around collective welfare provision and, by replacing local *government* with local *governance*, to mould a new local politics centred around local business interests? (cf. Cochrane, 1991).

Quality is certainly a normative, 'political' issue. Opposed to the Government's view, those who advocate the 'collective citizenship' perspective on quality are, in effect, arguing for an enhanced role for local government, representing *all* interests in localities, and having increased powers of general competence (e.g. Stewart and Stoker, 1988). The debate about quality encapsulates a debate about the legitimate and desirable purpose and role of local government in our society. It is a debate which extends beyond 'technical' issues; it is also a political debate and, in part, an ideological one. In this sense, it is likely to be perenially controversial.

References

ACC (1992) *Signposts to Quality — Local Authority Case Studies*, Association of County Councils with other Local Authority Associations, Association of Metropolitan Authorities, London.

AMA (1992) *Quality Services — An Introduction to Quality Assurance for Local Authorities*, Association of Metropolitan Authorities, London.

Atkinson, P. E. (1990) *Creating Culture Change: The Key to Successful Total Quality Management*, IFS Publications, Bedford.

Audit Commission (1988) *The Competitive Council*, Management Paper No. 1, Audit Commission, London.

Audit Commission (undated) *The Citizen's Charter — Local Authority Performance Indicators*, Audit Commission, London.

Barrett, S. and McMahon, L. (1990) Public management in uncertainty: a micro political perspective of the health service in the United Kingdom, *Policy and Politics*, Vol. 18, No. 4, pp. 257–68.

Berry, L. (1988) The rhetoric of consumerism and the exclusion of community, *Community Development Journal*, Vol. 23, No. 4, pp. 266–72.

Bewsher, J. (1990) Quality means a bigger menu, *Local Government Chronicle*, 2 November, 1990, p. 18.

Bone, C. (1992) *Modern Quality Management Manual*, Local Government Management Manuals, Longman, Harlow.

British Quality Association (1992) *Guidance on the Interpretation of BS 5750, Part 2 (1988) with Reference to Social Care Agencies*, British Quality Association, London.

Casson, S. and Humphrey, N. (1992) Quality assurance in social care — applying BS 5750 to the care of elderly people, in Blackman, T. (ed.) *Research for Policy*, Proceedings of the 1992 Annual Conference of the Local Authorities Research and Intelligence Association, Newcastle City Council, Newcastle.

Centre for Public Services (1992) *A Strategy for Quality*, Centre for Public Services, Sheffield.

Cochrane, A. (1991) The changing state of local government — restructuring for the 1990s, *Public Administration*, Vol. 69, No. 3 pp. 281–302.

Donabedian, A. (1980) *Explorations in Quality Assessment and Monitoring: Vol 1 The Definition of Quality and Approaches to its Assessment*, Health and Administration Press, Ann Arbor.

Edgar, D. (1991) Are you being served? *Marxism Today*, May, p. 28.

Feigenbaum, A. V. (1988) Total quality developments into the 1990s — an international perspective, in Chase R. L. (ed.) *Total Quality Management*, IFS Publications, pp. 3–9.

Flynn, N. (1990) *Public Sector Management*, Harvester Wheatsheaf, Hemel Hempstead.

Foster, M. and Whittle, S. (1989) The quality management maze, *Total Quality Management*, Vol. 1, No. 3, pp. 143–8.

Gaster, L. (1991a) Quality and decentralisation — are they connected?, *Policy and Politics*, Vol. 19, No. 4, pp. 257–67.

Gaster, L. (1991b) *Quality at the Front Line*, School for Advanced Urban Studies, University of Bristol.

Hambleton, R. (1988) Consumerism, decentralization and local democracy, *Public Administration*, Vol. 66, No. 2, pp. 125–47.

Hambleton, R. (1991) Beyond customer care, *Going Local*, Spring, pp. 18–20.

Hambleton, R. and Hoggett, P. (1990) *Beyond Excellence — Quality Local Government in the 1990s*, Working Paper No. 85, SAUS, University of Bristol.

HMSO (1991a) *The Citizen's Charter — Raising the Standard*, Cm 1599, HMSO, London.

HMSO, (1991b) *Competing for Quality — Buying Better Public Services*, Cm 1730, HM Treasury, London.

Hoggett, P. (1991) A new management in the public sector, *Policy and Politics*, Vol. 19, No. 4, pp. 243–56.

Isaac-Henry, K. and Painter, C. (1991) The management challenge in local government — emerging themes and trends, *Local Government Studies*, Vol. 17, No. 3, pp. 69–90.

Jessome, P. (1988) The application of total quality to a hospital setting, in Chase R. L. (ed.) *Total Quality Management*, IFS Publications, pp. 175–80.

Labour Party, (1991a) *Opportunity, Quality, Accountability — The Better Way for Local Government*, Labour Party, London.

Labour Party, (1991b) *The Quality Commission — A Consultation Paper*, Labour Party Policy Directorate, London.

Legrand, J. and Robinson, R. (1984) *The Economics of Social*

Problems — The Market Versus the State, Macmillan, London.

Levacic, R. (1987) *Economic Policy-Making — Its Theory and Practice*, Wheatsheaf, Sussex.

Mather, G. (1991) Serving you rights, *Marxism Today*, May, p. 29.

Mulgan, G. (1991) Power to the public, *Marxism Today*, May, pp. 14–19.

Pfeffer, N. and Coote, A. (1991) *Is quality good for you?* Social Policy Paper No. 5, Institute for Public Policy Research, London.

Pollitt, C. (1987) Performance measurement and the consumer: hijacking a bandwagon?, in *Performance Measurement and the Consumer*, National Consumer Council, London, pp. 42–55.

Pollitt, C. (1990) Doing business in the temple? Managers and quality assurance in the public services, *Public Administration*, Vol. 68, No. 4, pp. 435–52.

Rhodes, R. A. W. (1987) Developing the public service orientation, *Local Government Studies*, Vol. 13, No. 3, pp. 63–73.

Stewart, J. and Clarke, M. (1987) The public service orientation — issues and dilemmas, *Public Administration*, Vol. 65, No. 2, pp. 161–77.

Stewart, J. and Stoker, G. (1988) *From Local Administration to Community Government*, Fabian Research Series 351, Fabian Society, London.

Stewart, J. and Walsh, K. (1989) *The Search for Quality*, Local Government Training Board, Luton.

Walsh, K. (1991) Quality and public services, *Public Administration*, Vol. 69, No. 4, pp. 503–14.

Walsh, K. (1992) Quality, contracts and care, *Contracting In or Out?*, Spring 1992, p. 4.

3 Quality, decentralisation and devolution

Lucy Gaster

Introduction

If 'quality' is the buzz-word for the 1990s, then it might be said that 'decentralisation' was the word of the 1980s. Too often in local government, it seems as if big 'new' ideas have to supersede the old ones, with a terrible loss of knowledge and experience, and the devaluation of the work and commitment put into making the previous idea work. So the aim of this chapter is to identify whether, where and how those past developments can inform the next round.

The proposition to be examined is that, in at least some areas of local government activity, a decentralised, devolved service is likely to improve the service quality to the consumer and community. In other words, the organisational structures produced through a process of decentralisation, and the policies and processes of devolving power and decision making have the potential to provide a pre-eminently suitable framework for improving the quality of services. It is suggested that this proposition applies, whether services are being provided directly or through contractual arrangements.

It is important to stress that such a proposition is not meant to imply either that decentralisation and devolution are a panacea, nor that they are *sine qua non* for quality developments. As will be seen from the discussion below, both concepts need to be examined carefully, both for their potential benefits and for their possible disadvantages, in the light of the objectives to be achieved. They need to be viewed as two out of a range of possible options, bearing in mind the issues raised elsewhere in this book such as the need for an appropriate organisational culture (chapter 7) and developments towards the 'enabling' authority (chapter 4).

The framework for understanding quality introduced in chapter two suggests that two important dimensions need to be considered. These are how quality is defined; and who the key 'stakeholders' are. In addition, the introduction and improvement of service quality depends on an appropriate organisational environment, almost inevitably involving processes of organisational change. These are the starting points for the analysis in this chapter.

First, in defining quality we need to distinguish between technical, 'fitness for purpose' characteristics and non-technical characteristics such as the service relationship and the service environment. These distinctions are highly relevant to the analysis both of potential dangers and of what can be achieved through decentralisation and devolution. Perhaps the key element of this definition is that a high quality service is one that meets needs. It is the definition of these needs — individual and collective — based on knowledge, understanding and negotiation, that are the key factors in determining the 'purpose' for which the service must be 'fit'. At the same time, especially for those services where there is little choice for the user, either because they are 'universal' (generally environmental) services or because consumers are bound, through statute or tenure for example, to receive them, the mode and environment for delivery are of great significance. This means that issues like accessibility and equity, choice (of options if not of the service itself) and accountability, sensitivity, timeliness and responsiveness are all vital elements in the kind of 'quality' we are discussing here. And while the individual characteristics of each service will necessarily mean that the exact definition of 'technical' quality is bound to vary, it is these sorts of characteristics — the non-technical and environmental — which will be common to many services. Their significance for this discussion is that they will also be intertwined both with their location — where they are delivered — and with how and by whom decisions are made.

Second, for any service there will be a range of key players who will have a greater or lesser influence in defining the organisation's value base, deciding service objectives, standards and targets, delivering and receiving the service, monitoring and evaluating it. In this chapter the focus is on two sets of these players — the direct service providers, and the direct (users and consumers) and indirect (non-users, referrers, community) service receivers. Apart from financial resources, the front-line staff are, in a service industry, probably the most important 'input' into the quality process. The importance of individual and collective service 'users' in defining need has already been outlined above. So, while policy makers at all levels have an important role in relation to decentralisation and quality, and politicians and senior managers are equally crucial in determining the extent of managerial and political devolution, it is on the interaction at the front line that this chapter concentrates.

In addition, new concepts often require new ways of working. Past rules and procedures, 'custom and practice', attitudes and behaviour may be totally inappropriate for the implementation of any policy that is to be more than just a structural change — a shift of the famous deck chairs.

While decentralisation as defined here does not necessarily require more than just such a shift, there would be little point in pursuing what is always a major upheaval if some benefits, in the form of at least a more efficient and, preferably, a more responsive service, were not intended to be the result. Although decentralisation has often been introduced on the assumption that structural change alone will bring the benefits being sought, it is clear from subsequent analysis that more is required: leadership and staff commitment; changed working practices — including, most importantly, devolved decision making — and new relationships with the public are just as necessary. And these, the reader will note, are exactly the ingredients of organisational change needed for the effective introduction of quality programmes, whatever model is chosen.

So, at the very least, there is much in common between quality, decentralisation and devolved decision making. All require changes in organisational style and culture, all emphasise the interaction between front-line staff and public. On the other hand, there is not necessarily a causal relationship: decentralisation will not inevitably lead to improved service quality, and there are some circumstances where it certainly will not. (For an initial analysis of these connections, see Gaster, 1991a.) So different aspects of decentralisation and devolution need to be looked at in more detail. What are they intended to achieve, what forms do they take, what are their advantages and disadvantages as potential agents in the development of a quality service?

In this chapter we look, in turn, at decentralisation and devolution, based on recent research and experience by the author and other writers. Policy and management objectives, implied and explicit, are examined, and quality-related factors — relating mainly, as explained above, to such non-technical and environmental dimensions of quality as accessibility, responsiveness and choice — are tested. Is quality likely to be improved through decentralisation and devolution, or are there counter-balancing difficulties and disadvantages? In conclusion we attempt to draw together the threads of the analysis, returning to the central question of service quality and assessing how far decentralisation and devolution are relevant concepts for the local government manager.

Decentralisation

If managers wishing to improve the quality of their services are to draw on ideas about decentralisation and devolution, it is obviously necessary to have a common understanding of what these terms might mean in the context of British local government, both in theory and in practice. Certainly, both terms can be variously interpreted, if only because their currency extends far beyond local government and into the national and international political arenas.

So let us exclude some uses of these terms. First, although the European Community idea of 'subsidiarity' may be useful insofar as it conveys the notion of pushing decision making down to the lowest level, this version of decentralisation, that is, the division of powers between the Community and member countries will not be considered here. Nor shall we examine the French version of decentralisation, which takes the form both of a handover of some powers by central to regional and departmental administrations and the retention of other central powers which are then subject to the process known as 'deconcentration' — the devolution of central government administrative power to locally based but centrally accountable prefects (see, for example Ashford, 1990). Nor, finally, will the process of establishing direct but 'decentralised' relationships between central government and new forms of service delivery, such as opted out schools and hospital trusts, be addressed.

Forms and Purposes of Decentralisation

Turning to the context, British local government, in which these terms will be used in this chapter, further questions of definition emerge. Decentralisation can be used as a portmanteau word for a range of characteristics — a more localised service, a more integrated service, a service where decisions are taken closer to the user, a service which is more closely accountable to the community. However, it has often been confined in practice to a much narrower interpretation: the localised, accessible service. The discussion in this chapter will take the latter definition as its starting point, moving on to look at the links between a localised and an integrated, accountable service.

Decentralisation can, therefore, be contrasted with devolution, which covers the idea of a devolved service where decisions, political and/or managerial, are taken by people lower down the management hierarchy, possibly assisted, informed, advised or made accountable by committees involving local people and local councillors.

As the 1980s progressed, and more and more local authorities developed some form of 'decentralised' service — departmental or authority-wide (Stoker, Wedgwood Oppenheim and Davies, 1988) — attempts were made to identify the main characteristics of such changes. The two questions were: what are they for, and what are they like?

At the beginning of the 1980s when the current conception of decentralisation in its portmanteau sense began to be introduced, many local Labour politicians appeared to hope that decentralisation would help achieve the political objectives of, on the one hand, making local government more popular and thereby more defensible against central government attacks, or, on the other, of empowering local people by these changes (Beuret and Stoker, 1986). In similar vein the Liberals of Tower Hamlets wanted to bring the council bureaucracy under the control of local politicians through powerful neighbourhood committees. However, objectives were in many cases neither clear nor agreed, often being the pet theory of one or two leading councillors alone; equally, even where there was a reasonable consensus about the ultimate aim, the means of getting there had rarely been discussed, agreed or made explicit (see, for example, Hoggett and Hambleton, 1987; Gaster 1991b, 1991c).

Despite these quite considerable drawbacks, the idea of neighbourhood-based services continues to attract attention and local authorities of all political complexions continue in the early 1990s to establish one-stop shops and service-led neighbourhood and area offices. Decentralisation has indeed not turned out to be a passing fad (Hoggett and Hambleton, op cit), and is increasingly entrenched, in a variety of forms, right across the local government structure.

Because different authorities and localities have different needs, different political values, different objectives, it is not surprising that no two systems are alike. While the survey by Stoker *et al.* (op cit) showed that a large number of authorities claimed that they had 'decentralised' in some sense, often just within one department, the detail of what this has meant in practice is lacking. Even more remarkable is the dearth of information about the effects of decentralisation on the rest of the organisation, especially the 'centre'. However, it would require a major — and regularly updated — national survey to document the changes and, most important, their effects on the organisation and the community. So Table 3.1 is based on information collected in the course of working relationships between decentralising authorities and the Decentralisation Research and Information Centre since 1983 and with the School for Advanced Urban Studies over about the same period. It is therefore neither systematic nor comprehensive.

Table 3.1 shows that decentralisation takes many forms and can serve a considerable range of purposes. It should be noted that this table does not attempt to portray a continuum: decentralised services may demonstrate several — or none — of these characteristics. But

Geographical coverage

- Local offices provide the main, or only point of contact for the public across the whole local authority area; or
- Local offices provide an additional point of contact targeted, as in Fife Region for example, to areas of high social need or, in rural areas, to provide physical access where public transport is inadequate and/or expensive.

Services offered

- Information and advice
- Referral to services elsewhere (enquirer goes to that service in future)
- Local 'ownership' of enquiries, with follow-up of referrals to other departments or agencies (enquirer maintains contact through the decentralised office)
- Delivery of some services at the decentralised office through peripatetic working and surgeries (generally departmental: welfare rights, housing benefit or planning — development control — but may include services provided by other organisations or, in two-tier local authority areas, by both councils)
- Delivery of a wide range of services by staff permanently based at the decentralised office
- Outreach, support for local groups, and community development based at decentralised office
- Development of local plans, service priorities and standards to meet local needs
- Forums of local workers from different services and other organisations, statutory and voluntary to identify local needs and coordinate service delivery

Democratic structures

- Tenants' committees and forums (area/neighbourhood wide or estate based)
- Residents' committees and forums
- User groups for specified services
- Management committees for local facilities
- Area committees of councillors — reporting to main service committees
- Area committees of councillors responsible for council policy at the local level, making all decisions about local services and raising corporate issues centrally

Table 3.1: Forms of decentralised service

there is one key feature common to all the different approaches: the emphasis on the role of the front-line staff as the visible boundary of the organisation, and the consequent significance of their formal and informal relationships with local consumers and residents.

Even where local offices are initially established for a fairly narrow purpose — and, whatever their formal role, they will anyway tend to be perceived as 'the Council' — as they take root and begin to respond to local circumstances and as workers in other departments and organisations begin to see the advantages of local working (to which they may well have been resistant at first) there will be a strong tendency to branch out into new areas.

The shortage of space in so many neighbourhood offices is perhaps a testimony to this trend. Initial enthusiasts, pressured by lack of interest (or positive resistance) from staff and other councillors and by the dangers of over-spending, have often been forced into a cautious mode, particularly as far as the capital costs of the initiative are concerned. If, subsequently, demands for services are more than was predicted — and they generally have been — it becomes a cause of concern, either that employees are forced to work in sub-standard conditions (and because of their good will, agree to do so), or that such offices are constrained in their ability to respond.

Decentralisation and Quality

The aspects of service quality identified earlier as particularly relevant to this discussion will now be examined in turn. How far can a decentralised, localised service improve the overall operations of a local authority along these dimensions?

Accessibility

The fundamental characteristic of a localised service must, by definition, be its geographical accessibility. An important question is, therefore, the size and nature of the area served. And there is in fact wide variation in what different authorities have termed a 'neighbourhood'. In Islington, for example, the original concept was for no office to be further away than half a mile — that is, walking distance — from the residents it was intended to serve, thereby arriving at areas with between 5,000 and 9,000 population. This size, or even smaller neighbourhoods can be found in some district councils — Harlow or Basildon for instance — while other decentralised authorities, Birmingham, Bristol or Manchester for example, have much larger areas, sometimes even as large as parliamentary constituencies.

As well as deciding whether to put offices or sub-offices into small enough areas for residents to reach on foot, decisions about the size of an area to be served appear to have been influenced by such considerations as: the number of properties one estate officer is to manage; the need to maintain enough officer 'cover' to keep the office open; perhaps the desire to have common boundaries with other services or, particularly where local democratic structures are being established alongside the bureaucratic structures, the use of ward boundaries to enable local councillors to play a maximum role.

> Locality does not prescribe in some magical way a recipe for etching or constructing all-purpose spatial boundaries: these must depend on the context of what is to be contained therein.
>
> (Gyford, 1991, p. 8)

Hambleton, Hoggett and Burns (1993, forthcoming), discussing their research findings in Tower Hamlets, point out that there is in fact something of a trade-off, at any rate in offices offering direct service delivery, between size and accessibility. Very local offices are likely to be quite small because of the need to spread officers evenly round the whole area. They thus become dependent on the local staff turning up — or on the availability of peripatetic staff who are likely to be less familiar with the area. This could mean that local people receive a less good service, either because the office has to close more frequently because of staff shortages, or because staff are trying to spread themselves too thinly, on the basis of broadened job descriptions or of goodwill. It is a difficult equation: greater accessibility could actually undermine greater reliability and comprehensiveness.

A further dimension to the issue of accessibility is whether neighbourhood boundaries should be fixed or fluid. Birmingham's 43 neighbourhood offices, depending heavily on an increasingly intricate system of information technology, offer a service to anyone coming to them, wherever they live (including outside the city boundaries). This is probably unusual: the problems of 'co-terminosity' often loom large for councils examining possibilities for more co-ordinated local delivery of services (see, for example, Gaster and Rivers, 1991), where boundaries can seem almost immutable!

Returning to Islington, for example, a major effect was put into re-aligning all internal service boundaries to be co-terminous (and, later on, the police and health authorities did the same). However, when the first of the offices opened in 1985 the policy was established that, apart from the right to make payments to the Council in any of the twenty-four offices, residents could only receive service from 'their' local office. So people on their first visit were often redirected to another office, resulting in a considerable amount of frustration and, sometimes, anger.

Responsiveness and choice

Traditional paternalistic bureaucracy (Local Government Management Board, 1991), with its attendant characteristics of rule-bound inflexibility and lack of choice will not necessarily be changed simply by a physical relocation of some services out of the town hall, but it is ironic that increased accessibility might actually limit choice.

The placing of council offices to make them more accessible to local residents carries with it assumptions that such offices will:

- *be less intimidating than traditional offices*
- *enable positive relationships to be built up between service providers and users*
- *for the break down of the traditional professional and departmental barriers that have tended to lead people to deny rather than to take responsibility; this break down would/should lead to a more integrated service, better able to respond holistically to local individual and community issues*
- *build up knowledge and understanding of local needs*
- *respond to local needs more flexibly and appropriately.*

If all this actually happens, then it is likely that each office will develop differently, taking on different styles and characteristics. This is because the recognition and analysis of different local needs, through the responsiveness explicitly required at local level, is almost bound to produce different service patterns. Such differences are likely to be reinforced and perhaps exaggerated, partly through the use of the street level bureaucratic mechanisms identified by Lipsky (1980), partly by explicit levels of delegated authority (a question to which we shall return below). However, such differences could produce disadvantages. Are people needing or simply preferring a service provided elsewhere, not within their own areas, to be denied it on the grounds of bureaucratically determined boundaries?

Local accountability and equal opportunities

A further issue, partly related to the question of delegated authority, partly to localisation, is that of accountability, both to individual consumers and to local residents. As part of the process of 'empowerment', many authorities in the 1980s established formal committees and forums as a channel for local views to supplement the democratic processes carried out through elected councillors. Eligibility for membership of these committees, whether by invitation or on a representative basis, was generally confined to people living in the designated area.

As a voice and channel of communication between the council and the people, such mechanisms have been quite effective. They are instructive for officers, who have perhaps never had to account for their actions before, to learn how they are seen through service consumers' eyes. They can stimulate officers and elected members to develop more imaginative approaches to public consultation and participation. They can also provide an opportunity, often for the first time, not only for people to enter the democratic process but also to gain the courage to speak about their concerns in public. They can demonstrate the council's commitment to an area or neighbourhood and to the democratic process. And they can provide an arena for discussing and negotiating about detailed service priorities and quality.

They do, however, have a major limitation. Geographical restriction of participation to a particular neighbourhood risks weakening the voice and power of minorities of all kinds. Yet, as is stressed in the Local Government Management Board's useful publication 'Quality and Equality' (1991, op cit), a vital dimension of quality services is the ability to respond to the needs of different groups within society.

Islington Council tried to redress the balance by requiring each neighbourhood forum to include people from 'under-represented groups' — blacks and ethnic minorities, old people, young people, people with disabilities, women looking after someone at home, for example. Hambleton *et al.* (1993, op cit) found that this has not proved a very effective method of widening the base of accountability. While the strength of individual, authoritative voices at local discussions, representing a point a view if not a particular identifiable group of people, should not be underestimated, council-wide forums, enabling people from or representing particular groups to speak directly to the council, are likely to give more power to such groups. Many councils have encouraged and supported such initiatives (Taylor, 1991).

What has to be avoided is an over-dependence on just one mechanism for local consultation and participation, particularly if it is exclusively neighbourhood-based. The local factor will often be appropriate — but should not be exclusively relied on.

Informal accountability

Formal mechanisms are not the only way to increase local accountability. Equally important is the informal accountability — responding to need and taking personal responsibility — built up through day-to-day contact at the local level.

Even those staff who, perhaps against their will, have been required to work in neighbourhood offices, who may be reluctant to take on new ways of relating to the public, may well find themselves changing their behaviour as they find that, through better knowledge of their consumers, community and local area, doing something quickly, sensitively and well brings a positive response from the public. Of course, far more needs to be done to help people make permanent changes in their ways of working, but the 'accountability through visibility' brought about simply by being local and personally accessible — and, in open plan offices such as those built or converted by many decentralising authorities, literally visible — should not be discounted.

Nevertheless, it is not safe to assume that simply putting people into locally based offices will bring its own reward. It is perfectly possible to be local and inaccessible and unaccountable. In many traditional housing area offices, for example, the ethos has been that the least valued function is that of reception, while promotion depends on — or brings the reward of — distance from the front line. Surprisingly long hierarchies, even in very small offices, can often be found as a result.

Equally, good will and commitment from locally based staff are not enough. The 'charm-school' approach can lead to disappointment. Because of the complexity of the services they offer, local 'technical' quality of service will only be effective through the cooperation and back-up of the rest of the organisation. So those at the edge of the organisation may have excellent relations with the public — providing a high quality 'non-technical' service — but little influence on what goes on inside the organisation itself, leading to frustration and disappointment not only for local residents, who may have been led to expect great things of the new local offices, but also for local staff.

This raises questions both of integration (discussed in the next section) and local control (discussed in the context of 'devolution').

An Holistic Service Approach?

Annual reports from local authorities, questionnaires designed to find out what people think of their services, and actual service design, tend all too often to symbolise the following relationship with the public: we provide these services, if you can find out what they are, use them if you are eligible or can find your way round the system, but don't have complicated needs which do not fit what we have on offer! The user, in other words, has to fit the service, not vice versa.

While one aim of decentralisation has generally been to increase accessibility of services, another has been to provide that access through a single access point so that, at the very minimum, people would not be physically passed round the system. Moving on from that minimum, a further aim would be to respond not to problems, but to people, and to help identify and then obtain access to the most appropriate combination of services — to 'look behind the problem', as is stressed in the induction training of Birmingham neighbourhood office workers. In other words, one aim of decentralisation was to create a more integrated, less compartmentalised and therefore a 'better' service to meet local individual and collective needs: to 'break down the barriers'.

Integration can be achieved in several different ways, but it generally has to be purposefully developed, not left to chance and the goodwill and enthusiasm of individuals. Several ways exist of developing the 'seamless whole' suggested by the idea of 'community government' (Hambleton, Stewart and Taylor, 1991). These include:

- *flexible job descriptions (generic working)*
- *working as part of a team*
- *joint working in relation to specific issues (e.g. homelessness, pre-school children and so on) — across divisions and departments*
- *joint service planning and evaluation*
- *working across organisational boundaries, developing 'partnerships'.*

Generic and flexible working

The division of tasks in some areas of local government has long tended to promote a vary narrow view of what work should or should not be undertaken. During the 1970s and 1980s, the concept of a broadly trained worker with perhaps one or two specialist areas of knowledge developed quite substantially, for example in some decentralised housing departments and in social services.

Generic working of this kind could, of course, be introduced into any service structure. Its advantages in a decentralised context are several. First on grounds of efficiency and economy, it is difficult in a small, localised office, where there is fluctuating and unpredictable demand for the whole range of services provided by the council(s), to justify the retention of a great number of people with different specialisms. It therefore becomes practical and logical that individual staff widen their range of ability and experience so that better use can be made of their time.

If this were the only justification of generic working, it might be better argued that larger offices, where specialisms could be retained, would be even more efficient. An argument relating to service quality, however, is that not only can generic working be grounded in efficiency as defined by the Audit Commission (i.e. maximum outputs for minimum inputs), it is also more efficient in the everyday sense of the word, with the benefit going mainly to the consumer (but thereby to the organisation too). This benefit is that, rather than being referred to several people, who do not necessarily know exactly what the others do and may not make accurate referrals, they see one person only: there is then a much better chance of the consumer's needs seen as a whole, leading to a more sensitive and appropriate response. At the same time, members of the same team can cover for each other, thus ensuring better continuity of service, in itself another important element of quality.

What often seems to happen in practice — and to the extent that those establishing local offices hoped for this result, they were right — is that, even where staff have been appointed on traditional job descriptions, they take on tasks to help both their colleagues and the public, with whom they are in much closer contact than ever before. This is highly laudable, naturally, but it is uncontrolled, unpredictable and dependent on good will. If one attribute of a quality service is reliability — knowing what to expect and fulfilling that expectation — then such haphazard development of generic working will not be effective in the long run.

It is also a form of exploitation of the workforce. If there is no formal recognition or support (e.g. through training, regrading and so on) the results are likely to be both the discrediting of the concept and the loss, through burn-out, diminished job satisfaction and departure, of those people most valuable to the service. So it is important both to identify the service areas where some form of generic working is appropriate and then to ensure that training and staff development, together with specialist back-up, systematically support staff in those jobs.

However, generic working is only one form of service integration. It is perhaps in those other forms of integrated service listed above that decentralisation can play the greatest part.

Teamwork and Joint Work

One of the anxieties experienced by managers of decentralised offices concerns those members of staff who are 'loners', who do not want to be part of a team and who will make no effort to overcome their reluctance. There are, no doubt, a series of reasons why this should be so, including the possibility that, for these people (who have often been relocated against their will), it is a form of resistance to the new order, as well as a protection of their individual styles and content of work. The direct evidence from staff working in decentralised offices studies by the author and her colleagues suggest that teams are more effective than individuals: staff can learn from each other, give mutual support and cover, and bring a total approach to problem-solving, all of which seem likely to enhance the quality of the service.

Similarly, the potential for people from different teams and disciplines to work across traditional boundaries is much greater when contact and communication is simple and direct, backed by trust built up from past experience. All this, especially the mutual trust that is the essential foundation for effective team working, takes time to develop — and has to be built not just by faith but by positive action and leadership. Team-building activities, formal and informal, multi-disciplinary project groups, joint training and policy development, peer discussion and away-days for identifying issues and programmes, all play their part.

Research in Harlow and in Birmingham neighbourhood offices (Gaster, 1991b, 1991c, op cit) shows that, even if the positive effects of teamwork and joint working cannot be conclusively demonstrated, bad staff working relationships have a negative effect both on staff morale (and therefore commitment to the job) and on the ability to offer a comprehensive, user-friendly service.

Working Across Boundaries

Factors inhibiting cooperation have been well described elsewhere (e.g. Webb, 1991). Performance indicators, used as a tool of control and regulation, also tend to pin people down into narrow, target-fulfilling and non-risk taking habits (Carter, 1991, op cit). Can decentralised services encourage wider co-operation and collaboration with other organisations, statutory, voluntary and community?

The question is important, not only for the general and obvious reason that it is more helpful for the public if different service providers can work together — and not duplicate their efforts unnecessarily — but also because, in the era of compulsory competitive tendering and the mixed provision of Community Care, such joint working will be an increasing necessity for local government.

The issue of geographical boundaries, referred to earlier in the discussion of accessibility and choice, is important but not insuperable. Some organisations will have large and/or variable catchment areas, some will be highly centralised, others will favour a local approach. Relationships are likely to exist at different levels and to be mutually reinforcing, as a recent study of neighbourhood centres run by a large voluntary organisation in Liverpool shows (Gaster, 1992, forthcoming): members of the same organisation sit on city-wide planning committees at the same time as local staff work with local health visitors, social workers, police and the churches to provide an integrated service for their users and community, thus linking local knowledge with strategic planning.

Client-contractor co-operation at local level has been developed in

Harlow. 'Community inspectors', located in the neighbourhood offices, are employed by the client services department to monitor non-building work contracts (street cleansing, grounds maintenance and so on). They have proved very effective, not only in giving local people access to normally inaccessible and unresponsive services, but in creating local relationships with the contract services.

So the existence of local offices, with people in them who are committed to and knowledgeable about 'their' area, makes overall improvement — meeting local needs more exactly, better co-ordination — in the planning and delivery of some services possible. However, like all the forms of integration mentioned in this section, it requires considerable organisational and personal commitment to make it work. It also requires at least some measure of devolved power. This is discussed in the next section.

Devolution

'Devolution' requires some definition. Its general meaning is to pass down the power of making decisions to a level lower than that formally accountable through the processes of representative democracy or appointment, but, like decentralisation, the word has special connotations which are not the subject of this discussion. It has, in particular, a special meaning in Scotland.

Rationale for devolved decision making

In this chapter, and relating in particular to the local government setting, three aspects of the concept of devolution will be identified and inspected for their potential relationship to service quality. These are:

- *devolved political power*
- *devolved managerial power*
- *devolved financial power.*

It can be argued that all three types of devolved power are interdependent. However, in the early days of decentralisation, the idea of empowering local people by devolving power through different forms of 'participative democracy' (area committees of local tenants, neighbourhood forums of residents, user or management groups for local facilities) was not accompanied by devolved decision making within the bureaucracy. Indeed, experiments with some forms of devolved decision making, especially financial 'cost centres' and 'responsibility centres', began their lives in the public sector in counties such as Berkshire and Cambridgeshire, which were not decentralised in the sense used in this chapter. Cost centres represent 'accounts for collecting data on inputs and outputs at the lowest distinct level of activity

. . .', and responsibility centres 'provide the basis for budgetary control by clearly defining the area of responsibility of individual managers' (Jones and Pendlebury, 1988, pp. 25–6). The stimulus for such devolution was more the notion of economy and efficiency, borrowing standard financial control methods from the private sector rather than the ideals of accountability and empowerment driving political devolution.

Accountability — taking responsibility and explaining your decisions to those to whom you are (or feel) responsible — is not, of course, a new concept. In the past the emphasis tended to be on defending actions and decisions. Now it can allow those closest to the front line to respond to needs more effectively and immediately. Devolved power can bring resources and needs more closely in line with each other: local managers can take into account local conditions, negotiate local priorities and respond accordingly, developing a sense of ownership and commitment in the process. In the long run, devolved decision-making could within a clear policy framework, encourage experimentation and innovation without the fear of retribution normal in a hierarchical, non-risk-taking culture.

At the same time, devolving decision-making inevitably implies high levels of trust in the budget-holders and decision-makers. Senior managers must not only have confidence in front-line managers, they must, as a logical consequence, back up and support decisions which they themselves might not have taken. They must restrain themselves from continually checking what has been done, but not stand so far back that local managers feel isolated and unsupported. It is a very hard balance to keep!

Devolution of Political Power

Earlier in this chapter, in the discussion of the locality-based approach, we looked briefly at the issue of local accountability in terms of local choice and representation. Here the question of power arises.

If political power is to be devolved effectively and visibly, clear policies are needed:

- *are local committees and groups promoted and encouraged for the purpose of having a real effect on councillors' decisions? Are they capable of making decisions, giving advice, receiving and responding to consultation papers or are they merely tokenistic gestures towards 'empowerment'?*
- *how much weight is given to their views?*
- *what support are they given to ensure their effectiveness – community development, resources, training and advice?*
- *what are they excluded from discussing?*

- *what is their access to detailed information about local services (priorities and centrally set targets, staffing matters, resources)?*
- *how clear is the policy and value framework within which they are operating?*

In relation to service quality, the last three questions are perhaps the most important. At the beginning of this chapter (and in chapter two), the framework for understanding quality was set out. A crucial element is, we argued, the role of consumers and citizens, individually and, in the present context, collectively. In theory, the devolution of political power, whether to localities or to wider special interest forums, ought to be an enormous help in developing the appropriate context for collectively discussing quality.

A major difficulty arises, therefore, if key issues of service content and priorities, or the nature and numbers of staff, are excluded from discussion. Yet it is precisely these issues which are often the most difficult to get onto the agenda. 'Professionalism' is a useful cloak for preventing discussion — the idea that you can only legitimately be assessed by your peers (Pollitt, 1990) — which, added to traditional public sector defensiveness and secrecy, can make it very hard for local people to get 'inside' the machine.

Yet job descriptions are not state secrets, neither are performance measures. And a local forum, rather than the cold publication of figures recommended by the various citizen's charters published in 1991–2, provide the opportunity for explanation, discussion and review of local priorities. This is not available through individualistic complaints procedures or consumer surveys.

Devolved Managerial Power

The credibility of devolved political power must, as implied above, rest on the response of the council and of its representatives, in this case the local managers. Although the existence of forums and other means of influencing the council can demonstrate good intentions, tangible results are needed if cynicism and non-involvement are to be avoided.

Much will depend on elected councillors' response. But the role of local managers in establishing and maintaining a positive relationship is important: and although much can be achieved by force of personality, personal commitment, and the day-to-day responsiveness of the local office, it is, as Paul Hoggett suggests, 'the ability to create locally-specific policies or to interpret and adapt corporate policies to local requirements' that in the long run is likely to encourage consumer involvement:

> Without managerial devolution there really was very little point in
> users becoming involved in service delivery matters except as com-
> plainants and antagonists, but once real power over decisions and
> resources had been located at the point of delivery, user-based forms
> of local democracy became a more tangible possibility.
>
> (Hoggett, 1991, p. 254)

The 'loose-tight' organisational form in the private sector appeared
to be a factor in the success of America's best-run companies, according to Peters and Waterman (1982, chapter 12). It encourages, they
argued, autonomy, innovation, excitement and hence quality (with a
bottom line) — but it is also unusual, because most companies do not
trust their employees enough to allow the necessary levels of relative
independence.

Kastelein (1987) and his colleagues have since the early 1960s,
been auditing and analysing public and private sector organisations in
Holland in terms of the relationship between 'the centre' and individual units of production. They distinguish between organisations where
the centre exercises considerable control from a variety of central
points, focusing on processes and throughput; and those where, within
centrally set or negotiated targets, the units take responsibility for and
are judged by their results. They suggest that the latter are more likely
to be able to meet needs, to be more productive and to involve consumers and communities more effectively, but they also chart a whole
range of conditions that need to be fulfilled before such a 'results-
responsible' organisation can fully develop. Some of these are technical (the availability of appropriate information technology and monitoring systems, for example), but others are 'human' factors — the
motivation of support staff the doubts of middle management, the exist-
ance of long hierarchies, and the presence of a leader with charisma
(Burger and Kastelein, 1990, p. 10). It is difficult to point to public
sector organisations in the UK where these conditions are yet fulfilled.

Budgetary devolution

Many of the same factors apply to the issue of devolved budgets. As
already mentioned, this is by no means a new concept in the private
sector. It is now beginning to appear in the public sector. Several
decentralised local authorities have, since the early 1980s, given
neighbourhood forums or area committees 'community' or environmental budgets for local decision. Not only are locally appropriate and
practical decisions made, but the process of deciding also gives local
residents insight into the realities of local government resource allocation. It thus raises the general levels of information exchange, mutual

honesty and, ultimately, the credibility of the structures themselves. This creates a base for realistic discussion of services and service standards (such as those described by Wendy Thomson in chapter 9 later), in contrast with unrealistic demands and/or hopelessly low expectations (based on previous experience) that may have existed before.

Similarly, the ability to make budgetary decisions locally gives both freedom and a sense of responsibility to local managers (Blake, Bolan, Burns and Gaster, 1991). However, such devolution, to be satisfactory and effective, needs a suitable policy framework and organisational infrastructure: support and incentives to good financial management, such as the power of virement and carrying over monies from one year to the next; user-friendly, accurate and up to date information technology — and written manuals and procedures where necessary; training and ongoing support from financial specialists.

Devolution and Accountability

If local managers have the power to make decisions and spend (and, sometimes, raise) money, who has the power to control such spending, to ensure that it is in line with central values, corporate policies (such as equal opportunities, or environmental protection) and political priorities? How — and this is a key quality issue — can consistency of standards and equity of provision be maintained while at the same time enabling local and possibly quite strongly variable needs to be met?

The logical step is for managerial devolution and political devolution to go hand in hand. In a tight-loose organisational model, local semi-autonomous management units should have a parallel line of political accountability at the locality or neighbourhood level, giving a higher profile to elected ward councillors working within Council-wide policy frameworks. This would create the conditions for the introduction of programmes to improve service quality at all levels of the organisation, enabling local flexibility and responsiveness and dramatically improving the quality of government itself.

Bringing it all together

Quality, as will have been said many times before the end of this book, is a complex issue. So are decentralisation and devolution. Within the public sector, and particularly within local government, they may well complement and enhance each other. It is very important not only to have an idea of reinforcement to a quality service that a decentralised, devolved approach may provide, but also of the possible drawbacks and difficulties.

Standards and Standardisation

The American quality gurus — mainly talking about manufacturing industry — underline the need for standardisation (right first time, conformance to specification) in the attempt to beat off Japanese competition (see, for example, Deming, 1986). This might seem to contradict the notions of local variation implicit throughout this chapter. Certainly there is a question to be asked: how far, in local government, is it desirable to formulate and publish consistent 'standards' for each of the services if offers, so that actual and potential consumers, referrers and relatives, tax-payers and electors can form an accurate expectation of the service to be provided and have grounds for complaint if it does not meet that standard?

In terms of equity, it might be argued that everyone should have access to the same service if it is wanted, but in terms of the whole range of what is known as 'equal opportunities', the likelihood is that there will be different needs that should be met in different ways, even to the point of supplying a service in some areas but not in others.

One function of a decentralised, devolved service is to be able to respond more exactly and sensitively to the variety of needs in the community. Such variation is likely for inter-personal services; it may be equally appropriate for the 'universal', technical services, responding both to individual and community priorities and to differences in the local environment. Such responsiveness may consequently increase the confidence of the community in the local authority.

However, a balance is needed between overall, recognisable quality and local variation. The differences between local offices within one authority can run the danger of being too great. So the role of the centre, of politicians and senior management, is vital in establishing clear policy frameworks and suitable mechanisms for monitoring and supporting staff in local offices and residents in local forums. Otherwise the dangers of isolation and perhaps even inappropriate competition for what should be common resources, may undermine the benefits of accessibility and responsiveness.

Quality Systems and Front-line Staff

Quality assurance (QA) and 'total quality management' (TQM) systems emphasise the need for the whole workforce to be involved in quality for it to work. In a service organisation the quality of staff is a major, even the main, input into the quality of the overall service. So the commitment of front-line staff is necessary for success.

Staff in small, devolved units can bring their knowledge of consumer needs and expectations into the organisation, and they can contribute their experience of delivering services into the mainstream of thinking. At the same time, the 'tight–loose' organisational model enables them to develop not only responsiveness, flexibility and commitment to improving quality, but also the power and ability to achieve results.

Conversely, if front-line staff are not involved in the development of policies about quality and have no power over its implementation, they are unlikely to put energy into making them work. As Peters and Waterman (op cit) and others have pointed out, employees have seen many management fashions come and go: what is so different about this one?

Quality Systems and Consumers

Quality systems such as TQM or QA (formalised in the BS 5750) do not build in the involvement of consumers, far less citizens. But for local government, we would argue that the only way to develop services truly 'fit for purpose' is to ensure as full an input by consumers and citizens as possible. Localised service delivery, particularly if it is of a high standard, can increase the credibility of the local authority as a whole. Local people, in different sections of the community, may then believe it is worth becoming involved in more formal consultation mechanisms necessary for real negotiation about quality priorities and standards. At the same time, the decentralisation and devolution of power provides the opportunity for local consultation, feedback and decision-making. Services can thus become more responsive to need and more accountable in their operation.

For reasons of equity and equal opportunities spelt out earlier, local consultation and decision-making should not be the only way of involving local people in developing quality. They can, however, form one part of a wider participation strategy.

Technical and Non-technical Quality

One danger of local, devolved units of service delivery is that attention is diverted from the nature of the services to be provided — their fitness for purpose — and concentrates disproportionately on how and where the services are to be provided. In the process of developing new ways of working and relating to the public, the actual content of the work, protected as it often is by professional or union interests, can appear to be immune from comment and change.

Certainly, the provision of local offices and the establishment of local democratic mechanisms is, through the process of personal and collective accountability, a possible and even probable impetus towards improving the non-technical aspects of service quality. But although the interface between service providers and receivers and the overall environment of service delivery can be changed for the better, improvements do not automatically result from geographically local offices, as has been stressed throughout this chapter. Locally-based workers need to be clear exactly how they may need to change their approach to delivering services, they need to be aware of what aspects of the office environment will enhance the overall quality, and they need recognition, support, co-operation and encouragement from the rest of the organisation to achieve the necessary changes.

As far as technical quality is concerned, two aspects need to be mentioned. First, front-line workers and local groups and committees need power to influence the services provided by the rest of the organisation. Co-operation is likely to develop when others see that local offices can actually help them to do their job better. The build-up of mutual trust, based on good information and effective internal communication, may take time — longer than the idealists want — but, as the foundation for real improvements in service content, it is indispensable.

But if the informal power to intervene, make suggestions, and give feedback to colleagues is important — and implies a quite different culture from that traditionally experienced — so, too, is formal power acquired through devolution. Within a broad policy framework, and with 'the centre' having a clear strategic role, devolved service units (whether decentralised or not) have the opportunity not only to examine the design and quality of their services, but also to do something about it. Rather like the much talked of quality circles, they need clear objectives, leadership and facilitation to be effective, but with suitable support and encouragement, it seems highly likely that such units, ideally accountable to parallel devolved democratic structures, could be the leading edge of technical improvement for the whole organisation.

Conclusion

The structures of decentralisation, as defined here, have many advantages and some disadvantages: they can provide a context for the development of sensitive, appropriate, responsive and integrated services, which are also likely to be more efficient (less time and effort spent providing inappropriate services) and effective (more likely to be able to meet objectives if they have been formulated on the basis of local need). If geographical boundaries are not rigid, they can also provide more choice for the consumer.

The processes of devolving political and managerial power, and managing by results, give a sense of ownership and responsibility crucial in any quality assurance model. They also allow the possibility of a more 'bottom-up' approach to policy development and decision making, bringing the realities of experience and local knowledge nearer to the levels of strategic policy.

Decentralisation and devolution are both means to an end. Historically, that 'end' may not always have been clear in the minds of those introducing them. But now, with quality at the top of the political and management agendas, these new structures and processes could — and maybe should — provide a launch-pad for the next, crucial stage in the future of local government: the development of reliable, consistent, high quality services responsive to consumer and community need.

References

Ashford, D. (1990) Decentralising France: how Socialists discovered pluralism, *West European Politics*, Vol. 13, No. 4, pp. 46–64.

Beuret, K. and Stoker, G. (1986) The Labour Party and neighbourhood decentralisation: Flirtation or Commitment?, *Critical Social Policy*, Vol. 17, pp. 4–22.

Blake, W., Bolan, P., Burns, D. and Gaster, L. (eds.) (1991) *Local Budgeting in Practice*, Decentralisation Research and Information Centre, Paper 3, School for Advanced Urban Studies, University of Bristol.

Burger, Y. D. and Kastelein, J. (1990) *Success and failure factors of decentralisation and automisation processes in larger (inter) organisations: report of an enquiry*, Paper to International Conference on Participation, Organisational Effectiveness and Quality of Life, Piraeus.

Carter, N. (1991) Learning to measure performance: the use of indicators in organisations, *Public Administration*, Vol. 69, Spring, pp. 85–101.

Deming, W. E. (1986) *Out of the Crisis*, Press Syndicate, University of Cambridge, Massachusetts.

Gaster, L. (1991a) Quality and decentralisation: are they connected?, *Policy and Politics*, Vol. 19, No. 4, pp. 257–267.

Gaster, L. (1991b) *Quality at the Front Line*, Decentralisation Research and Information Centre, Paper 2, School for Advanced Urban Studies, University of Bristol.

Gaster, L. (1993, forthcoming) Organisational change and political will: a case study. Monitoring and evaluating decentralisation and democratisation in Harlow, Decentralisation Research and Information Centre, Paper 4, School for Advanced Urban Studies, University of Bristol.

Gaster, L. (1992, forthcoming) Neighbourhood centres and community care in Liverpool, chapter in Smith R. *et al. Working together for better community care*, SAUS Study, School for Advanced Urban Studies, University of Bristol.

Gaster, L. and Rivers, A. (1991) Liverpool City Council: day-to-day service delivery in Granby-Toxteth — analysis and city-wide implications, Interim report to the City Council (unpublished), Decentralisation Research and Information Centre, School for Advanced Urban Studies, University of Bristol.

Gyford, J. (1991) Does place matter? locality and local democracy, The Belgrave Papers No. 3, Local Government Management Board, Luton.

Hambleton, R. (1988) Consumerism, decentralisation and local democracy, *Public Administration*, reprinted as Working Paper 78, School for Advanced Urban Studies, University of Bristol.

Hambleton, R., Hoggett, P. and Burns, D. (1993, forthcoming) The politics of decentralisation (provisional title), Macmillan, London.

Hambleton, R., Stewart, M. and Taylor, M. (1991) The strategic role of local government in the community, discussion paper for the Local Government Management Board (unpublished).

Hoggett, P. (1991) A new management in the public sector? *Policy and Politics*, Vol. 19, No. 4, pp. 243–256.

Hoggett, P. and Hambleton, R. (1987) *Decentralisation and Democracy: Localising Public Services*, Occasional Paper 28, School for Advanced Urban Studies, University of Bristol.

Jones, R. and Pendlebury, M. (1988) (2nd edn) *Public Sector Accounting*, Pitman, London.

Kastelein, J. (1987) *Result-responsible units and central control in public and private organisations*, Paper to the European Group on Public Administration Conference, Valencia.

Lipsky, M. (1980) *Street-Level bureaucracy: Dilemmas of the Individual in Public Services*, Russell Sage Foundation, New York.

Local Government Management Board, (1991) *Quality and Equality: Service to the Whole Community*, LGMB/Institute of Local Government Studies, Luton/Birmingham.

Peters, T. J. and Waterman, R. H. (1982) *In Search of Excellence: Lessons from America's best-run Companies*, Harper Collins, New York.

Pollitt, C. (1990) Doing business in the temple? Managers and quality assurance in the public sector, *Public Administration*, Vol. 68, No. 4, pp. 435–452.

Stoker, G., Wedgwood Oppenheim, F. and Davies, M. (1988) *The Challenge of Change in Local Government: a Survey of Organisational and Management Innovation in the 1980s*, Institute of Local Government Studies, University of Birmingham.

Taylor, M. (1991) Participation: lessons and good practice, Appendix A in Gaster and Rivers, op cit.

Webb, A. (1991) Coordination: a problem in public sector management, *Policy and Politics*, Vol. 19, No. 4, pp. 229–241.

4 Quality in an enabling context

Mick Paddon

Introduction

The growing interest in the quality of local authority services in Britain is part of a wider debate about the role of local government. The terms for this debate have, to a significant extent, been set by legislation and government policies under the Conservative Governments since 1979 which have redefined or prescribed a local government role. Two of the most significant areas of change initiated by legislation have been in services subjected to Compulsory Competitive Tendering (CCT) and in 'Community Care' services. The changes require new forms of arrangements with external or non local authority agencies and, most extensively in the case of CCT, prescribe a legal framework for these arrangements. They have also contributed to a reformulation of the relationships between sections and departments *within* local authorities where structures, management and budgets have been separated. In so far as the external relationships are *contractual* they are also governed by a legal framework emerging at a European level in the form of Directives issued by the European Community.

This chapter reviews the implications of these related elements for the pursuit of quality in services. The first section examines the association between the concern with quality and the proposition that the future of local government will lie in a more 'enabling' role. It also investigates political debate about how competition and contractual arrangements enhance or detract from the pursuit of quality. The second and third sections focus on the practical issues of how quality is being inserted into managing and arranging the relationships *between* agencies under CCT and in Community Care and *within* local government as it separates into different functions. The final section reviews some of the issues raised by the EC Directives for the incorporation of quality into contractual arrangements.

The 'enabling authority': Quality and the role of local government

Quality and the restructuring of local government

The increasing interest in the 'quality' of local government services is directly related to the changes in the structure, functions and role of local authorities in the UK since 1979, and in particular in the second half of the 1980s (Stewart and Walsh, 1989, LGMBa, 1992; Centre for Public Services, 1992). Much of the legislation which has redefined the role of local government, such as in community care and social services, makes explicit reference to 'quality'. In other service areas, especially education and housing, provision in legislation for opting out of local authority control has reinforced concern with quality as a means of persuading institutions or tenants to remain with local councils. Emphasis on high quality specifications has been part of the strategy advocated by the Local Authority Associations and public sector unions in responding to Compulsory Competitive Tendering (CCT) for building work (after 1980 legislation) and for the services such as refuse collection and street cleaning which were 'defined' under the 1988 Local Government Act.

The increasingly tight financial constraints on local government have provoked first, a concern with greater efficiency, actively promoted by the Audit Commission, and second, an emphasis on quality, by the Audit Commission and others, as a response to the criticism that traditional 'value for money' measures extol efficiency and economy at the expense of effectiveness, equity and other 'quality' measures. It would be wrong, however, to regard the more extensive interest in quality as being generated solely by initiatives by the Conservative Governments. Many local authorities have consistently set high standards in specifications for their services, and in their current 'quality' initiatives are in reality extending or revising programmes already developed to place services closer to clients and users. Still less should it be assumed that *real* improvement in service quality has been the objective result of the reforms of local government imposed by the Conservative Governments, as this is very much the contested area between the proponents of these changes and their critics (as will be reviewed in greater detail below).

What the reforms have undoubtedly done is to provoke a debate about the present and future role of local government in which 'quality' is now a common part of the vocabulary, even if the meaning ascribed to the term may be imprecise. The debate also seems to have settled on a widespread agreement that this future will cast local government more in the role of 'enabler' than direct provider of services. Again, the common use of the same notion obscures important differences in what is meant by an 'enabling authority' which will be discussed further. What is common in the currency of the term is an apparent acceptance that there will be a greater plurality of organisations involved in the actual *provision* of services. In the analysis and promotion of the potential for improved quality of services this raises the questions of what is to be the relationship between the local authority and these other agencies and how it is to be managed. It also prompts a reconsideration of whether such arrangements make quality less or more easy to achieve in two senses. First, in so far as quality is defined in terms of the 'outputs' of services, how are the appropriate outputs to be determined and how is their achievement to be ensured? Second, if one of the characteristics of public services is the very close relationship between the production and consumption of services and in some areas the *interaction* between staff and users/clients (Stewart and Walsh, 1989, p. 4), how are the training, staffing and other employment considerations necessary for quality in delivery to be required of other agencies?

In identifying these issues, it is helpful to conceptualise approaches to quality in terms of six broad elements as suggested by the Centre for Public Services, each with a number of possible procedures or initiatives associated with them. The elements are (Centre for Public Services, 1992):

- *the management of the service*
- *the design planning and specification of the service*
- *the processes and procedures involved in ensuring service delivery*
- *monitoring and evaluating services*
- *user rights and information*
- *the quality of employment of those delivering the services.*

The 'Enabling' Local Authority

The terms 'enabling local authority' or 'enabling state' have been used both descriptively, in an attempt to capture the changes which have been taking place, and prescriptively, in propositions about how the role of local government *should* develop. The core notion of the 'enabling' local authority is that the activities of local government as they have developed in the period since the Second World War, as the sole provider of services in some areas of social and welfare policy, or as the major provider in others, are replaced and/or augmented by a range of other organisations, which may be voluntary organisations, not-for-profit bodies, or private companies. There are, however, important differences of emphasis among advocates of the 'enabling' role ranging from those who associate these changes with a diminishing role for local authorities, through those who see a new strategic role emerging, to those who argue for a more extensive and invigorated *community government* (Cochrane, 1991).

The more restricted or diminished role for local government has been articulated by Nicholas Ridley (Ridley, 1988) who, as a Conservative Cabinet Minister was most (in)famously associated with the view that British local authorities might move to a US model of meeting for the main purpose of awarding contracts to private contractors for the carrying out of services. However, his version of the new relationships does not deny a strategic role for local authorities:

> Authorities will need to operate in a more pluralistic way than in the past, alongside a wide variety of public, private and voluntary agencies. It will be their task to stimulate and assist these other agencies to play their part instead of, or as well as, making provision themselves.
> (Ridley, 1988)

This potential for a new strategic role for the 'enabling authority' has been embraced by Rodney Brooke on behalf of the local government community. He sees a future with a proliferation of single-service agencies in which local government acts as leader/planner/regulator with a wider facility for comment and intervention on issues of general interest to their communities (Brooke, 1989).

The most expansive vision of what enabling local government might look like is set out in the work of John Stewart writing with a number of associates. For Stewart, the forms of service provision dominant in UK local government since 1945 have aimed at uniform service provision requiring historically high levels of expenditure resulting in pressures within authorities for centralised control of budgets and policy. He argues for a difference in emphasis in local government which starts from the needs of communities and gives greater recognition to the diversity of these needs. Different forms of provision may then be appropriate, including direct provision by local authorities but not necessarily or exclusively so. This is a vision which requires both greater legal powers for autonomous action by local government (Stewart, 1991) and the empowerment of local communities through greater accountability and decentralisation. It is a view of local government which is also implicitly critical of the main thrust of the changes implemented by Conservative Governments which, in the name of 'enabling' local government, has taken control increasingly to central government. (This is a synthesis of a number of pieces of work in which Stewart has been involved: see, for example, Clarke and Stewart, 1988; Stewart and Stoker, 1988, 1989).

Quality and the 'Enabling' State in Political Programmes

The lexicon of the 'enabling' state, with an acceptance of a plurality of service providers and a focus on service quality is now shared by the main political parties in Britain. As might be anticipated, where they differ is on the mechanisms for introducing this plurality and the actual role of local government.

The 1991 White Paper, *The Citizen's Charter*, set out most comprehensively the Conservative Government's proposals for further reform of the public sector as a whole. 'Quality' is one of the Charter's four main themes — the others being choice, standards and value (HMSO, 1991, p. 4). Reforming local government to an enabling role close to the Ridley conception, is part of the programme set out for delivering these objectives.

The 'key tools' for this reformation are to be accountability and competition. Competition is to be extended by further compulsory competitive tendering to cover white collar local government employment. The Government was well advanced in implementing the proposals for local government before the General Election in April 1992 with a new Local Government Act providing the legal framework for the extension of CCT and a Consultation Paper, setting out which additional services might now be subjected to CCT (Department of the Environment, 1991 a and 1991 b).

The Labour Party also set out a specific programme for improving the quality of local government services (Labour Party, 1989). Its vision of the 'opportunity', 'enabling' or 'servant' state is one in which:

> The role of Government is to help people achieve their aspirations, support their efforts to improve their own quality of life — as well as their family and their community — and take action against institutions and vested interests which deny consumer choice and undermine citizens' rights.
>
> (Labour Party, 1991, p. 9)

The superficial similarity in terminology between the two sets of political proposals conveys something of the convergence of interest in the issues of quality and the apparent common acceptance of the enabling role of government (*Financial Times*, 1992), but it also confirms that there are differences in what is understood by the term quality. Behind the similarities in vocabulary there are clear and important differences between the programmes. In the Conservative Government's proposals the pluralism in providing agencies is enforced through greater competitive tendering and contracting out which, it is asserted, produce better quality services The Labour Party documents put greater emphasis on the autonomy of local government, would remove the compulsion of competition and would invoke a public regulatory body, a new Quality Commission, only in the last instance. The Labour proposals also implicitly acknowledge the relationship between production and consumption in public services. Finally, they seem to differ on the questions of the relationship between resources and service quality. In the Conservative programme, it appears that the desire for greater quality is pursued as part of an overall programme of obtaining better value for money from existing or more constrained budgets. In the Labour Party's propositions, lack of or constraints on resources are seen as a major impediment to the achievement of quality.

The election of a fourth consecutive Conservative administration in the General Election of April 1992 ensured that the various proposals to differentiate service planning from provision, in their particular version of the 'enabling' authority, will be put into effect. The legislative framework for further competitive tendering already in place will be applied to a new batch of services. Before reviewing what this means in practice for attempts by local authorities to continue to pursue and promote quality in their own practices, it is informative to examine what the existing framework is and what impact the measures already in place seem to have had on service quality.

Defining and applying quality in managing relationships with other agencies: compulsory competitive tendering

Compulsory Competitive Tendering and Service Quality

Writing at the end of the 1980s, John Stewart and Kieron Walsh claimed that: 'The requirements of competitive tendering are the immediate cause of quality being on the management agenda' (Stewart and Walsh, 1989). This can be understood in several senses. First, the debate about the introduction of the benefits and problems of CCT has brought the issue of 'quality' in focus, but also exposes further the differences in emphasis in defining what the term means. Second, the implication of CCT requires a number of procedures to be carried through at various stages of which 'quality' will be a vital consideration. Third, however, the legal framework which directs CCT in the UK, and indeed contracting in general by local authorities, sets limits to the 'quality' considerations which can be taken into account. This legal framework is in the process of being changed with a number of important consequences for the application of quality.

Compulsory Competitive Tendering was first introduced in UK local government for building and related work under the 1980 Planning and Land Act. Setting the pattern later followed for other 'defined' services, the legislation laid down advertising and contract award procedures which had to be followed if an authority wished to consider offering work to its own in-house department (Direct Labour Organisation — DLO). The legislation also established a framework for internal accounting of DLOs and set a financial target, or rate of return, to be achieved. The 1988 Local Government Act extended the same principles and general procedures to services which the Secretary of State was empowered to 'define', and brought the term CCT into common use in local government. The services initially defined in the Act were refuse collection, other cleaning (street cleansing), school and welfare catering, other catering, grounds maintenance and vehicle maintenance. Management of sport and leisure facilities was added to these services the following year. The 1988 Act also set out a general, but loosely defined, obligation on authorities not to act 'anti-competitively' in awarding contracts. Finally, the Government regulated the award of *any* contracts for goods or services entered into by local authorities by the prohibition of consideration, or insertion in any contract documentation, of 'non-commercial matters' including the composition of a contractor's workforce. This precluded consideration or stipulation of terms and conditions of employment, training or other opportunities and promotion (Cirell and Bennett, 1990).

In the academic literature, five benefits from competitive tendering have been identified, two of them quality-related (Parker, 1990). First, it is claimed that competition to be a service provider through contracting drives down costs and maximises efficiency. This is claimed to be true irrespective of whether the contract is awarded to an in-house service or to an outside contractor, since it either introduces lower cost external contractors or forces reorganisation of internal practices to compete with outside pressures. Second, the growth of providers/suppliers not limited by politically-determined local authority boundaries can promote specialisation and economies of scale. Third, by dividing service provision from quality regulation, it is argued that competitive tendering facilitates the establishment of quality standards and effective policing of standards. Fourth, competitive tendering supposedly shifts concern from inputs into services to the monitoring for the quality and quantity of outputs. Finally, there are claimed to be indirect public sector financial gains to the Exchequer from increased taxation levied on profitable private contracting companies.

On the other hand, critics of competitive tendering have argued that in general, where it is operated, service quality tends to decline. Secondly, private contractors tend to reduce pay and employment conditions. Third, tendering for contracts is open to collusion between potential suppliers. Fourth, competitive tendering introduces increased administrative costs through the drawing up, processing and monitoring of contracts (Parker, 1990).

In practice, the rationale for CCT in UK legislation has been overwhelmingly in terms of presumed wastage of resources by local government and the gains to be made in terms of two of the Audit Commission's measures of 'value for money': economy and efficiency. In its limited monitoring of the actual impact of CCT, the Government's major concern appears to have been with the savings which have been estimated in some authorities. Thus, it has publicised the findings of Department of the Environment funded research by the Institute of Local Government, which indicate average savings of 6 per cent overall in the annual cost of work subjected to the 1988 Act (Department of the Environment, 1991a), but without the caveats made by the researchers themselves about these findings. The financial savings from CCT are challenged by its critics who claim both that they fail to take account of the true total *costs* of introducing CCT and, that the savings are at the expense of poorer quality services (Manchester City Council, 1988; Centre for Public Services, 1992).

There has been little official monitoring of the impact of the legislation on service quality. Academic research on the effects of competition before the 1988 Act which claimed that there are no discernible indications of cost savings being accompanied by reductions in quality has been severely criticised (Paddon, 1991). The Public Services Privatisation Research Unit, which has monitored contracts awarded under CCT since 1989 on a national data base, argues that 'quality has been sacrificed by undermining a committed and stable workforce and imposing an inflexible financial regime' (Public Services Privatisation Research Unit, 1992). It cites as evidence of 'quality destroyed' the fact that private contractors who have won contracts have consistently performed less well than direct employees of local authorities. 'Failure rates' in terms of contract problems or terminations are four-and-a-half times higher with private contractors than for contracts held by the in-house workforce.

There are a number of aspects to these problems with contracts: falling standards, problems in recruiting and retaining staff, inadequate resources, and the suitability of contractors. Three arguments can be considered here, each with rather different implications for the assessment of how quality can be sustained or enforced through contracts. The first, and the possibility generally argued by those supportive of competitive tendering, is that contract failures result largely from inexperience and will decrease with increasing experience of contractors and the longer term establishment of contracting (Parker, 1990, p. 656). Unfortunately for this argument, data base material does not seem to indicate any lessening of failures over time. The second argument is that there are fundamental difficulties with ensuring 'conformance' with specifications in a contracting relationship (Walsh, 1988), even where these specifications are clearly spelt out. The third argument, which is suggested by the Public Services Privatisation Research Unit, is that the ability to deliver a good quality service is undermined by general features which have accompanied competitive tendering:

> Because of financial pressures, tender winners — whether private or in-house — often do not employ enough staff, or cannot recruit trained and experienced workers because of the poor conditions and rates of pay they offer.
>
> Breaking public services into 'purchasers' and 'providers' or 'clients' and 'contractors' forces the in-house team into the same position as the private contractor — to maintain profits at the expense of quality.
>
> (Public Services Privatisation Research Unit, 1992, pp. 4–5)

Quality in the Implementation of CCT

When the claim has been made that CCT has improved service quality, what is actually being asserted is that it has improved the management of services, largely because the requirements for the delivery of a service are clearly spelt out in a specification. In the practical management of CCT, procedures have been required which would be the first steps in establishing *quality control* for services, in the setting and monitoring of specifications. Many authorities have gone further and, following the strategy advised by a number of Local Authority Associations, have adopted a more comprehensive approach which has incorporated *quality assurance*. In some, this too has now been incorporated into a more extensive authority-wide approach to quality. The practice of implementing CCT has undoubtedly helped to push many authorities in these directions and to establish good practice in several. However, there are real questions about whether the restrictive framework of CCT actually allows quality in its widest sense to be pursued, and how the combined effects of these and other restrictions on local authorities constitute effective 'barriers to quality'.

The 1988 Local Government Act has marked a fundamental change in the way in which contracting arrangements are made, not only with non local government agencies, but also between different sections of the same authority. While it is impossible to distinguish precisely between the effects of a number of simultaneous processes, it is arguable that in the period up to 1988, financial restrictions on local authorities and the curtailment of public house building had a more substantial impact on local council building services than did enforced tendering under the terms of the 1980 Planning and Land Act (ADLO, 1987). In the first part of the 1980s a number of authorities also innovated in attempts to use contracts for building work, and in other areas, to pursue broader policies through 'contract compliance'. In so far as several of the issues covered by contract compliance concerned the terms under which goods and services were produced — such as Health and Safety, training, employment of women and black people, etc. — there was a definite, if indirect, link with the 'quality' of services. The 1988 Act extended the practice of CCT to the defined services but also severely restricted the ability of local authorities to take these quality-related employment issues into account or stipulate them in contracts.

At the most basic level, CCT has required local authorities 'to do a great deal of work on service specifications' which is 'essentially service design and should be seen as an integral part of the quality management system' (Walsh, 1988, pp. 5–6). This has been the first stage of the tendering process and necessary for all contracts. They have also been required to devise mechanisms to monitor and check that specifications have been met, and to devise penalties for failure to meet them. Although this is another basic requirement of good practice, it has not been policed universally; indeed, many authorities are said to have initially grossly underestimated the true costs of monitoring (Manchester City Council, 1988). These are the basic requirements for a system of quality control, the absence of which would question an ability to meet even a minimal commitment to quality of provision.

The more comprehensive strategy for CCT developed by the National Coordinating Committee on Competitive Tendering (whose membership includes the Local Authority Associations, ADLO, CLES and the LGIU) emphasises two major additional dimensions. First, the significance of involving service users in the drawing up of specifications; and second, the link between *how* and by whom services are provided and how they are used or 'consumed'. Since service delivery is people-, not technology-based, the way and circumstances in which services are delivered are an important part of how they are experienced, and, for these reasons, production and consumption of services are inseparable (Stewart and Walsh, 1989; AMA, 1992). In *public* services of the kind provided by local authorities, the multiplicity of needs makes the simple setting of single standards inappropriate. This, with the requirement that services are politically and publicly accountable, necessitates the direct involvement of service users.

The strategy sets out a systematic series of stages to be followed by local authorities in preparing the defining services for CCT (AMA, 1988). It is 'based on the provision of quality services, quality employment, and the principles of public service' (Centre for Public Services, 1992, p. 2) and builds quality into all the stages of the tendering process:

- *service profiling, as a prelude to drawing up specifications*
- *joint working between local councils, local authority trade unions and service users*
- *investigating the private companies who will compete for work, industrial sector by sector*
- *specifications drawn up to high standards*
- *stringent contract conditions*
- *comprehensive evaluation of tenders before contracts are awarded*
- *rigorous monitoring.*

Evidence from the first phases of the CCT schedule of contracts, has indicated that where authorities adopted this approach they were also more likely to win contracts for their in-house DSOs (LGMB, 1991a, 1991b, 1992a and 1992b).

Quality Assurance, through third party accreditation, has increasingly become an accepted part of this strategy for CCT.

> The application of techniques including Quality Assurance to contracting activities has intensified in the past three years partly to improve management systems and partly to gain competitive advantage over private contractors with accreditation to British Standards such as BS 5750.
>
> (Centre for Public Services, 1992, p. 2)

BS 5750 is a UK standard for quality systems introduced by the British Standards Institute in 1979. It has since provided the basis for European (EN 29000) and International Standards (ISO 9000) which makes it compatible with the EC Directives for Public Procurement discussed below. BS 5750 is essentially a framework for establishing that the management systems operating in an organisation enable it to perform consistently to quality targets. To proceed with BS 5750 an organisation must produce documentation, systems and procedures under a number of standard headings. Once the system is designed and is in place, it may seek certification from one of a number of independent, third party accrediting agencies which include BSI Quality Assurance, and the Lloyd's Register of Quality Assurance Ltd (LGMB, 1992a). The requirements for BS 5750 are set out in very general terms which have to be translated into the necessary detailed systems. This process takes months and possibly years requiring specifically dedi-

Service	Councils with contracts requiring BS 5750		Ave months to achieve	Range months to achieve
	No.	%		
Building Cleaning	28	10	24	12–60
Refuse Collection	21	6	25	18–36
Other Cleaning	15	7	23	12–24
Vehicle Maintenance	8	3	27	24–36
Education/Welfare Catering	8	9	25	12–48
Other Catering	6	5	30	24–48
Ground Maintenance	43	11	27	–
Sport & Leisure Management	24	19	28	–

Source: Local Government Management Board *CCT Information Service Survey Report No. 5*, April 1992

Table 4.1: Local authorities requiring BS 5750 in contracts

cated quality assurance staff, consultants or combinations of the two, to devise the systems. It assumes a contractual relationship between client and contractor and is being introduced on both sides of the CCT arrangements in local authorities.

In its role as a client awarding contracts, the local authority might either insist on accreditation under the Standard as a condition of contract, or set a requirement that contractors achieve certification within a specified period in the lifetime of the contract. Increasingly, and in each of the defined services, authorities are taking the latter course, largely because this form of certification is a recent development. Table 4.1 indicates the number of contracts which have specified periods for accreditation and the range of time period allowed.

As the process of seeking BS 5750 accreditation has developed on the client side, so an increasing number of authorities have sought certification for DSOs and DLOs. There are three strategic options being used here. First, some authorities have pursued BS 5750 for a discrete section or activity within their building or defined services, such as road surface dressing in Gloucestershire CC and Tayside Regional Council (see Table 4.2). This approach has the advantage of incrementalism with the possibility of transferring the expertise gained to other areas. Second, other authorities have committed themselves to acquiring BS 5750 for the whole of a service area, notably Manchester City Council which is certifying the whole of its Direct Works Department with over 4,000 employees, organised in 28 costs centres (AMA, 1991; Centre for Public Services, 1992). The third option, available to small

Local Authority	Services
Ashfield DC	All direct services
Avon CC	Fencing and vehicle crash barriers
Chester le Street DC	Refuse collection
Gloucestershire CC	Surveying and road surface dressing
Leeds City Council	Catering
Lewisham LB	Vehicle Maintenance
Newcastle City Council	Leisure
South Glamorgan CC	Building cleaning
Tayside Regional Council	Road surface dressing
Tunbridge Wells DC	Drainage and sewerage

Sources: Association of Direct Labour Organisations, *Direct News,* Winter 1991/92; AMA, *Signposts to Quality,* 1992

Table 4.2: Local Authority DLOs and DSOs with BS 5750 Certification

er authorities which have reorganised all their DSOs into a single organisation, is to gain certification for all the defined services. Thus Ashfield District Council has gained certification for building cleaning, building maintenance, highway maintenance, street cleaning, street lighting, grounds maintenance, refuse collection, transport and purchasing (LGMB, 1992b).

Despite the increasing use of BS 5750 and its attraction to many authorities, its application is not unproblematic. Certification under BS 5750 is gained either for only a part of an organisation or for a designated site or workplace. BS 5750 may not, therefore, cover either the specific service or workplace for the contract. Since the practice is still relatively recent, it remains to be seen whether any authority will terminate a contract because of the failure of a contractor to gain certification within the allotted time. The other reservation for some authorities has been that BS 5750 does not itself set standards. It is not 'output' based and leaves the onus on the client authority to set out its requirements in clear specifications. Nor does it substitute for systematic evaluation of contractors and tenders since many of the 'quality' related issues which should be taken account of are not covered; such as financial standing, experience, workload and other commitments, and health and safety at work (AMA, 1991c, p. 31)

Paradoxically, for some authorities, a decision not to seek BS 5750 accreditation derived from an assessment that this system of quality assurance is still most appropriate for services where the physical output can be measured in a relatively straightforward way. Islington adopted its own approach of quality service, which includes the CCT-defined services of refuse collection, meals on wheels and swimming pools, on the grounds that neither BS 5750 nor total quality Management approaches were wholly adequate.

> The BS 5750 system appeared to us in Islington to concentrate on the quality of inputs to a service. Establishing detailed procedures may assist an authority to deliver the service to the same specification everytime, but it cannot tell you whether the specification is appropriate and therefore, whether you are delivering a 'quality service'.
>
> (AMA, 1992, p. 34)

Similarly, Wolverhampton Council, while accepting the logic of applying standards to the management of sport and leisure facilities and employing many of the areas covered by the framework of BS 5750 in its own system, decided against formal accreditation on the grounds that 'as BS 5750 is based on physical production, it has shortcomings for a public service with no physical output' (AMA, 1992, p. 47). Despite the attempt with BS 5750 to provide a service-based framework for quality assurance, it is noticeable that it has been most widely (though not exclusively) adopted in 'those departments delivering front line services which are relatively easy to quantify and judge' (LGMB, 1992). This has tended to mean those CCT services, like refuse collection, which most closely approximate the production of a definite, tangible set of objects.

The cost of money and staff resources are other important considerations for authorities reviewing the BS 5750 route. The direct costs to Ashfield Council of obtaining certification were over £12,000 in consultancy costs, and £7,000 for certification with unspecified internal costs of staff time and training (LGMB, 1992b, p. 11). The costs to Manchester's Direct Works Department are a six person Quality Assurance Group, and a substantial departmental training programme. However, in a large department such as Manchester, this will comprise only a marginal increase in staffing costs. And against any additional costs should be set the savings achieved by the elimination of costs of re-doing poor quality work, which in Ashfield, for example, was estimated to be 25 per cent of total costs (LGMB, 1992b).

Overall, however, the ability to pursue quality as a real *objective* in the defined services is constrained in four ways. First, by the difficulty in, or exclusions from, taking some quality-related employment considerations into account when awarding a contract or including them in contract conditions. Second, central government has attempted to set increasingly restrictive interpretations on acceptable contract award procedures and conditions under the terms of the 1988 Act. The initial approach by many authorities and Local Authority Associations to implement the Act has been to argue that contract arrangements, on issues such as the size of contracts, the depots and equipment contractors are required to use, etc. are defensible if the client organisation is satisfied that they affect the ability to meet the specification, i.e. they are quality-related. The various circulars issued by the Government to interpret the Act have provided more restrictive guidelines on each of these issues. The 1992 Local Government Act now gives greater powers to the Secretary of State to give binding instruction on such areas which undoubtedly will be used to further limit the degree of client discretion on these criteria and conditions. The third constraint derives from the increasingly severe financial constraints facing authorities, exacerbated by the Community Charge and which will continue under the Council Tax. On the client side, an authority will specify the quality of service which it can afford to pay for, irrespective of whether its own DSO or a contractor delivers the service. Fourth, CCT has been accompanied by a number of changes in the internal organisation and management of services. The 1980 and 1988 Acts imply a separation of *function* within an authority between client and the contractor. The departmental and managerial structures chosen to achieve this have varied substantially, but in many authorities what were previously single departments have been separated with the functions divided off organisationally (Department of the Environment, 1991a). This clear splitting of client and contractor roles was indeed advocated by some commentators on the early requirements of CCT. However, for some authorities which have taken this route, the division between planning of service on the client side and provision of services on the contracting side has been experienced as artificial and detrimental to the quality of services. It is a clear division that is especially hard to make in smaller authorities.

Clear divisions of function need not, in principle, be detrimental to quality provision. The financial and accounting requirements of operating trading accounts for building and defined services has also meant new arrangements within authorities between DSOs/DLOs and central service departments such as finance, personnel, and legal services. Some authorities now formalise these internal arrangements in 'Service Level Agreements' which establish the normal service to be provided, how it will be charged for, how the services will be monitored, mechanisms for amending the level of service and how the agreement will be enforced (AMA, 1991b). While some critics see this approach as extending impracticable divisions between different parts of the same corporate identity (they are all, ultimately, part of the same authority), or potentially creating fragmented 'internal markets', others see this as an opportunity to establish quality-based arrangements inside the organisation. This can be achieved by (AMA, 1991b):

- *agreeing service specifications*
- *giving different internal users a choice of services to reflect their needs*

- *creating partnerships between services and departments to achieve corporate goals*
- *involving staff in defining and improving service delivery*
- *identifying the costs of failure*
- *recognising the role of central support services in contributing to the final services delivered to external users.*

New internal arrangements, where these are not artificial and where they are planned within a corporate structure, may, therefore, contribute to authority-wide quality programmes. However, there appear to be particular problems when the planning and delivery services are completely separated and the arrangements between these functions mediated by contracting arrangements, and, in so far as the four constraints indicated above constitute 'barriers to quality', the barriers will get higher over the next period of Conservative Government, especially the first three. Since the first and third are common to all services in which authorities contract with other agencies, they will also pose difficulties for ensuring quality provision in community care.

Quality in the Extension of CCT

While the Government's rationale for extending competitive tendering under the revised 1992 legislation remains, as it has previously been, to achieve cost savings, the proposals for white collar services indicate a shift in emphasis with a more explicit reference to quality considerations and, arguably, an inconsistency with the earlier approach. The 1991 Consultation paper indicated the Government's intention to extend CCT to four broad categories: first, direct to the public services, such as management of theatres and arts facilities and library support services; second, construction-related services such as architecture, engineering and property management; third, corporate services, including legal, financial and personnel services; and, finally, manual services covering, among others, cleaning and maintenance support to the police and fire services (LGIU, 1991).

The consultation paper introduced the idea of a 'quality threshold' for construction and engineering related professional services. What seems to be implied is a procedure borrowed from the franchising of commercial television in 1991, in which tenderers submit two envelopes, one of which deals with the service, the other with the price. The first envelope would be opened to assess whether a contractor crosses the 'quality threshold'. The second envelopes of all those crossing the threshold would then be opened and the contract awarded to the lowest bidder in price terms. The proposals have been criticised for an unjustified differentiation between those services to which quality criteria would be applied on direction from the Secretary of State, and others on which the legislation appears to take powers to further restrict local authorities from considering anything other than financial criteria (LGIU, 1991).

It is unclear what these new procedures will look like in practice, how quality will be defined, and where the 'threshold' will be set. The Independent Television Commission required over three years of consultation to devise the quality threshold in television franchising, the application of which still produced High Court Challenges by two unsuccessful bidders. Those with experience of dealing with the management of contract awards under CCT claim that most authorities have, in effect, been applying quality screening already. Moreover, quality and price should be evaluated together rather than sequentially, since an authority needs to be convinced that a tenderer's pricing enables him/her to deliver the quality of service required in the specification.

There was widespread condemnation from all parts and parties of local government of this selective approach to quality implied in the Government's consultation document. Professional bodies covering the architectural and civil engineering professions, for which 'double enveloping' was initially intended, were particularly vocal in their criticism. As a result, the whole timetable for this next phase of CCT appears to be under reconsideration in mid-1992. However, service quality will remain one of the major focuses for debate and disagreement in the application of the new phase of CCT and the way in which it is defined will be one of the crucial issues for local government.

Defining and applying quality in managing relationships with other agencies: community care

Quality and Contracts in Community Care

The Conservative Government's intention to change the role of local government to that of service 'enabler' is more explicitly set out in the Community Care legislation than in the earlier phases of enforced tendering:

> The role of an enabling authority is to identify the needs for care among the population it serves, plan how best to meet those needs, set overall strategies, priorities and targets, commission and purchase as well as provide necessary services and *ensure their quality and value.*
>
> (Department of Health, 1991, my emphasis)

The broad intention of the 1990 NHS and Community Care Act is to introduce a 'mixed economy of care' (Department of Health, 1991), for residential, nursing home, day care, and domiciliary care for those requiring services because of ageing or disability. It requires local authorities to prepare and publish plans by April 1992 for the ways in which community care services are provided. April 1993 is the target date for assessment procedures for all the clients who 'look to the local authority for support' (Department of Health, 1991), and for contracting or other arrangements with the agencies who will deliver these services. The local authority becomes a 'purchaser' or 'commissioner' of services, a role which certainly includes overall planning of services and may include the assessment and management of individual care. Service 'providers' in the mixed economy will include the local authority itself and a diverse 'independent sector' including voluntary, not-for-profit and private organisation. Authorities are required to consult with these bodies in the preparation of community care plans, as well as using them for the delivery of services.

In the Government's view, it has written 'quality' into these new arrangements by requiring that authorities indicate in their plans how they intend to ensure and to monitor quality, and by the stipulation that they must have put in place, by April 1991, inspection units and complaints procedures. However, there are doubts, articulated by the House of Commons Select Committee on Social Services, that quality of provision can be maintained in community care contracts without other procedures:

> We believe that without other regulatory or quality assurance mechanisms, there is a danger that community care contracts will be awarded primarily on cost grounds, thus leading to compromise on the quality of services provided.
>
> (House of Commons, 1990)

The community care legislation does not make competitive tendering between prospective providers compulsory, although there is a requirement that authorities promote it. Indeed, the Government itself envisages a range of options, firstly in terms of what precisely is assigned to the respective roles of purchaser/commissioner and provider (Department of Heath, undated) and, secondly, in terms of how the relationship between them is managed. The Department of Health suggests four possibilities for selecting providers: open tendering, select list tendering (the practice most widely used in CCT), direct negotiation and setting up 'new' organisations (Department of Health, 1991, p. 4).

Those in local government tend to regard the competitive tendering option as particularly inappropriate. First, it would encourage bids from national agencies and undermine local knowledge and access to client groups. Second, it would require a strict separation between the purchaser and provider functions. Community care arrangements are more likely to be effective when drawn up by the purchaser and provider sides jointly. Third, tendering would lead to an emphasis on cost rather than quality. Fourth, moving to a contractual relationship with voluntary organisations with whom authorities already work will threaten to undermine the innovations of some voluntary sector organisations in involving local people in community projects and also their *advocacy* role. It is emphasised by many, who question its extensive use in public services, that the contract is an inflexible and often static form of relationship (Stewart and Walsh, 1989). Fifth, there is a particular danger that less well established voluntary organisations would fare especially badly in the competition for contracts, particularly those representing black and ethnic minority interests and those with fragmentary and changing client groups, while the contractual process might discourage some community groups, such as those representing lesbian and gay interests (AMA, 1990). Finally, any formal contracts will be covered by those sections of the Local Government Act which severely limit 'contract compliance' clauses. In community care services there is particular concern about the nature, training and qualifications of the work-force of potential providers and an even greater emphasis on a practical commitment to equality of opportunity in delivering services and in organising staff.

Since the provider arrangements do not have to be in force until 1993, most authorities are still in the process of determining what they will look like. There are, therefore, only limited illustrations of good (or bad) practice, and guidance for the management of quality in purchaser/provider relationships tends to focus on general principles and procedures. There are two considerations here relating, firstly, to the nature of the providing organisation or agency and, secondly, to the procedures to be followed in making some formal arrangement for the delivery of services. For the reasons discussed above, it is likely that authorities will predominantly reject competitive tendering as a means of making these arrangements. However, the framework of procedures, stages and issues now followed in most authorities for managing CCT does provide essential guidance on how quality-related issues can be dealt with in purchaser/provider arrangements.

Many localities lack an extensive range of agencies other than the local authority or the health authority for delivering community care services. (AMA, 1990, p. 15). Financial pressures on, and inducements to, local authorities have therefore generated an interest in several authorities, under quite different political controlling groups, in establishing new organisations or arrangements. There are a number of possibilities: trusts; arrangements with housing associations; not-for-profit companies (such as that established by Tameside Council to run its elderly persons' homes); consortia between local authorities, health authorities and housing associations; and management 'buy outs' of particular operating facilities or homes (although this has not been as widespread as at one time anticipated).

There is a suggestion that the nature of the agency may itself suggest the appropriate form of relationship with the 'purchasing' body and the way in which quality should be pursued. Kieron Walsh envisages three approaches in working with other agencies. First, quality management standards will need to be clearly defined where there are contracts with providers. Second, there may be joint approaches to quality management, for example in joint inspection with other public agencies, such as health authorities. Third, with agencies such as voluntary bodies, it may be important to assist in the development of appropriate quality systems, for example by providing training (LGMB, 1992a). The AMA also draws a 'clear distinction between cases where the local authority jointly agrees to enter a contract with a voluntary organisation and cases where it invites competitive tender to provide services' (AMA, 1990, p. 15). It suggests that there are alternatives to formal contracts which are already used in many authorities. Per capita fee paying for individual users is used for residential or day care placements; grants are made to support advice and advocacy work; partnership arrangements have been made in combined nursing and care homes; and Service Level Agreements, which are discussed fully below (AMA, 1990, p.16). Where the voluntary agencies have been significant contributors to service provision, part of the local authority role in ensuring quality and continuity may be to contribute to the 'infrastructure' of the voluntary sector, by providing or paying for training, administration, equipment, legal and financial advice, etc.

Birmingham City Council provides an illustration of a renegotiation of arrangements with voluntary sector organisations *before* the Community Care legislation, for example in day care and provision for a multi-handicap group. The Council moved from grant aiding to Service Level Agreements (SLAs) with the agencies. SLAs in this context were clear agreements on target groups and objectives, service availability, criteria for receiving the service, and user consultation. They provide the basis for a funding agreement. The voluntary sector agencies have also agreed to quality statements which cover staffing and complaints and which commit the organisations to introduce quality assurance systems consistent with a framework provided by the Social Service Department of the Council (AMA, 1992).

This example of the modified arrangements made with voluntary organisations in Birmingham indicates how the logic and basic principles of the procedures adopted for CCT can be used to pursue service quality in community care arrangements, even where competitive tendering is not adopted and, therefore, arrangements are not contractual in the true sense. There are a number of factors of relevance to the achievement of quality. First, quality can be a requirement of the value and organisational structure of any providing agency, indicated in a quality policy and staff training. Second, the specification of the service to be provided in the contract or agreement should give an explicit statement of the standards to be achieved. There are a number of practical issues to be addressed in setting these standards. Who is to set them and what factors will be taken into account? Any adequate approach to quality in community care will involve users in designing and setting standards. How can standards be defined so that they both achieve policy objectives and allow for flexibility and potential innovation in the way services are delivered? Once the standard is set, what performance measure will be established to ensure that it is being met? How is equality of opportunity integrated into the quality standards?

A third consideration relates to the incorporation of quality assurance procedures into the contract or agreement. The example above from Birmingham City Council's revised arrangements indicates how this can be achieved with some agencies without the formality of BS 5750 type procedures, although these may be appropriate where there are formal contracting arrangements with profit-making bodies. Fourth, the contract or agreement will need to be monitored. Monitoring should ensure that the specification is being complied with (i.e. 'conformance'); it should evaluate the outcomes of the service (i.e. is the service actually achieving the policy intentions — 'fit for purpose'?). Moreover, quality assurance procedures will require specific monitoring. The most effective monitoring procedures will combine and co-ordinate the independent Inspection Units required under the community care arrangements, the purchasing agency, and the users of the service, both through the established complaints procedures and through other more direct forms of involvement (information, consultation, participation and control, AMA, 1991a). Finally, contracts or agreements can include 'quality clauses' which, in addition to the specifications, will indicate the nature of the service to be provided. Of importance here will be issues around staffing, covering qualifications, training, ratios to users and residents, and requirements that the workforce composition reflect the ethnic composition of the catchment area or prospective user groups (AMA, 1990). However, where there are formal contracting arrangements with providing agencies, these will be subject to the restrictions of 1988 Local Government Act.

In mid-1992, before the new purchaser/provider arrangements have been carried through, these suggestions about mechanisms for ensuring quality merely represent proposals for good practice. The practical obstacles and difficulties in implementing the new structure for community care has already resulted in local and heath authorities falling behind the schedule set down by the Government. The practical difficulties of putting these approaches to quality into practice will therefore be substantial. They will also be subject to the more general 'barriers to quality' which central government constraints on, and changes to, the public sector will impose.

Quality, contracting and EC directives

Where local authorities do enter into formal contracts with other agencies, the procedures and criteria they use are subject to EC directives in addition to domestic legislation. This framework of Public Procurement Directives originated in the 1970s but has been substantially revised and extended as part of the programme for the Single European Market. The original directives covered building works (from 1971) and purchasing of supplies (initially from 1977). These have been revised at EC level with effect from 1989 for building work and 1990 for supplies, and both Directives have now been codified into UK law through statutory instruments in December 1991. In 1993 they will be joined by a further directive of even wider significance for local authorities *and* other bodies either acting as their agents or with whom they contract. The Services Directive effectively extends the EC regime to all remaining services 'procured' by local authorities and, indeed, all 'bodies governed by public law'.

The EC framework has three basic requirements: the first deals with advertising of contracts and reporting of contracts awarded; the second prohibits the specification of technical standards only used nationally which would have the effect of discriminating against contractors based in other member states: the third establishes 'objective' criteria for the award of contracts. The second and third requirements have an obvious significance for the various ways discussed earlier in which authorities may attempt to implement 'quality' in their contracting arrangements. They do not, in principle, make the achievement of quality in contracting any more difficult. Indeed, 'quality' is a consideration explicitly endorsed as part of the process of awarding contracts.

However, there are fundamental differences of emphasis between the EC Directives and UK legislation (Paddon, 1992, Digings, 1991). Compliance with one does not necessarily ensure that the requirements of the other are being met. In some areas, notably those relating to employment and production issues, the EC framework arguably gives greater facility for pursuing the full range of quality-related issues, especially for those services 'defined' under the 1988 Local Government Act which are also covered by EC Directives. However, for services and areas of community care not covered in the same way by UK legislation, the Directives lay down a set of procedures to be followed with some restrictions on their application. The application of EC Directives to all 'bodies governed by public law' may mean that some organisations acting as agents for local authorities have to apply the Directives as client bodies when they purchase goods, services or building work.

For technical specifications, or contract inputs, the Directives essentially set out a hierarchy of preference. Ideally, specifications should conform to European-wide standards. Alternatively, they may conform to national standards which implement the European standards. Only where this is not possible may use be made of national or other standards, and always within the general requirement of the Directives viz that procedures do not, in principle, disadvantage potential contractors or suppliers from other member states. The references to quality assurance in the Services Directive follow this same logic. Contracting authorities are to refer to the EN 29000 European standard if they require conformity to quality assurance but must also accept equivalent certification from bodies established in other member states. And where potential service providers have no access to certification, they must also accept other evidence of equivalent quality assurance.

Contracts may be awarded on the basis of 'open', 'restricted' or 'negotiated' procedures, with restrictions placed on the use of the latter. In the award of contracts, where these are not negotiated, there are two basic elements. The first, 'qualitative selection', sets criteria against which potential contractors or service providers may be judged. These include bankruptcy, professional misconduct, failure to meet social security and taxation obligations, and falsification of information; the list in each Directive is exhaustive. The second covers the basis on which tenders are evaluated and offers two options. Selection may be on price alone, with the contract awarded to the lowest tenderer without qualification, or on the basis of the 'economically most advantageous' tender. No comprehensive definition is given of the latter, and the list of illustrative criteria in each Directive differs slightly. However, 'quality' is explicitly listed in the most recent of the Directives (the Services Directive) alongside other 'quality related' considerations such as after-sales service, and delivery periods (European Commission, 1992).

Taking the wider application of quality of services to cover employment conditions and considerations, the Directives are less clear. The European Commission appears to see no difficulty in the inclusions of wider 'social' and 'regional' considerations in contracts, such as requiring employment of the unemployed, women or black people, provided this does not contravene the ultimate requirement for all EC Law, that contractors from other member states should not, in principle, find it more difficult to comply (European Commission, 1989). This is confirmed in the one piece of European case law on contracting under the Directives — the 'Beentjes' case (Common Market Law Reports, 1990). It is less clear how these considerations might be included in the process of selecting between contractors. At present, and in the foreseeable future, it is in any case the more restrictive proscriptions of the 1988 Local Government Act which prevent inclusion of several of these issues in the award of contracts.

The Beentjes ruling also illustrates the implication of the wider application to non-government or local government bodies which are governed by 'public Law' since it was judged that the Directives applied to a non local government body because it fulfilled the *functions* of the state though not part of the formal state administration (Common Market Law Reports, 1990). It is unlikely that many of the organisations established by local authorities or other bodies will fall even within this broader definition of the state. However, it would imply an obligation on any such body to carry out the directives when it was itself a client for goods and services in contracts with other third parties.

Conclusions

The EC Directives are illustrative of two general themes in this paper. The first is the importance of legislative frameworks, at domestic and European level, in structuring the relationships between local authorities and those other agencies which may, in the future, provide an increasing number of services. The second is that 'quality' is one of the key terms used both in debating the merits of these changes in service delivery and in determining their outcomes. It is now accepted as an appropriate consideration in deciding the outcome· of contracting processes and awarding contracts. In so far as the division of service provision into the two functions of client and contractor or purchaser and provider requires a clear specification by the former of what is required, there is some expectation that *clarity* will produce improvement in quality. Many of the positive proposals for implementing explicit measures or determinants of quality in the relationship between client authorities and contracting or providing agencies have focused on this.

Judged in terms of the outcomes of the new arrangements of CCT, however, real evidence of any improvements in service quality is scant. In part, this reflects the imprecision in the uses of the term quality when discussing or making proposals about local authority services. This imprecision is likely to come under increasing challenge with the phase of competitive tendering starting from 1992, when the contracting and other arrangements for community care are in operation from 1993, and when EC Directives apply to all service contracts. However, the legal frameworks operating at a UK level also provide effective barriers to a complete approach to quality in the services they cover, given the restrictions on issues that may be contained in the contractual relationship. Without a quite fundamental review of this framework in the context of EC Directives, it is unlikely that clarity of terminology on quality, or the clarity of role and objectives that moving to a more 'enabling' role for local government can bring, will be simply translated into better or improved services.

References

Association of Direct Labour Organisations (ADLO) (1987) *Proposals for a Comprehensive Construction Industry Bill*, ADLO, Manchester.

Association of Direct Labour Organisations (ADLO) (1991) *Direct News*, Winter, 1991/92, ADLO, Manchester.

AMA (1988) *Don't Panic*, Association of Metropolitan Authorities, LGIU, LSPU, ADLO, London.

AMA (1990) *Contracts for Social Care: the Local Authority View*, Association of Metropolitan Authorities, London.

AMA (1991a) *Quality Services: An Introduction to Quality Assurance for Local Authorities*, Association of Metropolitan Authorities, London.

AMA (1991b) *Service Level Agreements: Agreeing on Quality?* Association of Metropolitan Authorities, London.

AMA (1991c) *Quality and Contracts in the Personal Social Services*, Association of Metropolitan Authorities, London.

AMA (1992) *Signposts to Quality: Local Authority Case Studies*, Association of Metropolitan Authorities, London.

Brooke, R. (1989) *Managing the Enabling Authority*, Longman, London.

Centre for Public Services (1992) *A Strategy for Quality*, Centre for Public Services, Sheffield.

HMSO, (1991) *Citizen's Charter*, Cm 1599, HMSO, London.

Clarke, M. and Stewart, J. (1988) *The Enabling Council*, Local Government Training Board, Luton.

Cirrell, S. and Bennett, J. (1990) *Compulsory Competitive Tendering: Law and Practice*, Longman, London.

CIPFA (1988) *Accounting Code of Practice for DSOs*, Chartered Institute of Public Finance and Accountancy, London.

Common Market Law Reports (1990) Gebroeders Beentjes BV v. the State (Netherlands), 6 February.

Cochrane, A. (1991) The changing role of local government: restructuring for the 1990s, *Public Administration*, Vol. 69, Autumn, pp. 281–302.

Department of Health (1991) *Community Care in the Next Decade and Beyond*, HMSO, London.

Department of the Environment (1991a) *Competitive Tendering for Local Government Services*, HMSO, London.

Department of the Environment (1991b) *Competing for Quality: Competition in the Provision of Local Services*, DoE, London.

Digings, L. (1991) *Competitive Tendering and the European Communities*, Association of Metropolitan Authorities, London.

European Commission (EC) (1989) *Public Procurement: Regional and Social Aspects*, COM (89) Final, EC, Brussels.

European Commission (EC) (1992) *Procedures for the Award of Public Services Contracts*, Common Position adopted by the Council on 25 May 1992 with a view to adoption of a Directive, Brussels, EC.

Financial Times (1992) Three cultures converge in concern for consumer, 6 March.

House of Commons (1990) *Community Care: Quality*, House of Commons Social Services Committee, London.

Labour Party (1989) *Quality Street: Labour's Quality Programme for Local Government*, Labour Party, London.

Labour Party, (1991) *Citizen's Charter*, Labour Party, London.

LGMB (1991a) *CCT Information Service Survey Report No. 1*, Local Government Management Board, Luton.

LGMB (1991b) *CCT Information Service Survey Report No. 2*, Local Government Management Board, Luton.

LGMB (1992a) *Quality: A Councillor's Guide*, Local Government Management Board, Luton.

LGMB (1992b) *CCT Information Service Survey Report No. 3*, Local Government Management Board, Luton.

Manchester City Council (1988) *Contractors' Audit Volumes 1–3*, Manchester City Council, Manchester.

Paddon, M. (1991) *The Real Costs of Contracting*, Discussion Paper 22, Public Sector Research Centre, New South Wales.

Paddon, M. (1992) EC Public Procurement Directives and the competition from European contractors for local authority contracts in the UK, in Clarke, T. and Pitellis, C. *International Privatisation: Strategies and Practices*, Routledge, London.

Parker, D. (1990) The 1988 Local Government Act and compulsory competitive tendering, *Urban Studies*, Vol. 27, No. 5, pp. 653–668.

Public Services Privatisation Research Unit (1992) *Privatisation: Disaster for Quality*, PSPRU, London.

Ridley, N. (1988) *The Local Right: enabling not providing*, Centre for Policy Studies, London.

Stewart, J. (1991) *An Experiment in Freedom: the Case for Free Local Authorities in Britain*, Institute for Public Policy Research, London.

Stewart, J. and Walsh, K. (1989) *The Search for Quality*, Local Government Training Board, Luton.

Stewart, J. and Stoker, G. (1988) *From Local Administration to Community Government*, Fabian Society, London.

Stewart, J. and Stoker, G. (eds.) (1989) *The Future of Local Government*, Macmillan, London.

Walsh, K. (1988) *Quality and Competition*, Local Government Training Board, Luton.

5 Quality, strategic planning and performance review

Ian Sanderson

Introduction

There has recently been a resurgence of enthusiasm for 'rationality' in the form of strategic planning and performance review in local government and these activities are widely seen as prerequisites for the achievement of quality. This new enthusiasm can be seen as related to the increasingly widespread adoption of quality assurance (QA) approaches in local government (see chapter two). QA places the focus, on the one hand, on assessing needs and setting objectives, standards and targets and, on the other hand, on the development of 'rational' processes and systems to ensure that standards are achieved. Therefore, a serious commitment to QA in a sense *requires* a process of planning, monitoring and evaluation.

Nevertheless, the approaches which are being developed in this context look rather different from previous attempts to achieve rational planning and management. This is essentially because it is recognised that quality strategies must address key 'organisational parameters' — the structures, processes and the 'culture' of the authority. Consequently, strategic planning and performance review processes must be an integral part of the *management* process, adapted to the particular organisational context, and not operated as an activity 'abstracted' from this context as has been the case in the past.

The purpose of this chapter is to discuss the role of strategic planning and performance review in the achievement of quality. In the next section we consider briefly issues relating to the development of a strategic planning process as the basis for a quality strategy. We then consider the rationale for performance review in this context before

moving on to discuss the concepts and principles involved, considerations in developing an effective system for performance review, and
organisational issues. Finally, we conclude by drawing together the
main themes and issues.

Strategic planning for quality

As discussed in chapter two, a key component of the quality of a service is the extent to which it achieves the purpose for which it is
intended or, more specifically, meets the requirements of those who are
intended to benefit from it. Effective management for quality therefore
involves three main elements: first, specifying purpose and requirements clearly; secondly, organising the service to achieve these
requirements; and, thirdly, assessing the extent to which the service
provided actually does achieve the requirements. Strategic planning
plays an important role in defining purpose, in identifying the needs of
the local community, in specifying objectives for services to meet
those needs, and in developing action plans for services to meet objectives and targets. Performance review processes assess the degree of
success achieved through monitoring relative to targets and through
evaluation which will seek to measure the extent to which needs and
requirements of the service are met and to identify how the authority
can be more successful.

There are two particular aspects of the contemporary concern for
quality which have implications for the role and form of strategic planning. The first is the requirement to obtain the views of those who use
and potentially need services as to their expectations and needs. This
imperative derives from the critique of public services as 'producer driven', operating in the interests of those who work in them rather than
those who need to use them which was an important factor behind the
Thatcher Government's programme of reform, culminating in the present Government's perspective on quality, emphasising the 'empowerment of the consumer' (HMSO, 1991).

However, generalised discussion of 'empowerment of the consumer' neglects the plurality of interests in local communities.
People's relationship with a local authority may be as actual or potential users: they may choose to use a service; they may have a statutory
right to use a service; they may be compelled to use a service; or they
may be refused a service on the grounds that they do not meet the criteria of need (Stewart and Clarke, 1987). People also have other important relationships with local authorities: as an employee; as a local tax-
payer; as a member of a particular community; as a representative of
local business; or as a member of a group concerned to promote a particular set of interests. Critics of consumerism emphasise the broader

role of people as *citizens* in local communities, which goes beyond the consumption of specific services in an individualised relationship, to incorporate active participation in the process of local government on a collective basis (Hambleton and Hoggett, 1990; Gaster, 1991a). Consequently, there is a wide range of local 'stakeholders', each with their own wants and expectations, needs and criteria for judging the performance of the authority. Authorities will need to give considerable attention to how they are involved in the strategic planning process since, as Bryson (1988, p. 52) argues, 'the key to success in public . . . organisations is the satisfaction of key stakeholders'. We return to this issue later.

A second key aspect of the debate about quality concerns the organisational structures and processes which promote the achievement of quality. Of importance here is what Hoggett (1991) calls '. . . the crisis of bureaucratic regulation . . .', the demise of bureaucratic control and of mechanistic and rationalistic approaches to management, and the development of devolved and decentralised approaches to organisational control which are now widely seen as essential to the achievement of quality. A key feature of post-bureaucratic control is that while operational functions are decentralised, strategic command becomes more centralised. The organisation becomes 'loose–tight' in nature, to use Peters and Waterman's (1982) phrase. Thus, operational units gain devolved power to make decisions within a framework of strategic priorities and objectives set by the centre. In addition, organisational control in this context is achieved more through specifications of results and performance requirements than through conformance to operating methods and procedures. This is seen particularly in the development of 'control by contract' where a purchaser/provider split is introduced and control is achieved through the specification of output standards which define contract compliance (Hoggett, op cit, p. 250).

This trend towards the centralisation of strategic command can also be seen as arising due to uncertainty deriving both from central government policy and from the economic and social environment. Barrett and McMahon (1990) argue that uncertainty affects all the various 'stakeholders' or interests in the organisation, '. . . all scanning, anticipating, planning and adapting; all seeing how the primary changes will either be disadvantageous or offer opportunities for advancement' (ibid, p. 262). If management is seen as a process of negotiating and bargaining between the various interests, rather than controlling a hierarchy which integrates functional elements of the organisation, then managing under uncertainty can be seen as requiring the definition of strategic direction. Such direction is based upon a 'deep seated set of values about organisational purpose . . .' (ibid, p. 261); it constitutes a 'vision' or 'mission' which provides both a 'template' against which operational decisions can be made and a means for steering and co-ordinating incremental change so as to achieve longer-term objectives (ibid, pp. 262–3).

These developments imply a strong role for the 'centre' in local authorities in exercising strategic command', in specifying the mission, the strategic direction, the corporate priorities and objectives which provide the framework for operational management by service departments or units. In addition, this strategic role requires monitoring of performance against defined objectives and evaluating the degree of success achieved by the authority in relation to its defined mission and purpose.

In a context of uncertainty and change, planning is important for a number of reasons (Caulfield and Schultz, 1989). It helps in clarifying the authority's purpose and in translating this into purposeful action. It promotes greater awareness of the strengths and weaknesses of the authority. It helps in recognising and capitalising on opportunities and in defending against threats in the process of adapting to change. It promotes effectiveness in the use of resources in achieving the priority objectives of the authority. It can help in the process of communicating to 'stakeholders' what the authority is seeking to achieve. Moreover, strategic planning helps managers in various ways: it promotes thinking about priorities; it brings managers together so they can share problems and perspectives; and it improves communication and coordination (Thompson, 1990).

As indicated earlier, emerging approaches to strategic planning in the context of quality strategies in local government are rather different from the discredited approaches of the 1970s. Attempts at corporate planning at that time were too prescriptive and rigid, too detailed and ambitious, they failed to focus on key strategic issues, they were 'imposed' by the centre and failed to 'mesh' with broader management processes, culture and political processes. It is now widely recognised that planning must be part of a broader approach to strategic management, adapted to an authority's particular circumstances and, in particular, guided by political processes.

Therefore, approaches to strategic planning will vary between authorities depending upon the perception of purpose and role and the attendant structure, culture and approach to achieving quality. In particular, the character of strategic planning will vary according to the relative power of the 'centre' and individual departments. We have indicated that the devolution of power and management responsibility is widely accepted as a pre-requisite for quality. However, the degree of power retained by the centre will vary according to the perceived need to establish corporate priorities in relation to collective concerns for the broader welfare of local communities. In chapter two, we argued that this issue distinguishes perspectives on quality. The 'consumerist' perspective focuses on the provision of services to customers, primarily through contracts with other agencies, and therefore tends to devalue the broader potential role of local government in developing a strategic view of the overall economic, social and political well-being of the community and in seeking to promote such well-being through a wide variety of means.

In authorities pursuing the 'consumerist' road, the corporate management role of the centre will be minimised and the emphasis placed on devolved responsibility to managers in operational departments or 'business units' who are held accountable for performance. Examples of such authorities are Kent and Lincolnshire County Councils. In such a context strategic planning is essentially reduced to business planning, with all operational units (whether providing 'external' or 'internal' services) preparing individual Business Plans within minimal corporate guidelines (Delderfield, Puffit and Watts, 1991).

On the other hand, if an authority chooses to adopt responsibility for a more broadly-defined well-being of the community, it will need to address issues relating to the assessment of needs on a collective level, the identification of corporate issues and the co-ordination of services and activities. These requirements imply a stronger role for the centre in setting corporate priorities and guidelines. Examples of authorities pursuing this path are provided by Metropolitan District authorities such as Birmingham, Kirklees, Bradford and Tameside. In such authorities the strategic planning process aims to elaborate key corporate objectives and issues relating, for example, to economic regeneration, poverty, health and the environment. The corporate strategy then provides the framework for individual service committees to prepare plans expressing their own objectives, priorities and targets which are consistent with the achievement of the corporate objectives. The specific characteristics of the process vary between authorities who have developed approaches appropriate to their particular political and organisational circumstances rather than attempting to adopt a 'blueprint'.

If an approach to strategic planning is developed out of, as an integral part of, broader strategic management processes, this will ensure that it makes a real contribution to increasing the effectiveness of the management of the authority and promoting quality. It should provide clear, positive objectives and the basis for effective action to achieve those objectives. There are a number of aspects of importance here. First, the process must provide the basis for elected members to focus on their role in defining key values and priorities and in the strategic management of the authority and must, therefore, be an integral part of the process of political management. Second, to promote quality in services, the assessment of needs and the setting of objectives and priorities should incorporate the views of all 'stakeholders', in particular those of customers, communities and front-line workers. Third, the process should be fully integrated with resource planning and budgeting processes; in particular, the annual revenue budget should be formulated within the context of the objectives, priorities and targets set in the strategic planning process. Finally, the process should incorporate an approach to monitoring the progress which is being achieved towards objectives and targets and evaluating the performance of the authority as a basis for learning and action to improve performance. We now discuss the importance of performance review to the achievement of quality in more detail.

The rationale for performance review

Performance review (PR) is conventionally viewed as a 'technique' of policy analysis, a stage in the rational model of the policy process which contributes to organisational *effectiveness*. This technical perspective is evident in the Audit Commission's approach which emphasises the role of PR in developing better management in local government to promote more effective and efficient use of resources and in demonstrating success in this respect to those to whom local authorities are accountable (Audit Commission, 1986). This perspective is widely expressed in local government. An article by Taylor (1988) introduced PR as '. . . the essential tool for modern management . . .' and argues that it is:

> . . . systematic continuous and analytical approach to management, based on the principle that a structured appraisal of departmental performance is likely to result in improving performance on the ground.
>
> (op cit, p. 2026)

The argument that performance assessment is essential to the promotion of efficiency and effectiveness in the public sector has an economic basis. Since customer choice cannot provide the basis for the regulation of supply and demand for many public services, performance assessment is necessary as a substitute for the market mechanism (Healey and Potter, 1987). However, just as the notion of the 'allocative efficiency' of the market cannot be seen as purely technical, neither can the notion of 'effective performance' in the public sector context. The managerialist perspective neglects the issue of *whose* view is to count in relation to the relevant attributes of performance and what constitutes 'successful' performance.

Performance review also has an important role to play in promoting accountability by demonstrating performance achievements to those to whom local authorities are accountable. Again, this cannot be seen as a technical, managerial issue. Local authorities are accountable both to central government and to a variety of interests in the local community. Different interests will have a stake in, and will emphasise, different aspects of a local authority's performance. What is to be the relative influence of these various interests in defining performance? Clearly, this is a political issue.

In promoting accountability, performance review systems permit stakeholders in local government a degree of *control* through an influence on the criteria used to judge performance and through an involvement in the review process. However, according to Pollitt (1987, p. 43):

> . . . the majority of performance measurement schemes appear to have been 'top-down' affairs, propelled by the interests of politicians and senior officials in controlling both expenditure and the range of types of activities engaged in by lower level officials, particularly the 'street level' service deliverers. . . .

The control function of performance review systems reflects the distribution of power in local authorities: the power of central government to control their expenditure and activities and the relative power of politicians, senior managers, front-line workers and 'customer'. The devolution of power in the context of strategies to achieve quality in local government has implications for performance assessment systems. The devolution of operational power to front-line workers implies, as we have seen, a strong role for the centre in setting the parameters for 'control by results', whereby control is achieved through the assessment of performance of staff against defined targets (Hoggett, 1991).

Central government exercises a considerable degree of control over local authorities and this has important implications for approaches to the assessment of the performance of local authorities. Thus, in the context of housing management, Clapham and Satsangi (1992) argue that the interest of central government lies mainly in the extent to which the service is provided in an efficient and economic manner. This is seen as consistent with a focus on restricting service inputs and achieving control over the objectives of the service by emphasising particular service outputs. They see central government interests as promoted by the approach to performance assessment 'imposed' on local government through the Audit Commission:

> Their type of approach focusing on economy and efficiency does little to promote the direct accountability of housing management to tenants. Good performance is seen as an apolitical, managerial issue which does not take into account the impact of services on the needs, demands and aspirations of customers. The measures that are made

do, however, make a clear contribution in improving the accountability of the service to central government.

(op cit, p. 68)

While this criticism may overstate the degree of insensitivity to local needs in the Audit Commission's model of performance review, it does emphasise the political significance of approaches to performance assessment. From this perspective it is possible to question the role of the uniform system of performance indicators which is being developed by the Audit Commission as part of the Government's Citizen's Charter quality programme (HMSO, 1991) with the intention '. . . to inform the public about standards of performance of their council, and to facilitate comparisons with other councils, and from one year to another' (Audit Commission, undated, p. 1). By definition such a system will give little attention to specific local needs and will be likely to emphasise quantifiable service outputs. This implies enhanced central control over the objectives which will be seen as relevant to the measurement of the degree of 'success' achieved by local authorities.

However, within the constraints set by central government policy and legislation, local authorities have discretion to determine an approach to assessing performance which gives a voice to various local interests in accordance with local political circumstances. We discussed earlier the wide range of local stakeholders and the implications in terms of potential conflict over criteria for judging performance. We shall return to this issue of the involvement of local people in the performance review process. However, we now turn to a discussion of the concepts and principles of performance review and this is followed by a discussion of practical issues in the development of performance review systems to promote quality in local government.

Concepts and principles of performance review

We indicated above that there may be different viewpoints on what constitutes 'successful performance' for a local authority due to the varying interests of stakeholders. The concepts of relevance to defining performance are summarised in Figure 5.1. These have been discussed extensively (Audit Commission, 1986, 1989; Flynn, 1986, 1990; Klein and Carter, 1988) so we will outline them only briefly here.

In seeking to achieve its purpose and objectives an organisation uses various *resource inputs* (staff, materials, office space, energy, etc.) to produce *service outputs* designed to meet the needs of its customers or clients. Outputs are services provided for the public e.g. the care provided to a social services client, the education provided to a child, bus services provided for passengers, etc. However, it is helpful to distinguish, following Flynn (1986, 1990) between capacity provid-

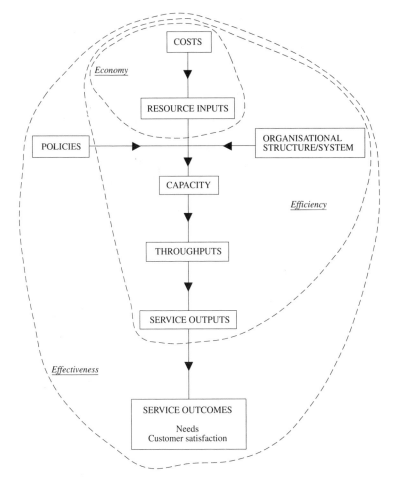

Source: Adapted from Flynn, 1990, p. 101.

Figure 5.1: Concepts of performance

ed (e.g. facilities, places), throughputs (customers/clients using facilities and occupying places) and outputs. These outputs have an impact on people's well-being and quality of life which is defined as the *final outcome* (e.g. improved economic and social conditions, improved environment, better personal mobility, satisfied customers/clients). It is this impact which defines the true 'value added' by an authority in relation to the intentions expressed in its objectives.

Various definitions of performance are derived from these concepts. First, *economy* refers to the cost of acquiring resource inputs. Performance can therefore be assessed in relation to the objective: 'the purchase and provision of services at the lowest possible cost consistent with a specified quality and quantity' (Klein and Carter, 1988, p. 6). An example of an economy measure would be average staff costs.

Second, the concept of *efficiency* refers to the relationship between resource inputs and service outputs. Efficiency objectives can refer either to the maximisation of output for a given resource input or to the minimisation of resource input for a specified level of service output. Measures of efficiency include unit costs (output per pound), productivity (output per person), and processing times. Flynn (1990, p. 101) defines two possible measures of efficiency. 'Efficiency 1' is the ratio of inputs to capacity (e.g. cost per place) while 'Efficiency 2' is the ratio of inputs to service outputs (e.g. cost per child educated).

Economy and efficiency can be seen as 'technical' measures of performance in that they take the value of an authority's activities as given. In order to assess the extent to which these activities are achieving the defined purposes and objectives of the authority, we need to refer to a third definition of performance: *effectiveness*. This is defined as the extent to which outputs achieve the impacts which are intended, i.e. the relationship between outputs and outcomes. Effectiveness addresses the difficult question of the value of an authority's activities and services. Does the social care provided actually address people's problems and needs? Does the education provided meet the needs of personal development and of the economy? Are roads swept to a standard which produces public satisfaction?

The assessment of effectiveness requires a clear statement of the authority's purpose and objectives and their relative priority, in order that the value of the authority's services and activities can be determined. Various aspects of the value of local government services have been outlined by Healey and Potter (1987) in a framework of performance review from the consumer's perspective which is illustrated, in a form adapted to health services in Figure 5.2. This indicates that the assessment of effectiveness must go beyond the benefits to users and the community to incorporate objectives relating to access, equity, choice, participation and representation, and *quality*. However, the definition of the latter is, in our view, too restrictive and the evaluation of performance in terms of the achievement of quality should incorporate both the extent to which services are meeting the needs of communities and the requirements of users on the one hand, and issues relating to the question 'What is it like to use?' on the other (cf. chapter two). The latter requires an assessment of the 'quality of interaction' between an authority and the public in terms of such factors as information provision, staff/public contact and opportunities for representation and participation. In chapter two, we defined this interaction as the 'service relationship'.

There are, of course, a number of well-known difficulties in measuring effectiveness and therefore assessing quality in outcome terms. For many services, especially those which impact upon personal and social needs, outcomes are difficult to measure directly. Moreover, outcomes are often not totally under the control of local authorities, but are subject to a wide range of influences, and impacts of services may become evident only in the long term. Finally, problems arise due to different interpretations as to what constitute acceptable and legitimate outcomes. We have indicated that the views of 'customers' are central to the assessment of quality, especially where the service relationship

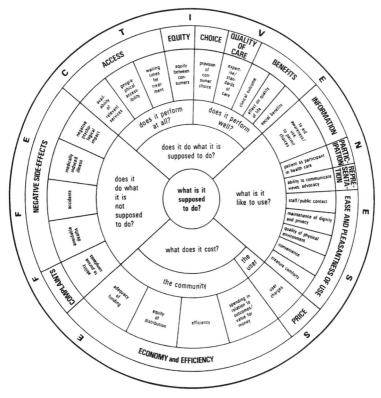

Source: Healey and Potter (1987, p. 16).

Figure 5.2: Evaluating health services: the consumer criteria

is important. Nevertheless, these views must be treated with appropriate caution in cases where services over-ride individuals' wishes and expectations in the wider 'collective interest'.

Because of these problems, it is necessary to refer to 'procedural' aspects of performance — the 'service organisation' aspect of quality defined in chapter two. Strategies for the achievement of quality involve the reform of organisational structures, systems and processes in order to secure the procedural basis for quality outcomes. At present there is a lack of evidence as to the contribution of various types of organisational reform to the achievement of attributes of quality. Therefore, an important aspect of performance review is the researching and evaluation of various organisational parameters in order to identify factors which contribute to 'success' or 'failure', and to inform learning about how to improve performance. Such evaluation should address the way the authority goes about planning, organising and delivering its services and activities in terms of such 'formal' aspects as the process of planning and performance review, research and information collection, the provision of support services, contract specification and control, the provision of management information and also 'informal' aspects related to the organisational culture. Recognition of this dimension of performance assessment is leading many authorities to adopt more formal quality assurance (QA) approaches although these tend to focus on the more formal systems and processes.

Consequently, there is a range of possible measures of the performance of local authorities and it is clear that the evaluation of performance is by no means a straightforward task. 'Performance' is a complex, multi-faceted concept and its measurement cannot be reduced to a set of simple, unambiguous indicators. Evaluation is not an objective, 'technical' exercise but involves value judgements in relation to trade-offs between objectives. The development of an effective performance review system requires, in our view, a multi-dimensional approach which combines input, output, outcome and process measures, focusing on the key dimensions of effectiveness and quality. We now discuss more practical considerations in the development of such a system.

Developing an effective performance review system

The fundamental requirement for a performance review system is self-evident: it must be useful. It should provide a clear picture of how successful an authority is in relation to its defined purpose and objectives and it should feed into the planning of programmes and activities and thereby provide the basis for improving performance.

The evaluation of performance should be an integral part of the process of planning and management, indeed, a commitment to evaluation, learning and improvement should be central to the 'culture' of the authority. What is required is a commitment on the part of all in the authority to a 'performance orientation' as part of a 'quality culture' — constantly to strive for success, to know and demonstrate what degree of success is being achieved, and to learn how to be more successful. In this sense, performance review can be seen as an integral part of a QA approach. It is unlikely to be effective in promoting quality if it is merely 'bolted on' to existing processes and ways of thinking and seen as a 'technical fix'. The commitment involved may require changes to values and basic assumptions. On the other hand, the development of an effective performance review framework which is seen as legitimate and beneficial by staff can be an important means to gaining the commitment to the assumptions, values and attitudes which represent a 'quality culture'.

An important dimension of the value of a performance system must be its cost-effectiveness. The approach to performance review should itself be evaluated for its contribution to the effectiveness of the authority, as a 'process' element of the framework. This implies that trade-offs will be required between the capabilities of the system and the cost of maintaining it. Consideration of cost-effectiveness points to the need to ensure maximum simplicity consistent with the effective demonstration of performance. Simplicity is also implied in the need to avoid 'information overload' and to ensure that the system captures key aspects of performance and permits the important lessons to be learned which will result in improved performance.

A basic requirement for the evaluation of quality is an assessment of the problems, needs and preferences of 'consumers' and communities (Healey and Potter, 1987). Such an assessment provides a 'baseline' against which the impact of programmes can be evaluated. Traditionally, approaches to needs assessment have been dominated by professionals and elected members but it is increasingly recognised that the achievement of quality requires an enhanced role for the public. There are two aspects to this: firstly, a need to find out directly the public's views on services, their problems and their expectations; and, secondly, a need to involve the public in the process of need assessment both as individuals and on a collective basis. The process of 'community needs auditing' seeks to achieve these objectives in attempting to establish a pluralistic framework for needs assessment involving all relevant interests (Percy-Smith and Sanderson, 1992). This issue is discussed in more detail by Blackman in the next chapter.

Given an assessment of the problems, needs and preferences of local communities, priorities can be established for addressing them and objectives drawn up expressing what the activities and services of the authority should achieve for local people as individuals and on a collective basis. Clear and unambiguous objectives are essential to the evaluation of performance since they express the value of the authority's activities. However, there has been a traditional reluctance to specify clear objectives in local government. One reason for this may be political expediency — fear of criticism of failure to achieve stated objectives. This is symptomatic of the 'defensive mentality' which must be overcome in the pursuit of quality. Another possible reason for such reluctance is the existence of many conflicting objectives for local government services and activities due, for example, to the 'tension' between providing for individual choice on the one hand and accommodating 'externalities' on the other. The existence of conflicting objectives requires priorities and trade-offs to be specified; this involves value judgements and therefore raises the awkward issue of whose values are to count. Finally, there is a danger, in specifying objectives, of stating what services do rather than what they should achieve thus reinforcing the status quo rather than promoting the development of more effective and better quality services.

Again, the specification of objectives for the achievement of quality services will require the views of the public to be incorporated. Indeed all stakeholders should be involved in defining what services should aim to achieve for those who have an interest in them either as customers/clients (individually and collectively), as representatives of customer interests, as deliverers of the services, or as representatives of the broader interests of the community as a whole. Conflicts of viewpoint and interests will arise which will require the development of approaches to resolving them by establishing priorities:

> The democratic nature of local government means that elected members have the perhaps unenviable task of deciding between the interests of all the different stakeholders in determining policies and goals. It will still be necessary to ensure that the different interests are clearly and separately identified, and that precise objectives are made public.
>
> (Healey and Potter, 1987, p. 21)

Clear objectives are essential, then, to the specification of relevant performance measures or indicators which allow the impact of services and activities on objectives, and therefore their 'value', to be assessed. Performance measures should be derived from objectives and should not be determined on the basis of current activity and available information. They should measure what is important — what the authority is seeking to achieve — not merely what is done at the present time (Horton and Smith, 1988). The emphasis should be on identifying key measures of performance which capture the value expressed by objectives, seeking simplicity and relevance and avoiding 'information over-load' which can actually detract from effective management. This will be important to securing the commitment of staff throughout the authority to performance review and avoiding the cynicism which can result in the manipulation of the system.

Performance measures should also relate to aspects of services and activities over which the authority has control if they are to provide a meaningful guide to improved performance (Klein and Carter, 1988). In a system of devolved responsibilities the performance of operational units or cost centres must be assessed against measures which are sus-ceptible to managerial influence. As Flynn (1986, p. 401) argues: 'Nothing but frustration can result from a set of performance indicators over which a manager has no control'. Performance measures are more likely to be unambiguous, relevant and controllable if they are devised with the full participation of all staff in the authority, particularly those who are close to the front-line of service delivery (Horton and Smith, 1988). Participation of front-line staff will also help to ensure that per-formance indicators measure attributes of services and activities which are of particular concern to the local public — a key requirement for quality.

We referred earlier to the tension between local discretion and cen-tral control in relation to the determination of criteria of 'success'. There is indeed something of a contradiction between the requirement for 'local relevance' and the present Government's proposals for cen-trally-imposed performance indicators which will be used to construct 'league tables'. Unless such indicators capture the *value* of services for local people (i.e. relate to outcomes), they will be less about promoting quality than about extending the scope of central control over local government.

The specification of relevant performance measures and targets to define 'successful' performance is not an easy task. Without targets or standards it is not possible to say whether performance is good or bad, or better or worse than expected. Comparisons can be made on various bases: year on year; between similar units within the authority; and between authorities (Klein and Carter, 1988, pp. 12–13; Flynn, 1990, pp. 102–4). The controversy over performance league tables both for schools and authorities as a whole indicates the need for considerable caution in using inter-authority comparisons. Ideally, targets should be set so as to be achievable with a continuous and concerted effort to improve performance; if they are set too high or too low they may gen-erate cynicism, disillusionment and manipulation. Where impacts are influenced by factors beyond the authority's control it should be clear to what extent the authority can exercise influence and the reasons for any failure to achieve targets should be made explicit. Targets should promote a culture which encourages a commitment to, and the reward of, success and which seeks to improve quality.

The specification of explicit and consistent measures and standards of attainment for services is important to the achievement of quality. According to Pollitt (1990, p. 437) '. . . quality assurance in the public services has to do with establishing explicit — and transparently arrived at — standards, which reflect the defined or stated need of service users'. The importance of standards is emphasised in the Citizen's Charter and standards take on particular significance in the context of contracted services. However, most progress with the specification of standards has been made in relation to the more 'technical' and 'product-oriented' services such as refuse collection, street sweeping, housing repair, etc., where the definition of outcome measures and standards is more straightforward. Most of the 'customer charters' which have been developed in such authorities as York, Lewisham and Leicester refer to these services, providing customers with an entitlement and a basis for complaint or redress.

On the other hand, in the 'social' and 'people-orientated' services, such as social services and education the specification of outcome measures and standards is more problematical. In such services, which are more orientated to specific identified personal and social needs, the interaction between provider and recipient is more important and in some cases (e.g. counselling) may define the service and it is difficult to derive standards, either qualitative or quantitative, which will provide an unambiguous measure of 'success'. In this case, 'procedural' standards may be easier to define than outcome standards, referring to the way in which people are treated in the service relationship.

The views of customers and those affected by services must be of central importance in the process of establishing performance indicators and standards and in the evaluation of performance against standards (Flynn, 1986; Klein and Carter, 1988). Many local authorities are now committed to finding out what consumers themselves think about services through market research exercises and other forms of public consultation. Nevertheless, in relation to housing services, Clapham and Satsangi (1992) argue that most of these initiatives have been developed from a 'consumerist perspective' which does little to empower people as citizens. It is less clear to what extent local authorities are prepared to encourage real participation by their publics, both as individuals and on a collective basis, in the development and operation of performance review systems. Clapham and Satsangi (op cit, pp. 71–2) argue that:

> Not only should the views of tenants be used as indicators of performance, but tenants should be involved in choosing appropriate indicators and therefore in defining the criteria of success. Also, as well as

seeking the views of tenants individually through questionnaire surveys and group interviews, the collective views of tenants' associations and other democratically representative bodies of tenants would have to be sought.

The measurement of quality, particularly in relation to the collective views and perceptions of the public, will require considerable attention to be given to qualitative methods of data collection (Gaster, 1991a, 1991b; Healey and Potter, 1987; Pollitt, 1987). In order to understand the 'meaning' of people's situations, to get a rounded picture of their perceptions of services and expectations, and to appreciate the broader impact of services on people's quality of life and well-being, it is necessary to obtain qualitative information through structured discussions with individuals and with representative community-based groups. Also of importance, as indicated above, are the views of front-line staff who work at the point of service delivery and who have valuable (but usually neglected) insights into the impact of services. Although caution must be used in the collection and use of qualitative information, it can nevertheless be of considerable value in supplementing quantitative indicators particularly in relation to the measurement of service quality. (This argument is developed further by Tim Blackman in chapter six.)

There are various limitations, however, on the use of user perceptions in the evaluation of performance. We have already referred to the need to ensure that the collective dimension of impact is assessed. In particular, the perceptions of individuals must be treated with care in relation to services which address externalities and public interests considerations (e.g. traffic management, environmental health, police) precisely because a purpose of such services is to control and over-rule the wishes of some individuals in the wider public interest. Moreover, local authorities must ration services to match constrained resources and must decide priorities between competing claims. Consequently, many people will be dissatisfied because outcomes do not meet expectations.

Therefore, we would argue that there is a need to ensure a balance in a performance review system between different types of measures and the influence of different interests and perceptions. There should be a balance between input, output, outcome, quality and process measures, between quantitative and qualitative measures, and between the perspectives of the public (as individuals and collectively), professionals and politicians. There has been a tendency in the past for performance measurement to focus on the quantifiable, on inputs and outputs (and therefore on efficiency) and on the perspectives of professionals and politicians. In our view, the achievement of quality in local government requires that these biases are redressed and a more pluralistic approach to performance assessment is adopted, recognising the importance, but also the limitations, of measures of 'customer satisfaction'.

Organising for performance review

According to Caulfield and Schultz (1989, p. 61), '. . . performance review needs to become an integral part of the well-run authority's set of managerial processes'. However, there can be no blueprint; authorities must develop their own systems tailored specifically to their own needs (Taylor, 1988). An important issue concerns the respective power and roles of the centre and service departments or operational units in reviewed performance. Eiles and Ellsworth (1988) argue that there has been a tendency in the past towards a standard 'centralist' model characterised by a central review team, usually reporting to the Chief Executive and then to a performance review committee. However, this model has not been successful because central staff often lack a service perspective and due to resentment in the service departments at the perceived 'imposition' of a review process.

The traditional pattern in local authorities is, as Goss (1990, p. 17) argues, that '. . . power rests with the service committees and departments rather than the centre'. If performance review systems are to mesh with this structure of power, service committees and departments must be given a strong role, setting service objectives and targets and reviewing performance against them. However, the danger is that such an approach will '. . . obscure the strategic. The attainment of key objectives will be masked in a plethora of data about the attainment of service objectives generally.' (Caulfield and Schultz, 1989, p. 62).

These arguments suggest that a balance is required between the respective roles of the centre and service department in the performance review process. We discussed earlier the implications of the trend towards devolved and decentralised approaches to organisational control for strategic planning systems. Thus, a 'dualistic approach' emerges with the centre specifying the mission, strategic direction, corporate priorities and objectives which provide the framework for operational management by service departments or units. In such a context, performance review systems embody this 'dualistic' character. On one level, key corporate objectives and priorities are established by the centre and these result in indicators of performance and targets for achievement by all service departments through their policies and programmes. At the second level the service committees and departments formulate their specific objectives in the context of the broader strategy and within a consistent framework, and have responsibility for reviewing the performance of their activities and services against these objectives and targets.

This 'two-tier' approach has been adopted in several authorities, for example, Solihull MBC, Avon CC, Wiltshire CC, Redditch and Wolverhampton MBC. In the latter authority, for example, corporate objectives for the authority as a whole arise from a specific planning process and service committees annually prepare statements of objectives for three years ahead within centrally-defined criteria. Targets for the year ahead must also be specified and each service committee reviews performance against targets annually as a basis for reviewing its objectives:

> In reviewing targets the aim is both to assess the extent to which they contribute to meeting objectives and to draw out lessons which can be used for improving services. In this way they act as a mechanism for determining priorities, clarifying actions and pre-planning and aids accountability by providing members with information on achievement.
>
> (Wolverhampton MBC, 1992)

An issue of considerable importance concerns the respective roles of elected members and officers in performance review. It is now widely acknowledged that in the past members have become rather too involved in day-to-day management and operational matters at the expense of focusing on strategy, policy and results (Clark and Stewart, 1990). The trend towards post-bureaucratic forms of organisation strengthens the case for an increased focus by elected members on strategic management and the delegation to officers of operational detail. Following this argument, elected members should play a strong role in setting the strategic objectives and priorities and in reviewing performance in terms of the key strategic indicators of both corporate and service performance which measure the extent to which an authority is 'successful' in relation to its obligations, intentions and aspirations. Thus, Goss (1990, p. 17) argues that performance review is most successful:

> . . . when the policy framework is driven by members, who spend time and energy making sure the objectives reflect the political realities they face and the priorities they wish to establish. This requires new skills from members, to think strategically and develop corporate political decision making.

Such a focus by elected members has implications for committee structures. Thus, the Audit Commission (1990, p. 12) poses two questions for authorities concerned to encourage member focus on policy issues. First, does the committee structure focus centrally on policy and strategy, delegating resource and service management where possible to service committees/departments? Second, do service committees need to focus more on performance and results and the impact of service delivery on customers? Greater use of sub-committees with delegated powers is recommended and an example of reform along these lines is provided by Avon County Council (Latham, 1988). A distinction was made between policy making, policy implementation and reviews of policy and implementation. The role of policy and performance review was strengthened by the creation of Policy and Review Sub-Committees both for the Corporate Resources Coordination Committee and for each service committee.

However, the development of an effective approach to performance review which will contribute to making local government more 'successful' (and widely recognised as such) involves more than structural change. What is more important is change in the 'culture' of local authorities, in 'the set of attitudes, beliefs, ideas, understandings, procedures and everyday rules that make an organisation what it is . . .' (Walsh, 1989, p.7). We have argued that a commitment to performance review is a commitment to being open and critical, to being explicit about what the authority stands for and is seeking to achieve, to continuous learning about why performance is good or not so good, to a continuous striving to be more successful. Hicks (1991) refers to reforms achieved in Solihull MBC as seeking to achieve a 'performance related culture', seen as central to the achievement of quality. The importance of culture change as a basis for the development of an effective and successful performance review system is widely recognised (cf. Flynn, 1986; Goss, 1990; Klein and Carter, 1988) and is being addressed by an increasing number of local authorities (Caulfield and Schultz, 1989).

An important aspect of the culture of local authorities relevant to the development of performance review systems is the extent to which staff throughout the authority participate in their formulation and operation. We have indicated that the devolution of management responsibility is now widely recognised as an important pre-requisite for the achievement of quality. There are various aspects to the 'empowerment' of front-line staff: providing delegated powers of decision-making with a devolved budget; setting achievement targets with the responsibility to monitor and evaluate progress towards them; providing the opportunity for all staff to participate in the wider process of decision making and performance review. The latter is seen by Taylor (1988) as an important element in a performance review system:

> Most of the best ideas for improvement on the ground will come from individual members of staff. Regular job consultation and/or performance appraisal schemes might be considered, along with finding other imaginative ways of further unlocking and unleashing the drive, energy and enthusiasm of the workforce.

(op cit, p. 2027).

Therefore, in the quest for quality, local authorities will look for ways to incorporate the view of customers and the public on the one hand and front-line staff on the other in the process of performance review. It is worth emphasising again that the development of participative, 'pluralistic' approaches to the assessment of performance and quality is much more a matter of 'culture' than one of 'structure'. Structures and systems are relatively easily reformed but are unlikely to be effective unless there is the necessary change in values, attitudes, shared assumptions and commitments — in the attributes of culture. Assuming that the latter factors are supportive of a participative, pluralistic approach, then the 'Quality Audit' may play an important potential role in assessing quality in performance in local government.

The notion of a Quality Audit has been advocated by the Labour Party, and developed by various local authorities as an approach to assessing performance which goes beyond value for money to incorporate quality considerations in a way which involves all relevant stakeholders (Labour Party, 1991). As part of the quality auditing process, the views of service users, community representatives, councillors, employees and managers, and trade union representatives would be obtained on the impact and outcomes of services, and such measures would supplement consideration of performance in terms of costs, efficiency and quantitative indicators. This principle has broad applicability in planning and decision making in the public sector. It has been applied in the context of need assessment (Percy-Smith and Sanderson, 1992) and provides a framework for a participative, pluralistic approach to policy making in local government to promote the achievement of quality.

The principles of quality auditing have been implemented by a number of local authorities. Examples of applications in recreation, transport and information technology are given in a recent publication by the Centre for Public Services (1992), which also presents guidelines for best practice based on developments by York City Council. A fundamental principle of quality auditing is the involvement of service users and front-line staff in assessing the extent to which the service satisfies the needs of current and potential customers and achieves quality standards (op cit, p. 37). An example of a quality audit brief is as follows:

1. Examine and analyse the existing specification and cost.
2. Assess the quality of service provided and compare that quality against:
   – customer feedback;
   – feedback from other interested parties (e.g. employees, trade unionists, . . . experts, etc);
   – levels of provision in a number of other authorities.

3. Identify potential improvements to the quality of the service and assess the implications of those improvements for working methods, procedures and costs.
4. Recommend a framework within which the provision of a quality service can be assured.

(op cit, p. 46)

Therefore, quality audits represent an approach to performance review which can promote a Quality Assurance strategy as an integral part of a management process which continually seeks to assure, improve and review quality.

Conclusion

In the contemporary environment of uncertainty, change and controversy about the value of public services, effective systems of strategic planning and performance review are essential components of management for quality in local government. Such systems address a number of key requirements for quality: an assessment of the needs and expectations of the local public; clear purpose and objectives specifying intended impacts and benefits in relation to needs and expectations; an assessment of the capacity of the authority to deliver these benefits now and over the years ahead; the establishment of priorities for the available resources; targets against which the effectiveness of the authority can be assessed; monitoring of progress in achieving targets and objectives; evaluation of success in meeting the needs and expectations of the public and the reasons for shortfalls; and learning on the basis of evaluation so that action can be taken to improve performance.

Strategic planning and performance review systems must be an integral part of the broader process of strategic management of the authority. Lessons have been learned from previous attempts to introduce 'rational' systems which were essentially separate 'intellectual' activities, inadequately linked to structures of power and processes of control, both political and managerial. Any successful approach to achieving quality must address key aspects of service organisation and culture and therefore address such issues of power and control. In order to make a real contribution, strategic planning and performance review must be part of the quality management system.

As part of a broader quality management strategy, strategic planning and performance review must, of course, accommodate and promote the balance of power between stakeholders which the authority seeks to achieve in its perspective on quality. Again, authorities vary in their perspectives on the empowerment of the customer/citizen according to their politically-negotiated mission, purpose and role. Measures to involve service users in needs assessment, in priority-setting, in the determination of performance indicators, and in the assessment of performance are now universally seen as obligatory. However, authorities can choose to extend involvement and participation to provide local people with greater power to influence services and to seek to promote an active citizenship.

The scope for according local interests an influence over the criteria of 'success' will be determined in a context of increasing central government control over local authorities. Key components of the Government's programme for quality, as set out in the Citizen's Charter, reduce the scope of local discretion: the extension of CCT; provisions for 'opting out' in housing and education services; and the imposition of a uniform system of performance indicators for local authorities. These provisions in effect push local authorities down the 'consumerist' road and, coupled with spending restrictions, make it progressively more difficult to adopt a broader governmental role which emphasises the promotion of collective well-being and citizenship.

Quality audits provide a means by which a participative, pluralistic approach to performance review can be promoted, allowing authorities to achieve a balance of interests appropriate to their circumstances. A fundamental principle of quality audits is the involvement of service users and front-line staff in assessing performance. Clearly, where it is seen as appropriate authorities can include representatives of trade unions and various community and interest groups and quality audits could be developed as part of broader arrangements for citizen participation in the management of quality in local government.

References

Audit Commission (1986) *Performance Review in Local Government,* HMSO, London.

Audit Commission (1989) *Managing Services Effectively — Performance Review,* Management Paper No. 5, Audit Commission, London.

Audit Commission (1990) *We Can't Go On Meeting Like This — The Changing Role of Local Authority Members,* Management Paper No. 8, Audit Commission, London.

Audit Commission (undated) *The Citizen's Charter — Local Authority Performance Indicators,* Audit Commission, London.

Barrett, S. and McMahon, L. (1990) Public management in uncertainty: A micro-political perspective of the health service in the United Kingdom, *Policy and Politics,* Vol. 18, No. 4, pp. 257–68.

Bryson, J. M. (1988) *Strategic Planning for Public and Nonprofit Organisations,* Jossey-Bass, San Francisco.

Caulfield, I. and Schultz, J. (1989) *Planning for Change: Strategic Planning in Local Government,* Longman, Harlow.

Centre for Public Services (1992) *A Strategy for Quality,* Centre for Public Services, Sheffield.

Clapham, D. and Satsangi, M. (1992) Performance assessment and accountability in British housing management, *Policy and Politics,* Vol. 20, No. 1, pp. 63–74.

Clarke, M. and Stewart, J. (1990) *General Management in Local Government — Getting the Balance Right,* Longman, Harlow.

Delderfield, J., Puffit, R. and Watts, G. (1991) *Business Planning in Local Government,* Longman, Harlow.

Eiles, C. and Ellsworth, R. (1988) Performance in review — an activity for managers not councillors, *Local Government Chronicle,* 19 August, pp. 14–15.

Flynn, N. (1986) Performance measurement in public sector services, *Policy and Politics,* Vol. 14, No. 3, pp. 389–404.

Flynn, N. (1990) *Public Sector Management,* Harvester Wheatsheaf, Hemel Hempstead.

Gaster, L. (1991a) Quality and decentralisation — are they connected? *Policy and Politics,* Vol. 19, No. 4, pp. 257–67.

Gaster, L. (1991b) *Quality at the Front Line,* School for Advanced Urban Studies, University of Bristol.

Goss, S. (1990) Line of accountability, *Local Government Chronicle,* 23 November, p. 17.

Hambleton, R. and Hoggett, P. (1990) *Beyond Excellence — Quality Local Government in the 1990s,* Working Paper No. 85, School for Advanced Urban Studies, University of Bristol.

Healey, M. and Potter, J. (1987) Making performance measurement work for consumers in *Performance Measurement and the Consumer,* National Consumer Council, London, pp. 8–35.

Hicks, C. (1991) Strategy for shared success, *Local Government Chronicle,* 8 March, pp. 18–19.

HMSO (1991) *The Citizen's Charter — Raising the Standard,* Cm 1599, HMSO, London.

Hoggett, P. (1991) A new management in the public sector, *Policy and Politics,* Vol. 19, No. 4, pp. 243–56.

Horton, C. and Smith, D. (1988) *Evaluating Police Performance — An Action Research Project,* Policy Studies Institute, London.

Klein, R. and Carter, N. (1988) Performance measurement: a review of concepts and issues, in Beeton, D. (ed.) *Performance Measurement — Getting the Concepts Right,* Discussion Paper 18, Public Finance Foundation, London, pp. 5–20.

Labour Party (1991) *The Quality Commission – A Consultative Paper,* Labour Party Policy Directorate, London.

Latham, D. (1988) Reforming performance review, *Public Finance and Accountancy,* 15 July, pp. 9–12.

Percy-Smith, J. and Sanderson, I. (1992) *Understanding Local Needs,* Institute for Public Policy Research, London.

Peters, T. J. and Waterman, R. H. (1982) *In Search of Excellence,* Harper and Row, New York.

Pollitt, C. (1987) Performance measurement and the consumer: hijacking a bandwagon? in *Performance Measurement and the Consumer,* National Consumer Council, London, pp. 42–55.

Pollitt, C. (1990) Doing business in the temple? Managers and quality assurance in the public sector, *Public Administration,* Vol. 68, No. 4, pp. 435–52.

Stewart, J. and Clarke, M. (1987) The public service orientation — issues and dilemmas, *Public Administration,* Vol. 65, No. 2, pp. 161–77.

Stewart, J. and Stoker, G. (1988) *From Local Administration to Community Government,* Fabian Research Series 351, Fabian Society, London.

Taylor, W. (1988) Performance review is essential in today's world, *Municipal Journal,* 23 September, pp. 2026–27.

Thompson J. L. (1990) *Strategic Management: Awareness and Change,* Chapman and Hall, London.

Walsh, K. (1989) *Marketing in Local Government,* Longman, Harlow.

Wolverhampton MBC (1992) *Strategy Document 1992–95,* Wolverhampton Metropolitan District Council.

6 Improving quality through research

Tim Blackman

Introduction

The last few years have seen the development of new forms of management in the public sector with potentially major implications for the role of information and research. The bureaucratic model of the direct provision of services by large public sector organisations controlled by centralised hierarchies has increasingly lost favour among managers and politicians. Taking its place are decentralisation, contracting, devolved budgeting and a variety of initiatives centred on consumerism and citizenship.

The alternatives to the bureaucratic model differ significantly according to political ideology, particularly regarding the role of competition and the extent to which local authorities should provide services directly. However, there is broad agreement that services should be needs-led rather than needs being fitted to available services. Resulting from this is an emphasis on defining service levels and standards through a client–contractor relationship.

Hoggett (1991) suggests that while the bureaucratic model of control by hierarchy placed emphasis on methods and procedures within the organisation, control by contract puts the emphasis on results. As promoted by Conservative governments in legislation requiring local councils and health authorities to contract out, results have been seen very much in terms of containing costs and controlling expenditure. More recently, the issue of quality from the user's perspective has been highlighted in political debate about public services.

The Conservative approach to quality is one of targeting public services on individualised consumers rather than providing services on a collective basis. The Left's view of quality appears to be more wide-ranging. The Labour Party's consultation paper on its Quality Commission proposal refers to: 'Assessments of performance, analyses of outputs, perceptions of customers, surveys of unmet needs, reviews of standards and ideas of employees . . .', whilst emphasising that all of this has to be 'related to the efficient use of available resources' (Labour Party Policy Directorate, 1991, pp. 5–6). In assessing quality, this document states that:

> . . . skills in social and policy analysis, market research, community and quality development and customer care would be as important as financial skills.
>
> (Labour Party Policy Directorate, 1991, p. 14)

This is a radical approach. In local government, it suggests a role for research and intelligence on a par with local treasurers! Certainly the skills required at senior level in local authorities are changing, and this applies to both Labour and Conservative agendas for local government. Bob Chilton, Director of Local Government Studies in the Audit Commission, argued recently that local councils' current managerial skills base reflects the past dominance of personnel, finance and land rather than contemporary needs for chief executives and directors who are comfortable with marshalling and applying information from many sources.[1]

New forms of management in the public sector and the quest for quality have given rise to a number of important developments:

- *Citizen's Charters:* the prime features of these documents are to set targets openly and to define the councils' values in order to 'empower' users and citizens with information;
- *Customer Contracts or Service Guarantees:* these provide the public with clear statements of the level of service that will be provided and how to complain. Analysis of complaints is an important source of intelligence for managers;
- *Customer Care and Quality Audits:* both of these emphasise placing the user firmly at the centre of service provision. The views of consumers become important performance data;
- *Customer and Citizen Research:* consumer surveys of the general public and people with special needs have become more common. Some authorities are making use of qualitative research, previously largely confined to market and academic research;
- *Purchasing:* this function, which is replacing direct provision in areas such as community care and leisure services, is making demands for information on local needs, the nature, availability and inputs of services, their costs, the performance of services and consumer views;

- *Internal customers:* there is increasing use of Service Level Agreements (SLAs) between departments, especially between central services, such as accountancy, and service departments or locally managed units. These usually require the provider service to supply a service description and possibly a service guarantee, and to charge the purchasing department on the basis of time recording.

All of these developments increase the importance of information to evaluate the relevance and quality of public services. Much useful data is already available, but a significant part of the information needs involved require special surveys, the analysis of secondary data such as the Census or existing administrative records, and qualitative research.

A central argument of this chapter is that information has to be turned into intelligence: the capacity for perceiving and comprehending the meaning in information. This chapter attempts to demonstrate the key role for research in turning information into intelligence for quality management. The argument is developed in three main stages. First, the role of research in assessing needs and evaluating services is discussed. Secondly, the relationship between research and consultation is considered, especially in terms of whether research is part of a *consumerist* strategy or one which *empowers* and supports *citizenship*. Thirdly, issues in interpreting information and research are reviewed. In conclusion, the chapter argues for a commitment to research from managers and decision-makers.

The role of research in assessing needs and evaluating services

Research in local councils is discretionary and such expenditure must be justified by demonstrating added value in terms of improving performance, efficiency or attracting additional resources. Particularly important are the assessment of local needs, performance review and evaluation and competitive bidding for additional resources.

Need assessment is an essential part of service specification (whether internally or in relation to private contractors), including listening to local people's views on needs and the importance of different services or aspects of the same service. It is important to have a clear understanding of the type of needs which are being addressed. One of the most helpful frameworks in this respect is that of Bradshaw (1972) who distinguishes between:

- *Normative need:* need as defined by 'experts' and 'professionals';
- *Felt need:* an individual's subjective assessment of his or her need;
- *Expressed need:* this is felt need translated into demand for a service;

- *Comparative need:* need defined in relation to a standard such as a defined minimum.

Research is relevant to all these types of need but particularly to felt need and comparative need. Information about these needs can be used to set targets and standards for services.

Performance review is essential if services are to be monitored against contract specifications, and can include complaints procedures, user satisfaction studies and peer audits.

Need assessment and performance review require research to answer the following questions:

- *what are the current needs?*
- *what trends are occurring?*
- *what sub-areas and social groups are most in need?*
- *how effectively are services targeted on needs?*
- *what are residents' views about the specifications for services?*
- *what are their experience of using them?*
- *what are the priorities for new services?*
- *how successful are the council's policies and programmes in meeting its objectives?*
- *what resources exist within communities?*
- *what can be learnt from the successes and failures of past policies and actions?*

These questions are important enough to warrant the adoption of research programmes by local authorities, but a planned approach to research is rare. Much useful information is already held in administrative records but often the information systems in use make it difficult to utilise the data in policy-making, resource allocation or performance review. Progress on these fronts requires a strategic management style in which information systems and research services support the quality of the local authority's services.

In fact, research sits uneasily with the organisational culture of most local authorities. Research aims to produce rationally structured knowledge and information ideally on a continuous and consistent basis. By contrast, decision-making in local government is often founded on implicit beliefs and short-term pragmatism. But this does not mean the decision-making is irrational. Scepticism about research and information systems is often based on their perceived failure to deliver results of operational value. The recent emphasis on the consumer is helping to focus research and information much more on tangible questions, answers to which assist the development of user-led services.

Post-bureaucratic management in local government demands information and research to inform decision-making because it is expected that services will be clearly related to an assessment of the needs of users and citizens. For example, a community care plan based on informal theories and implicit beliefs is unlikely to be credible in today's environment; there has to be evidence that the plan will meet needs. This requires good systems and computerised records. The development of care management, for example, necessitates an explicit and sensitive assessment of vulnerable people's needs and those of their carers; this information should feed into resource planning as well as providing the basis for an individual client's care package.

Research can be applied to both operational detail and policy. Many local authorities have corporate anti-poverty and priority area policies which seek to favour deprived groups and localities in the distribution of services. But very few actually carry out research to evaluate their distributional impact. Bramley (1990) shows how surveys can reveal to what extent services are 'pro-poor' or 'pro-rich' by establishing who uses them, how much they use them, and what their spending preferences are. The mere existence of a library or swimming pool in a deprived area, for example, does not necessarily mean that these services are well targeted on poor people. The *utilisation* of resources is at least as important as the level of resources available if there are specific policy objectives about who should benefit from local authority services.

Geographical frameworks are a common basis for organising information in local government. Much information is recorded at small area level, and geographical units are an important basis for policy making, service delivery and local politics. Many factors of interest to local councils are geographically linked, such as leisure provision and usage, schools and pupils, housing and income, accidents and environment, land prices and land uses. This also means that meaningful typologies can be constructed geographically, such as neighbourhood types. Finally, people often identify strongly with districts and neighbourhoods.

It is particularly tempting to engage in geographical analysis from a quality of life perspective because people do not evaluate their quality of life in terms of the departmental compartments of local authorities. Sharp inequalities in quality of life have been found within urban areas on the basis of composite 'livability' indexes derived from geographical data on health, crime, housing and socio-economic conditions (Ley, 1983). This type of work is very relevant to many urban authorities' concerns with population loss and social polarisation, suggesting areas of intervention outside traditional local authority functions, such as crime prevention, combating social segregation through housing management and planning, and improving neighbourhood stability by addressing housing issues and weaknesses in support networks, including childcare and homecare.

However, geographical data can be misleading. Maps may reveal a geographical expression of symptoms whilst deflecting attention from the essentially non-spatial structural causes of inequality, such as decline in an industrial sector or social security benefit changes. They may provide an apparent rationale for area targeting based on the probability of deprivation or service usage in small areas, but a relative concentration of target groups in an area can lead to a redistribution of resources, which may then miss large numbers in the target groups who are more dispersed and include many people who are not poor. In other words, area targeting may be an efficient but not equitable way of allocating resources.

These qualifications must be borne in mind, and the need for explanations of the processes which show up in geographical patterns always highlighted to decision-makers who might otherwise be satisfied with an area targeting approach. The problem of the ecological fallacy can be ameliorated by expressing ratios for small areas as percentages of the total district-wide target group population and using point referenced data to analyse the actual spatial distribution of individuals or households in targets groups, rather than the numbers contained within fixed administrative units.

A recent development which could support the use of local authority data strategically on a spatial basis is geographical information systems (GIS). These are computer software packages which permit the integration, manipulation and presentation in maps of different datasets on the basis of common spatial referencing such as postcodes or grid references. Data can be viewed at different scales and information from different datasets can be merged together.

Currently, most GIS applications concern map-based inventories of land and infrastructure, but they have some possible applications in other fields. For example, they can assist in:

- *examining the changing spatial distribution of individual indicators, such as unemployment, housing voids, morbidity, crime or rent arrears*
- *investigating whether such phenomena are becoming increasingly concentrated in certain neighbourhoods*
- *developing and presenting composite needs indexes to assist in identifying social priorities or allocating resources, e.g. home help hours*

A GIS is not essential for this type of work, however, and at present the systems have limited value for local authorities outside land and infrastructure applications where there is a possibility of productivity returns or self-financing by increasing land charges. The major potential of GIS is probably yet to come with the development of on-line interrogation and analysis capacity.

Research and user consultation

Local authorities have certain statutory obligations to consult residents. Consultation is often regarded as fulfilling current expectations that local councils act in partnership with the community and adopt a 'consumer' orientation. Research cannot be a substitute for consultation, which usually has a commitment to everyone having their say and involving 'active citizens' in issues. It also cannot substitute for continuous processes such as monitoring and responding to complaints encouraged and solicited as part of quality assurance procedure. But it does provide essential intelligence about needs and services and the effectiveness of policies. Carefully designed, representative samples of target populations and the use of techniques such as control groups give valid and reliable information. Felt needs, usage and non-usage of services, and the degree of change following a particular action are all questions which local authorities frequently need to answer if quality services are to be provided.

Research can also be used to investigate the views of the majority who do not respond to consultation exercises. Newcastle City Council recently compared the results of public consultation about its draft Unitary Development Plan with the findings of a sample survey of residents' views across the city. During the consultation period, many comments were received from individuals and organisations arguing that public transport should have priority over accommodating car use. However, the residents survey indicated that most people's priority was to improve conditions and accessibility for pedestrians. Data from the survey also enabled residents' views to be analysed for differences arising from area of residence, age, socio-economic characteristics and other key variables which related to the council's policy priorities. For instance, whilst 50 per cent of employed and retired respondents opposed releasing Green Belt land for development, this declined to 28 per cent for unemployed respondents (Newcastle City Council 1992a).

Straight yes/no or agree/disagree questions in surveys can be of limited value to decision-makers if responses are split more-or-less fifty-fifty, as in the Green Belt example above. Qualitative research such as discussion groups can be used to find out the strength of feeling when survey results are inconclusive. Vittles (1991, p. 4) gives a good example from York, a local authority which has made unusually extensive use of qualitative research. A quantitative survey of views about a covered market showed 50 per cent in favour of a covered market and 50 per cent in favour of an open market. Follow-up qualitative research, however, revealed that those in favour of an open market held their views much more strongly, and for clear environmental reasons, compared with those in favour of a covered market.

The distinctive contribution of qualitative research is its focus on understanding rather than measurement: in other words, with 'why' and 'how' rather than the 'how many' questions which quantitative research seeks to answer with such techniques as questionnaire surveys and statistical analysis. Qualitative methods include group discussions which focus on a small number of topics, in-depth interviews, and participant observation, such as the 'mystery customer' technique when a researcher tests out a service by taking the role of a user. Qualitative data consist of detailed descriptions of what people say or do, including direct quotations about their experiences and attitudes, written accounts of events and passages from documents, letters or diaries. There can be substantial interaction between the interviewer or discussion group facilitator and the respondents to allow the probing of meanings, a focusing on particular aspects of the issue, or a full exploration of how people feel about a topic.

Although qualitative research cannot be used to make numerical generalisations, it does assist in enabling better understanding of people's needs and experiences. The main problem in this respect with consumer surveys, and the quantitative methods on which they are based, is that the level of detail they can collect is limited and it can be difficult for managers to decide precisely what practical steps are needed in response to the findings. As Bramley (1990, p. 49) writes, answers to questions about satisfaction with services can be ambiguous:

> . . . a given answer (especially dissatisfaction) could have a variety of opposing implications for service output levels, expenditure and taxes/charges. Dissatisfaction could imply that the service should be cut; or that it should be expanded; or that efficiency should be improved; or that the style of the service should be changed. Follow-up questions may narrow it down but still leave considerable indeterminacy.

In 1985, Newcastle City Council undertook a large-scale consumer survey in one of the city's most deprived wards to ascertain where service improvements could be made. A questionnaire and home interviews were used. The ambiguity which can arise with results from questionnaires is illustrated by the following commentary from the survey report about overall satisfaction with housing department services:

> . . . between 24% and 25% were dissatisfied to some degree with Housing Department services. Such dissatisfaction may have many meanings. Rather more than half of those interviewed were satisfied to some extent; approximately a quarter were dissatisfied to some extent. *Overall* perceptions of the Housing Department, then, do not reveal as much dissatisfaction as was found among people on the waiting/transfer lists. However, at the level of about a quarter of rele-

vant respondents, there is more dissatisfaction with Housing than with Education or Social Services. Of course, the local authority Housing Department affects the lives of *most people*, whereas Education and Social Services do not. Expectations of the services may be quite different. There are problems with comparisons between the three services. Notwithstanding these reservations, the level of dissatisfaction with Housing Department services is significant. . . . The negative comments overwhelmingly refer to *repairs*: largely to the time taken to have repairs carried out, but also to their perceived poor quality.

(Newcastle City Council, 1985, pp. 17–18)

Such a finding adds little to what housing managers would have known already — that housing services are judged very much by the quality of the repairs service — although regular surveys of this nature do give an indication of whether satisfaction is improving or deteriorating. Newcastle City Council has moved away from extensive consumer surveys because of their limitations in providing actionable findings for managers, and now targets consumer research on studies of individual facilities or services. For example, surveys of individual leisure centres are carried out, with interviews of people using the centre and of a sample of residents living in the centre's approximate catchment area to gather information from non-users. Questionnaires are designed on the basis of detailed briefs supplied by leisure services officers and the questions are focused on providing information which can be used in contract specification.

Qualitative research is not a substitute for quantitative research but can add value to quantitative survey data. A recent survey of satisfaction with housing repairs in Newcastle was followed up by discussion groups with tenants who reported dissatisfaction to find out in more depth what people felt was wrong — were the problems with the administrative systems or with the operatives for example? — and to assess tenants' expectations of the service. Survey results showing a high level of satisfaction were qualified by findings from the follow-up study which revealed serious inadequacies being experienced by a minority of tenants.

A survey by the Local Authorities Research and Intelligence Association (LARIA) revealed only 19 authorities that had undertaken qualitative research (Blackman, 1991). All were positive about the results, although the qualitative research was often combined with a quantitative study. The most common advantage of qualitative research was stated to be that it enables greater depth of awareness and understanding about people's needs, wants, perceptions and actions, and provides 'the feeling behind the figures'. Other common points were that qualitative research does not predetermine issues and that it generates ideas. It was found to be a useful preliminary before questionnaire design.

The presentation of qualitative findings can be very effective in bringing the message of the research to life. In a recent study of the problems of an inner city area in Newcastle, quantitative data from a survey were combined with qualitative reportage to bring to life the reality of children's experiences in the area (Hill, Blackman, Wallace and Woods, 1991). The survey showed that 68 per cent of respondents considered it a bad area for children. A percentage such as this can be brought home to the reader by results from qualitative research. In the report it was accompanied by this passage from an interview with a local mother:

> My first two weren't born here, and where we were before they got the chance to meet nicer kids. But my last ones were born here and them two are right little villains. They picked it all up. But I was still the same parent to them. I brought them up in the same way. And I knew it wasn't anything different I had done, it was just the society.
>
> (Hill *et al.* 1991, p. 23)

Other parts of the report present ideas for improving the area. Inevitably, responses in the survey to questions about how the area should be improved took the form of short replies, often instant reactions based on little thought. The group discussions, however, presented the opportunity for respondents to generate and test out ideas in a group. They could explain their beliefs and proposals to each other, and work towards agreement about what really mattered, such as 'bringing people together'.

A research design can make consultation more systematic and rigorous. Ritchie (1992) describes a one-day workshop to involve tenants on an estate management board in Leeds in deciding priorities for a modernisation scheme. Role playing was used to explore the advantages and disadvantages of different approaches from the perspectives of councillors, council officers and the Department of the Environment. All the participants were then involved in identifying the underlying criteria by which they were judging schemes. A final exercise involved everyone in putting different coloured stickers on flip charts to find out what priority they attached to the different criteria. The method was found to be 'effective and fun' and was used in four subsequent public meetings. Although Ritchie has reservations about the method's ability to handle complexity, it generated clear guidance for the capital finance bid:

> Crucially, the exercise showed that the main criteria for any bid were that spending should be directed to houses in greatest need of repair and should also be spread as widely as possible. This contrasted to

current Council policy of carrying out WHI (whole house improvements) on geographically defined areas on the estate.

(Ritchie, 1992, p. 18)

One of the commonest qualitative research techniques is the focus group. This is a small group discussion guided by a facilitator working from a topic guide. The participants are chosen from a target group such as users of a particular service or respondents who gave a particular answer to a survey question. They are usually selected so that they are of similar age and socio-economic background and the same sex, often using brief screening interviews. An observer/recorder takes notes of the sessions, backed up by a tape recording. The verbal/conversational data are analysed to highlight the structure of what people are saying, often linking together expressed ideas with relationships of 'may lead to' or 'affects'. Extensive use of quotes from participants is also usually made in write-ups of qualitative studies.

The rise of consumerism in public services, and its challenge to professional-dominated management by bureaucracy, has seen local authorities 'getting closer to the consumer'. As discussed above, surveys are often seen to be the most appropriate research response, but they have limitations. This is especially the case when the aim is consultation and participation:

> The pre-set questions express the council's agenda, not necessarily the service users. Moreover, surveys may indicate what people feel, but not why they feel this way. Only more interactive methods can help here, and this means getting out to people and engaging with them. . . .
>
> (Hambleton and Hoggett, 1990, p. 19)

Researching people in the aggregate is also far from satisfactory when there is a commitment to the subjective opinions of people rather than to the often dubious assumptions that law-like regularities can be the basis for deciding on levels and types of services. Qualitative studies carried out in some numbers can form the basis for judgements about the typicality of their findings and may thus be a more democratic alternative to surveys in many situations.

Hambleton and Hoggett suggest that research, by which they seem to mean survey and quantitative research, is part of a *consumerist* strategy but not of an *empowering* strategy, or one which supports *citizenship*. They argue that it puts the emphasis on individuals and reflects a power relationship between those providing and those receiving services.

Research in local government should, however, be about establishing knowledge about needs and services in order to serve democracy rather than displace it. What it seeks to do is to reduce the possibility of *misapprehension* about needs, policy effectiveness, and service efficiency and quality. Research aims to produce what Gregory (1978) terms an 'examined discourse'.

Anne Page, Director of the London Research Centre, has argued that the democratic role for research and intelligence should be in defining paths for policies and services through the tensions that exist between local and central government, citizens and officialdom, and political parties[2]. Its potential for doing this is in providing practical knowledge about what exists (needs, conditions, experiences, etc.), answers to why/how questions (causation and significant patterns), and evidence about the effectiveness of policies and services (evaluation). In other words, research in local government can be a counter-balance to ideology and image. Take, for example, a report in *Link*, the magazine of the Tyne & Wear Business Club, in June 1991 (p. 13):

> Decades of decline are being swept away as the foundations of a better future are being put in place throughout the region. . . . Today old is giving way to new and land which has lain waste for years is once again making a contribution, not only in economic terms but also to the quality of life of local people. . . . The task is being masterminded by the Tyne and Wear Development Corporation. . . . Achievements to date have been impressive and new development shows every sign of gathering pace throughout the 90s.

This passage can be contrasted with a research report which sought to establish the facts of progress in the Urban Development Area during its first four years:

> Between 1988 and 1991 there was a marginal increase in the proportion of land classed as developed. This increase was the net result of increases in commercial use (+47ha) residential land use (+18ha) and transport and other uses (+6ha) which outweighed the decline (–58ha) in industrial use. . . . (T)he UDA in March 1991 had slightly less vacant land (–9ha) and more derelict land (+6ha) and open space (+2ha) than at the base date of March 1988. . . . Many of the developments which took place in the early years of TWDC resulted from planning consents granted by the Metropolitan Districts. . . . Available sources indicate slight, if any, growth in employment in the UDA.
>
> (Tyne and Wear Research and Intelligence Unit, 1991, pp. 1, 5, 16)

In defining the paths which Anne Page described, the free flow of information is critical and an essential contribution to the health of local democracy. Large numbers of people experience the official structures and processes of local government as remote and have a hostile attitude to the local council, not least because information is used as part of a control function. This is particularly the case in deprived areas because so many services are experienced as control: housing management, social work, schools and benefits can treat people as objects of official decisions and as problems rather than as citizens. Research can also easily treat the people it studies as objects and problems without a commitment to provide information freely to support and enable user involvement, citizenship and community action.

It is often difficult to reach households in deprived inner and outer urban areas with survey research. Sampling frames such as electoral registers are more incomplete and out-of-date in these areas. Response rates, especially to postal questionnaires, can be low, making samples unrepresentative of the local population. Using local interviewers has been found to improve response rates in these circumstances, and provides training and income for local people (Wallman, 1982).

Survey research can be further improved by involving groups of local people in the design of the questionnaires, particularly so that questions are locally orientated, and by clearly linking the research with potential positive outcomes for the respondent and/or their community. This can increase respondents' identification with the aims of the survey and interest in the questions, thus improving response rates.

Whilst user surveys are now fairly common, surveys of employees are must less so. Any policy for quality must be informed about what happens at the point of contact between front-line employees and the public. It is unlikely to be successful if staff do not feel committed, involved and supported in providing a good quality service because of the level of discretion available to front-line employees in their day-to-day work. Gaster (1991) lists examples of the kind of topics which need to be examined: do staff have training in interactive skills such as non-verbal communication; do they have the information needed to answer enquiries from the public; do they feel that the public have reasonable expectations of what they can deliver; are they confident enough to deal with verbal or physical violence or threats; is the working environment demoralising or antagonising to the public; are employees isolated or do they feel supported; are they valued and kept informed; and what aspects of their work are rewarded, if any? Both surveys and focus groups are relevant to investigating these questions, but it is important that such research is conducted within a framework of support and openness.

Employee research is not just about staff's ability to do their job and the support they receive. It is also important to research the views of employees in carrying out evaluations of services. This is particularly important in developing indicators of performance and quality. These cannot just be policy driven; staff have to believe that the measures are useful and that they have the capacity and support to deliver on them and make improvements.

In the example of the Newcastle inner city study referred to above, local residents painted a picture of difficult relationships between themselves and council officers working in the area:

> When the professionals go into their jargon this puts the local people off, so therefore they lose them on the wayside. And then you'll find that everything local people want also goes by the wayside cause there's no one there to promote it and fight for exactly what they want on their Estate. Everything seems to be decided by the professionals and people on the ground don't get the chance to say what they want.
>
> (Hill *et al.* 1991, p. 19)

When council officers working in the area were interviewed, it was apparent that just as much frustration existed among many of them:

> The biggest resource in the area — the people — are not being used. There is a lot of good will in the area but it is not being channelled. Whatever is developed, local people need to be kept in control.
>
> Many policies appropriate to the area seem to be in place, the difficulty is with implementing them. It is important to have workers on the ground who can work within a community development framework. What is important is a shared philosophy between community and workers about what needs to be provided.
>
> (Hill *et al.* 1991, p. 41)

From the perspective of local residents, the problem was how officers working in the area operated. From the perspective of these officers, however, the problem was that their managers and councillors would not relinquish working in a traditional, hierarchical way. The result was low levels of trust and mutual confidence. This had to be addressed through a framework in which all the parties problem-solve together and which involves local people fully in what the council and other agencies are, or are not, doing in the area.

Using research to define people's needs directly, rather than having these needs represented through professionals, will also improve local people's identification with *their* services and interest in them. Developments in resource management information systems which enable managers to quantify the work done for users of services are encouraging, but they focus on numbers contacted and time spent with users rather than how services contribute to the quality of life goals of the people who choose to, or have to, use them. It is possible to use diaries completed by workers to obtain more sophisticated pictures of actual tasks done, but this still puts the emphasis on inputs rather than outcomes.

There can be little dispute over the view that outcomes should be assessed in terms of user's quality of life goals. Particular attention must be paid in research design to eliciting whether services contribute to or hinder the quality of life of people intended to benefit from them, for example, enabling a frail elderly person to continue living in his/her own home. This has special relevance in relation to minorities, such as minority ethnic groups, and sections of the population poorly represented by the political system, such as children. Perceptions of a good quality of life are likely to be related to the degree of control which people feel they have over their lives as both consumers and workers. Research into services and policies should always have full regard to this issue of control, and consider it as problematic in respect of its own methods. A person's experience of being a subject in a local authority research project should be one of a citizen contributing to the health of local democracy.

Problems arise in applying the quality of life and locus of control approach to services which have a high degree of social control, such as probation, where there are underlying possibilities of conflict between professionals and clients which make consumer assessment less appropriate. In these cases external benefits must be included in assessments of need. Indeed other services, particularly housing, education and social care, have significant external benefits which are received and valued by people other than direct users (Bramley, 1990). Research and policy should recognise this wider interest in services which people have, while not necessarily being direct users of them, by eliciting the views of users, employees *and* the wider public.

If research is about the free flow of information to inform democratic societies, then particular attention must be given to how results are disseminated. The research must be timely and the results must be relevant to decision-making needs, which means there must be a clear concept from the beginning of who is to use the results. Attractive presentation and eliminating jargon are important, and it may be necessary to prepare different versions of the results to suit different audiences.

Interpreting information

Qualitative research is no substitute for quantitative research and it is important to recognise that the nature of data from the two different research styles is vastly different. Qualitative research in government tends to be the poor cousin of quantitative studies because decision-makers want 'facts', and this usually means numbers. It is very difficult to make a case for resources without numbers. In the LARIA survey referred to above, a number of disadvantages of qualitative research were identified, almost all relating to a sceptical attitude to this style of research from managers who wanted statistics at short notice.

The problem with this attitude to qualitative data is that it implies that quantitative data is authoritative and largely free from bias. The attitude is much more a feature of public sector managers than in the private sector where qualitative research is more common. In fact, quantitative data must be interpreted with considerable care bearing in mind the essentially qualitative decisions that are made about what to research, how a concept like 'health' or 'education' is turned into measurable variables, the categories used in questions and analysis, the biases that may be introduced by low response rates or interviewer errors, the classifications used in coding schemes, mistakes in coding or data entry, and the tabulations and breakdowns chosen for analysis and presentation. It is hardly necessary to repeat the example of unemployment figures, where the frequency of changes in the definition of 'unemployed' people in the official count since 1990 has meant the 'same' figures keep measuring different things.

There are four main sources of quality problems with quantitative data:

- The wrong information is collected, e.g. data on inputs but not outcomes; under-reporting; reporting only users' views of services and ignoring non-users; and failing to collect certain data so that evaluations are biased towards the statistics which are available.
- The information is inaccurate and out-of-date, e.g. using 1981 Census data to allocate resources 10 years later; undertaking in-patient care surveys while respondents are still in hospital and may therefore be reluctant to voice criticisms; local authorities not following the definitions or guidelines of bodies such as the Local Government Management Board for statistical returns, thus producing misleading comparisons between authorities[3].
- The information is not disseminated effectively, e.g. statistical publications are slimmed down to save money.
- The information is interpreted wrongly, e.g. crude school examination results are used to draw conclusions about school effectiveness.

In essence, both quantitative and qualitative research require the same standards of scientific rigour. There are two main issues. Firstly, are the data valid? An interviewer asking 'do you have any problems understanding and filling in forms?' could well get a negative reply because the respondent is ashamed to tell a middle class interviewer that he or she has basic literacy problems. A focus group of long-term unemployed people could well tell a different story. Secondly, are the data reliable? Would a differently worded question get a different answer? Is the question ambiguous and therefore answered differently according to respondents' different understandings of it? For example, the question, 'Do you think that childrearing is predominantly the woman's role?' could be interpreted as asking about the current facts of the matter, in which case the answer is clearly 'yes', or it could be interpreted as asking, '*should* the responsibility be with the woman?', in which case the answer could be 'no' if the respondent believes the men should share equally in the care of children.

In qualitative research, this problem of the confidence with which inferences can be made from the data is just as real, but not worse. Qualitative analysis is also a logical process — taking care, for example, not to reduce the data down to categories too early in the analysis — and indeed computer programs which work with text are now available to assist with coding and analysing documents and interviews or group discussion transcripts (Tesch, 1990).

In using information for quality management, managers need answers to both the 'how many' and 'why' questions. This demands a combination of quantitative and qualitative research; consumer surveys and need assessment studies using Census data, for example, combined with complaints procedures, 'mystery customer' and other observation techniques, user panels and discussion groups.

It is important to conduct research rather than rely on possibly wrong conclusions drawn from information alone. Gaster illustrates this with her research on Birmingham neighbourhood housing offices. She found that one office treated a small number of returned 'satisfaction cards' as an issue for further investigation, and discovered many reasons why tenants were not completing the cards despite being dissatisfied. However, another office treated a similar response as a sign that tenants were satisfied with the repair service and took no further action.

Other recent research on housing management performance indicators shows that tenants can be confused by 'the welter of data' and that there needs to be consultation with tenants' groups or customer panels to make performance indicators of value to tenants (Passmore, 1991). This conclusion is echoed more generally in a recent publication by the Local Government Management Board (1992, p. 12):

> Formalising the relationship between the local authority and its consumers through standards and contracts of service, while empowering consumers to make informed judgements, has implications for performance measurement. Local authorities will not only have to produce and use internal data but develop ways of linking this assessment with the consumer's judgement.

As a recent TUC report on *The Quality Challenge* emphasises, it is not necessarily the case that an old person will regard five frozen meals a week as a substitute for a daily meals-on-wheels service, even though such a change may increase performance (TUC, 1992). Performance indicators should, where appropriate, be based on consumer research into specifications for the services. Clear service specifications based on consumer research and provided as public information give the user a basis for judging adequate performance. This facilitates much more targeted research on this performance which provides answers to specific questions rather than unfocused information with ambiguous meanings.

Also of relevance here are moves towards competitive league tables. Housing authorities now publish performance indicators that are supposed to enable comparisons in performance across housing management areas. Yet indicators such as empty properties measure a number of factors other than management performance, such as the age and condition of properties and therefore the number that are empty for repairs. It is essential that performance indicators are contextualised to control for the external factors known to affect them. The advocacy of league tables as a way of showing the relative performance of schools and local education authorities is a case in point.

A league table of school examination results across an authority may appear to measure school effectiveness. However, as Table 6.1 shows for schools in Newcastle Upon Tyne, it essentially ranks the socio-economic composition of the schools' intakes, given that in Newcastle over 72 per cent of the variation across schools in pupils leaving with five or more higher graded GCSEs is attributable to the variation in free school meal uptake. In some schools this has led to a change in examination entry policy, with children likely to achieve poorly in GCSEs being targeted for vocational examinations such as

School Examination Results and Free School Meals in Newcastle Upon Tyne, 1990				
	5 or more higher grade GCSE passes		Free school meals as % of rolls	
	Rank	Per cent	Rank	Per cent
School a	1	49	1	9
School b	2	48	3	16
School c	3	42	4	16
School d	4	29	5	19
School e	5	28	6	22
School f	6	28	2	15
School g	7	19	8	25
School h	8	18	7	23
School i	9	14	11	47
School j	10	14	9	26
School k	11	8	12	53
School l	12	2	13	54
School m	13	2	10	43

Table 6.1

City and Guilds qualifications more suited to their needs. A performance indicator based on GCSE results will fail to reflect this.

Consequently, examination results cannot measure the effectiveness of a school because the school effect is outweighed by the social composition of a school's intake in determining examination achievement: in other words, the social composition of pupils is a confounding variable which means that like is not being compared with like. This means that it is necessary to ask to what extent a school's examination achievements are better or worse than expected in the light of the social composition of its intake, rather than comparing crude results. If the data are available, more sophisticated methods can be used which measure actual school effects: the 'value added' attributable to schools and quantified by comparing pupil achievement in later years with achievement at intake. Even these methods, however, do not provide very useful guidance about how quality can be improved, especially if the data are not broken down by subject. Whilst differences in achievement can be shown quantitatively, the inter-personal and school ethos factors which appear to be the crucial factors in school effectiveness are difficult to measure statistically or even to observe (Shipman, 1988).

The need for a commitment to research

Research is a pointless task if there is no commitment to using it. This should also include a policy of making the findings freely available to local people. Such a commitment, however, requires a lead from chief officers in creating an organisational culture which expects recommendations to committees and operational decisions to be supported with appropriate research.

The Audit Commission (1991), for example, recently had to urge local councils to undertake rigorous analysis of 1991 Census data and to have in place 'the necessary managerial commitment to use the census'. Whilst census data have a very wide range of potential uses in local government, they can meet only a small proportion of the information needs of a quality approach. Some local authorities such as Newcastle have invested in inter-censual surveys to maintain a more up-to-date data source on their districts. Others such as Wrekin Council collect basic information on the sex, age and work status of household members as part of the annual electoral registration process in what has become termed an Enhanced Electoral Registration Population Survey (Worrall, 1989). Family Health Service Authorities' age/sex registers have also been tested for their usefulness as a continuous and comprehensive local demographic data source (Dobson, 1992).

The commitment to gather and use information also extends to exploiting local councils' vast collections of administrative data *as a resource* to meet the information needs of policy makers and service providers. Administrative registers support the day-to-day administration of services such as housing allocations, benefit payments, social services referrals and planning permissions. They contain up-to-date and detailed information which can be used to monitor and investigate key trends such as residential stability, low income, children in care and land use change. Such information can be used in the development of formulae for allocating budgets to areas and neighbourhoods, targeting services and evaluating the impact of programmes and projects. However, often only a very few officers are fully acquainted with the computerised information systems in their departments and do not have the time or reasons to interrogate the data for applied research purposes.

Special projects can be developed to look for new applications for local authority data. In Newcastle, the City Council's Research Section identified the potential of housing and Community Charge benefit databases for monitoring the incidence of low pay and poverty in local areas, using other variables in the data such as age, disability and household type to investigate this incidence in more depth. Realising this potential necessitated downloading the data into a flat computer file for analysis using a statistical package. A proposed joint study between Newcastle City Council and the University of Newcastle will use six monthly downloads of the data as a sampling frame to investigate relationships between poverty and employment.

Research and intelligence should play a much greater role in local government than in the past. This is not to suggest that research is a panacea for public sector management needs, and it is especially the case that no single piece of research is going to answer a policy problem, as Huxley *et al.* (1990, p. 187) point out:

> First, the results are usually less salient by the time the research is complete. Second, all researchers have 'angles' and all studies have defects, so several studies are needed before firm conclusions can be drawn. Third, policy problems usually involve more variables than are used in the research.

Recent changes in public sector management require authorities to have better quality information about the needs of their areas and the performance of their services. The NHS Management Executive (1991) recently identified three questions relevant to developing an intelligence function which are equally applicable to local government:

- *what do we know about the scope of services and needs in the District?*

- *what issues and changes in services should we focus on?*
- *what do we want to achieve?*

A research capacity will help to create the conditions for answering these questions but it is unfortunate that there is not the same investment in research in local government as in the National Health Service, where up to 1.5 per cent of NHS resources are earmarked for research and development (*Social Research Association News*, 1991).

Once a research problem is formulated, the research design stage should involve a review of the following broad methodologies:

- Focus groups and in-depth interviews with selected individuals. These techniques enable services and policies to be evaluated by members of target populations, but it is not possible to establish measures of the extent of particular findings.
- Social surveys using standardised questionnaires and samples. These enable representative generalisations to be made from the findings but often lack depth and small sample numbers can mean that local neighbourhood problems are not picked up.
- Social indicators from secondary data, such as census variables, benefit take-up, social services referrals, etc. Social indicators are commonly used in formulae for resource allocations but skew such allocations towards measures which may not be very sensitive to particular circumstances. Another type of social indicator is user complaints.

There are broadly three sources of research expertise available to local authorities: in-house research staff, professional research contractors, and academic research contractors. It is difficult to generalise about which is the best way of carrying out research. In a recent survey to local authorities about market research, respondents rated the performance of in-house staff and professional contractors about the same overall at an average of four out of a possible five points, although in-house staff were ranked higher for value for money and lower for technical competence (IPF, 1991). Academic research contractors received ratings of, on average, about three out of five.

The main concerns with using outside contractors are cost and the officer time that can be involved in working with consultants, but against this is the cost of managing and maintaining in-house research officers. Whether or not outside contractors are used, there is a strong case for local authorities to employ directly officers who are qualified and experienced in social and policy analysis, market research, community and quality development and customer care.

Research should not be confined to direct services. Local councils have a legitimate interest in all the factors that influence the well-being of the local population and are uniquely accountable to the local electorate in this respect. Some initiate research beyond their own services which asks questions about, for example, the effectiveness of Urban Development Corporations which operate within their boundaries or the costs and benefits of changes to local health services.

Indeed, local authorities have increasingly had to develop working relationships with the private sector and voluntary organisations. There is a strong argument for them to guide these partnerships in strategic directions by tapping the potential of research and intelligence to provide needs assessments and policy evaluations on the basis of which agreement regarding key objectives can be secured. This could range from quality audits of transitions from hospital to community care to citywide training and education strategies.

However, even if local government is seen purely as the organiser and deliverer of a (diminishing) range of services, there are two major obstacles to realising the full role for research and intelligence which the new public sector management demands.

Firstly, the resources available for research and intelligence in local government are tiny. There is a case for doing in local government what the Labour Party has advocated for the Audit Commission — that is, reorientating the accountancy-based approach to services towards quality by paying less for accountancy and auditing and more for policy analysis, market and social research, and quality audits. The research effort of relevant departments in institutions of higher education could be more closely linked with local authorities and joint research units established between authorities.

The second obstacle is that the organisational culture of most local councils is not one which provides political and managerial leadership for research and for marshalling the huge information resources of local authorities for policy planning, basic resource allocation and evaluating services. This seems in large measure to be an effect of the professional backgrounds of chief executives and other chief officers. There needs to be a commitment from local councils' senior executives to a research and intelligence strategy which supports improving the quality of local government.

Notes

[1]   Local Government Research and Intelligence Association Autumn Workshop, 'R & I for Good Decision Making', 10–11 November 1991, York.

[2]   See Note 1.

[3]   This problem was revealed in a recent Newcastle City Council committee report on staffing and spending levels in social services. The

wrong allocation of a number of areas of expenditure to fieldwork resulted in Newcastle's 1991/92 expenditure on fieldwork being 33 per cent above the metropolitan district average when a reallocation according to CIPFA guidelines reduced this to 25 per cent (Newcastle City Council, 1992b).

References

Audit Commission (1991) *Numbers that Count: Making Good Use of the 1991 Census,* HMSO, London.

Batley, R. and Stoker, G. (eds.) (1991) *Local Government in Europe,* Macmillan, London.

Blackman, T. (1991) The search for qualitative research, *Laria News,* No. 35, pp. 10–12.

Bradshaw, J. (1972) The concept of need, *New Society,* 30th March.

Bramley, G. (1990) The demand for local government services — survey evidence on usage, distribution and externalities, *Local Government Studies,* Vol. 16, No. 6, pp. 35–61.

Dobson, A. (1992) Using Family Health Service Authority data in local population estimates, in Blackman T. (ed.) *Research for Policy,* Local Authorities Research and Intelligence Association, London.

Gaster, L. (1991) Quality and decentralisation: are they connected? *Policy and Politics,* Vol. 19, No. 4, pp. 257–67.

Gregory, D. (1978) *Ideology, Science and Human Geography,* Hutchinson, London.

Hambleton, R. and Hoggett, P. (1990) *Beyond Excellence: Quality Local Government in the 1990s,* Working Paper 85, University of Bristol School for Advanced Urban Studies, Bristol.

Hill, M., Blackman, T., Wallace, B. and Woods, R. (1991) *The Walker Riverside Study,* Department of Social Policy, University of Newcastle Upon Tyne, Newcastle Upon Tyne.

Hoggett, P. (1991) A new management in the public sector? *Policy and Politics,* Vol. 19, No. 4, pp. 243–56.

Huxley, P., Hagan, T., Hennelly, R. and Hunt, J. (1990) *Effective Community Mental Health Services,* Avebury, Aldershot.

IPF, (1991) Market Research — Local Authority Services, Unpublished report of survey findings by IPF, a CIPFA company.

Labour Party (1989) *Quality Street: Labour's Quality Programme for Local Government,* The Labour Party, London.

Labour Party Policy Directorate (1991) *The Quality Commission: A Consultation Paper,* Labour Party, London.

Ley, D. (1983) *A Social Geography of the City,* Harper & Row, New York.

Local Government Management Board, (1992) *Citizens and Local Democracy: Charting a New Relationship,* LGMB, London.

Newcastle City Council (1985) *West City Consumer Survey, 1985, Second Report,* City of Newcastle Upon Tyne, Performance, Review and Efficiency Sub-Committee, 6 December.

Newcastle City Council (1992a) *Unitary Development Plan: Review of Consultation and Next Steps,* City of Newcastle Upon Tyne, Policy and Resources Committee, 26 February.

Newcastle City Council, (1992b) *Social Services Fieldwork, Interim Report,* City of Newcastle Upon Tyne Performance, Review and Efficiency Sub-Committee, 21 January.

NHS Management Executive (1991) *Purchasing Intelligence,* NHS Management Executive, London.

Passmore, J. (1991) A flawed performance, *Housing,* October, pp. 21–22.

Ritchie, C. (1992) An exercise in community consultation — devising general criteria, *Laria News,* No. 38.

Shipman, M. (1988) *The Limitations of Social Research,* Longman, London.

Social Research Association News, (1991) Report on a discussion with Jenny Griffin, Assistant Secretary Social Research, Research and Development Division, Department of Health, August, pp. 1–4.

Tesch, R. (1990) Software for the computer-assisted analysis of text, *Network: Newsletter of the British Sociological Association,* Vol. 47, pp. 10–11.

TUC (1992) *The Quality Challenge: A TUC Report on the Trade Union Response to Quality in Public Services,* TUC, London.

Tyne and Wear Research and Intelligence Unit (1991) *Tyne and Wear Urban Development Area Progress Report 1988–91,* Tyne and Wear Research and Intelligence Unit, Newcastle Upon Tyne.

Vittles, P. (1990) The Role of Research in a Democratic Framework, Unpublished paper, York, York City Council.

Vittles, P. (1991) The Principles and Techniques of Qualitative Research, Paper presented at the LARIA Autumn Workshop, Wakefield, 18th September.

Wallman, S. (1982) *Living in South London: Perspectives on Battersea 1871–1981,* Gower, Aldershot.

Worrall, L. (1989) Urban demographic information systems, in Congdon P. and Batey P. W. J. (eds.) *Advances in regional demography,* Belhaven Press, London.

Worrall, L. and Rao, L. (1991) The Telford Urban Policy Information Project, in Worrall, L. (ed.), *Spatial Analysis and Spatial Policy using Geographical Information Systems,* Belhaven Press, London.

7 Quality, culture and local government

Bill Cooke

Introduction

There is a mass of literature on culture, quality, and Quality Management. The main problem is not that there is nowhere to turn for guidance, but that it comes at one in profusion from every quarter: some write in a US context; some in a private sector context; some talk about the public sector as a whole; some see any one of these perspectives as directly applicable, barely modified, to local government in the UK; others see a need to understand local government as a distinctive institution and develop approaches accordingly; and some prescribe the one best approach to quality, others stress the need for pragmatism.

All may be of value. But is important to understand their potential weaknesses, as well as their suggested strengths. Tom Stephenson of Cheshire County Council (1989, p. 3) states:

> Let us assume that an authority has been convinced by all the talk that something radical is required. What is the first step? It is easy to be lured by those who provide ready-made solutions. From a menu of latest buzz-words, you simply choose the dish that suits your taste, and all that messy, unpopular preparation is done for you. If the meal proves unpalatable you can blame the chef.
>
> There is too much at stake here for the approach to be acceptable. The future style of an authority, its approach to service delivery and, on some arguments its very existence cannot be left to outside advisers. Nor can the course of events be dictated by the accident of a senior officer returning from a seminar having been impressed by a presentation on one of the current management concepts. The agenda is larger than that.

This chapter seeks to pick a path through the confusion, through that menu of buzzwords, and provide help with 'that messy unpopular preparation'. In the next section the problem of defining culture is discussed and a particular approach to definition is adopted. This is followed by an examination of culture in the local government context, in particular of bases for cultural variation. I then consider approaches to quality management in the service context, discussing the implications of quality assurance (QA) and total quality management (TQM) for culture change. In the final section approaches to achieving cultural change are discussed, focusing in particular on a comparison of TQM and organisational development approaches.

Defining culture

The problem of definition

When asked to define culture we often resort to illustrations, or use vague generalisations. Thus we hear: 'You can see culture in the way we treat people'; 'It's the atmosphere at work'; 'The state of the canteens/toilets/noticeboards tells you a lot about the culture'.

Pinning down exactly what 'culture' means is not easy. Yet a lack of clarity of meaning opens the way to action founded in ambiguity and confusion, more likely to fail and cause damage. The very first practical task for those addressing culture is to understand clearly what 'organisational culture' is. One of the most widely used definitions is: 'It's the way we do things round here'. This phrase begins to convey what we are talking about. It implies why culture is important, as a determinant of what happens within an organisation, what the organisation does. But it is simplistic and misleading.

An extensive variety of 'definitive' definitions can be found in management texts. This may be no bad thing, if all are considered and understood en route to a satisfactory working definition. But if a definition is selected by default, or at random there are dangers of an incomplete understanding of what is being dealt with. The choice is either to develop a new definition, adding to the list, or select an existing one to the exclusion of others. The latter option has been chosen here, but care has been taken in making the choice.

Edgar Schein's (1985) definition is used because consideration of the distinctions he makes in defining and explaining culture helps practical lessons to be drawn. Citing 13 different texts, Schein notes six different common meanings of culture, before presenting his own:

> the deeper level of assumptions and beliefs that are shared by members of an organisation, that operate unconsciously, and that define in a basic 'taken for granted fashion' an organisation's view of itself and its environment. These assumptions and beliefs are learned responses

to a group's problems of survival and its problems of external integration. They come to be taken for granted because they solve these problems repeatedly and reliably. This deeper level of assumptions is to be distinguished from the 'artifacts' and 'values' that are manifestations of the surface levels of culture but not the essence.

(Schein, 1985, p. 6)

Culture is explained at three levels. First, 'artifacts' (level 1) are defined as a culture's physical and constructed environment, evident in such things as physical space, overt behaviour (ibid, p. 14) — the way we do things, written and spoken language, easy to observe but hard to decipher owing to their plentiful and ambiguous nature. Second, 'values' (level 2) are the conscious, often written or spoken, shared views of how things ought to be. Harder to observe than artifacts, they can be inferred from frequently repeated phrases, which in their explicit articulation 'serve the normative or moral function of guiding members of the group in how to deal with certain key situations' (ibid, p. 15).

If over time the application of a particular value is collectively felt to have worked, it will, Schein suggests, undergo a process of 'cognitive transformation' and become a taken for granted belief that almost slips from consciousness — a 'basic assumption' (level 3). Not all sets of values go through this process, either because they are not felt to be valid, because they do not work, or because there is no way of satisfactorily agreeing that they are valid — they are not 'susceptible of physical or social validation' (ibid, p. 16).

The identification of what seems to be the 'level 2' major values of an organisation will not necessarily tell us all about its culture. They may be contradictory; they may not be reflected in actual observed behaviour; and they may not be comprehensive, with no allusion to significant areas of activity. We may well be left with the 'feeling that we understand a piece of the culture but still do not have the culture as such in hand' (ibid, p. 17). Hence the need to get at the deeper level of assumptions and beliefs — what Schein calls the 'essence'.

These deeper assumptions are even more difficult to identify and work with precisely because they are taken for granted, and not conscious. Their conscious understanding requires an examination of artifacts and values, from which initial inferrals about underlying assumptions can be drawn, but 'detective work and commitment' (ibid, p. 20) is required in working with organisations to bring assumptions and beliefs to the surface, and truly to understand the culture.

There are those who recognise that their working definition of culture is not as 'deep' as that of Schein. W. Warner Burke (1987) emphasises norms and values, which he accepts may be manifestations rather than the essence of culture, but 'constitute a more operational means for dealing with organisational change' (op cit, p. 10). There is some strength in this view, in that articulated values and visible artifacts are easier for managers to identify and deal with. The distinctions between Schein's levels 2 and 3 can be hard to understand and explain. Some writers on culture give 'values' a meaning equivalent to Schein's 'basic assumptions', which adds to the confusion. Indeed much of what follows here will be about work at levels 1 and 2, not least because that has been the focus of work by theorists, managers, and consultants.

There are however at least three practical lessons that consideration of Schein's definition helps us to draw out.

Customer care and culture change

First, making front-line staff wear name badges, or sending them on a customer care course does not mean culture has been changed. These are changes in observed behaviour, at the artifact level. Getting social workers to call clients 'customers' may achieve a change in behaviour, but not one that can be truly taken as a signal of change in values or beliefs. Most of us will act in a way which is at some variance with our underlying assumptions about the world if we think it necessary. Very early on in the debate on quality in local government Stewart and Clarke (1985a, p. 16) acknowledged 'the limitations of the "charm" approach'.

Of course, changes at this level may be a reflection of genuine changes in values and ultimately in underlying assumptions. They may be undertaken to symbolise and to promote an explicit set of values to which an authority aspires. In this case, they are important, although they will not necessarily be sufficient in themselves.

Resistance to change

Second, the profound nature of what we are doing when we try to change organisational culture must be understood. It means that the current 'learned responses' and 'taken for granted assumptions' are called into question. Such assumptions may include those linking the value of our worth as individuals to the value of the particular things we do at work; the contribution we feel we make to our communities and to society; and, fundamentally, the meaning of our lives. Management action which, intentionally or otherwise, confronts these assumptions, is capable of causing psychological pain.

This issue is often couched in terms of 'resistance to change', the argument being that opposition to change does not necessarily arise from bloody mindedness, nor even conscious rational self interest. However the phrase can be taken as implying that it is the resistance, or the resistors, that are the problem when it may be the nature of the change itself.

In his honest account of cultural change at Welwyn Hatfield Council, John Passmore writes (1990, p. 4):

> Resistance to change is a human reaction. Resistance may come about because of self interest, misunderstanding, different assessment of the need or desirability of the change and in some cases due to low tolerance for change in the individual. In local government, particularly in authorities subject to little previous change, the effects of low personal tolerance and differing assessments of change desirability can play a major part.

Those seeking culture change walk a fine line. Confrontation or challenge to an existing culture, or aspects of it, does have to happen if change is to occur. A certain level of anxiety helps motivate change. This must be high enough to cause a perceived need to change, but not so high as to paralyse action. It must also be balanced by accompanying levels of felt security and confidence, or tolerance for change. The difficulty is finding the right balance.

Actual versus espoused values

Third, managers must be aware that everyone in their organisation, and many of those coming into contact with it, will be able to distinguish between espoused values and actual values, if such a distinction exists. A set of espoused values suggests a certain set of behaviours. If different behaviours are seen to be accepted and rewarded, it will be apparent that a different set of true, actual, values exists. The message will be 'do as we do not as we say'.

This can be a particular problem in times of transition. As part of a programme to change an organisation's culture, a set of values to which the organisation aspires, ('core values') is often identified. Hence for example the 'Cheshire Values' adopted in 1987 by Cheshire County Council:

1. The purpose of the County Council is to serve the Cheshire people.
2. Councillors and employees are accountable to the Cheshire people.
3. The County Council will act with honesty, integrity and respect for the individual in its dealings with the public.
4. The County Council is a partnership between councillors and employees.
5. The County Council's most important resource is its employees
   (Stephenson, 1989, p. 4).

Insofar as an existing culture, and consequent behaviour, does not yet meet the aspirations of a set of core values, there will be a divergence between actual and espoused values. Individuals may be unconvinced of the core values, and not adapt their behaviour accordingly. The aspirational nature of such values at this stage does have to be stressed, and genuine steps to turn aspiration into reality do have to be seen to be taken. Moreover, those with responsibility for turning aspiration into reality must achieve a self awareness and self discipline that ensures that all they do is in keeping with the values they espouse.

The sometimes ambiguous or contradictory nature of values that are espoused does not make things any easier. For example, an espoused value similar to the last in the list from Cheshire above, in terms of 'we value our people, they are our greatest asset' is common to many authorities. If people are made redundant, in pursuit perhaps of another espoused value relating to efficiency, effectiveness or productivity, or for external reasons, then the 'people value' can justifiably be seen not to have real meaning, and the values per se may be undermined. Handling this dilemma is often the acid test for those who claim to be trying to develop a quality culture in the real world.

Finally, organisations for whom we are customers (or consumers or clients or passengers) in the private and the public sector increasingly espouse sets of values similar to those espoused within the authority in which we may work. If, as consumers, we commonly experience behaviour that contradicts espoused values, this can undermine their perceived validity per se in any context, including work. Care must be taken, therefore, to express values in language which avoids clichés and has real meaning for an organisation's members.

The nature of local government culture

A local government culture?

The purpose of this section is not to define 'the local authority culture', in terms of attitudes and beliefs common to every local authority. Rather, it is to identify those characteristics of local authorities' cultures which will help the local authority manager understand the culture, or cultures, of their own organisation.

This is not to suggest that a 'local government culture' does not exist. Its nature is implied in a range of sources (e.g. Bichard, 1990, p. 367). However, there are three pertinent issues for those tempted to use any such descriptions to inform the understanding of the culture of a given local government organisation. First, given the rate of change within local government there is a danger of such descriptions becoming rapidly dated. Second, what is often defined is not culture, but factors from which inferences about culture can be made, which may be incomplete or false. Third, in seeking what is common to all local authorities we may overlook elements unique to a particular local authority.

Differences between local authority cultures

One important source of cultural variation is professionalism. That strong professional cultures exist cannot be disputed. Indeed some might say that part of a profession's *raison d'etre* is to perpetuate a particular culture, a set of taken for granted attitudes and beliefs. However, it would be mistaken to assume that because all professional cultures have similar aspects that there are not differences, nor that such differences are important.

Local authorities contain a number of different professions — lawyers, accountants, planners, teachers, social workers, architects to name but a few. A particular profession, or mix of professionals, may dominate a particular department, which itself may be said to have its own culture. Each authority in turn has a mix of departments, which varies because of differing functional responsibilities and choices made with regard to organisational structure.

Moreover, there are other groups within local government likely to possess their own 'sub-culture'. There are other occupational groups besides those who would claim to fall into the formal definition of a profession. There are those officers who have either transcended or never had a particular professional orientation. The elected members as a whole and in political groups may form their own distinctive sub-cultures, as may different sets of trade union members. There is an extensive range of subcultures which form a particular whole in any one authority. Such subcultures may have elements in common, perhaps a commitment to public service, or to client/customer orientation, but they may also have unique aspects which are not always mutually reconcilable.

The definition of culture which we have used also applies to an 'extra-organisational' level – nationally and ethnically, or in terms of regional and urban/rural cultures. To the extent that a local authority is representative of the culture of the area it covers, this too will serve to influence the mix of cultural overlays affecting its overall culture.

There are a number of other factors which influence a particular organisational culture. History is one. The cultures of old organisations are likely to differ from those of new ones. Significant incidents in an organisation's past may have had a determining influence. Another is technology, broadly defined in terms of how work is organised and completed. In this sense, the bureaucratic aspect of local government might be included here, as might issues or centralised/decentralised service delivery. Size matters — cultures in large and small organisations will differ.

Leadership is relevant in at least two dimensions. First, the action and behaviours of individual leaders has a determining effect on organisational culture. This is implicit in the discussion of actual versus espoused value above. The second is in the way in which the concept of leadership is defined and acted upon within an organisation. Whether an organisation is led by one charismatic individual or by a consensus seeking team; whether individuals compete for leadership or avoid it; whether leaders are those with formal power or those with power from some other source are all factors which affect the culture of an organisation.

Political control is another factor. It is possible to question whether the political significance of organisational culture has been fully recognised. Paul Hoggett (1991, p. 243) sees a 'New Public Management' emerging. There is much more to this paradigm than a consideration of culture alone. However, central to it is the concept of post-bureaucratic control, which 'rides forth upon the rhetoric of "management excellence" in the 1980s' (ibid, p. 245), and new forms of organisation 'which rely heavily upon the power of socialisation processes to regulate behaviour', having cited 'the paramount importance given to the concept of "organisational culture" and "cultural change" within the literature of the 1980s'. These new organisational forms are, he argues, 'compatible with the full range of political values' (ibid, p. 243).

However, two problematic areas remain, for which solutions are not clear. First, although it may be possible to specify and then develop a culture which reflects particular political values, it may not always be acceptable to do so. For example, how free should local authorities be to define their role, their culture, and their notion of quality primarily as quasi-private sector deliverers of services, rather, say than in Rhodes' broad constitutional sense (1987, p. 67), discussed elsewhere in this book? (see chapter 2).

Consideration of whether local government has a constitutional role which individual authorities cannot choose to ignore, is beyond the remit of this chapter. However, there is a clear implication for officers, managers and consultants who work to establish particular definitions of quality, and associated cultures, within a given local authority. What they are doing can affect this constitutional role, or any other role which may be appropriate to local government. It may be that by focusing on service quality and service delivery alone, expectations of local government in Rhodes' terms, as an instrument of democracy, are being lowered. The will of the majority group, freely arrived at without officer guidance, is a source of legitimacy for this end only if it is accepted that that group itself has the requisite authority.

The second issue concerns what happens when political control changes in an authority. It may be possible, as Hoggett argues, to establish a culture, or at least articulate values, which adequately represents one or other set of political values. But what happens when the dominant set of values changes? For a set of core values and an organisational culture to be able to survive such a change implies an ability to identify and adopt a transcendent position acceptable in any political circumstance. The reality is, perhaps, that most authorities are sure enough of continuity of political control for the issue not to matter. But it is possible to foresee a majority group coming to power in an authority which has core values which it finds to be totally unacceptable. This will have profound implications within the organisation, if we accept the central significance of values as an indicator or a determinant of culture. Setting out core values, and defining quality on that basis, can provide a hostage to fortune. Those in a volatile political setting may be advised to take a completely different tack.

The potential for cultural diversity in local government means we would emphasise that those seeking to change their own organisational culture must adopt an approach grounded in an understanding of the idiosyncrasies of that culture and, moreover, must be seen to do so if they are to gain commitment to what they seek to achieve. Choices of those who are (and are not) involved in defining what a changed culture should look like, deciding on that process of definition, planning to achieve the new culture and carrying out that plan, must be carefully made. Defining a new culture requires the explicit specification of an organisation's *raison d'etre* and goals, in addition to its values (Schein, op cit, p. 52). It can explicitly or implicitly define how power and authority is distributed. In our context, it will also have a determining effect on the articulation of what 'quality' means, how it is defined conceptually and in terms of organisational processes and outcomes.

Quality management and culture change in a service context

Services and service management characteristics

The implication of the previous section is that finding a definition of quality can be problematic in a real organisational context, and is hard to divorce from the culture of that context. To complicate matters further local authorities deliver services, the characteristics of which have implications both for how quality is defined and for culture.

Three key characteristics which distinguish services from products are intangibility, heterogeneity and inseparability. (Parasuraman, Zeithaml and Berry, 1985). Thus, when one provides a service one provides the recipient with an experience — what might be seen as a performance. Both are intangible, albeit combinable with tangible factors. Heterogeneity refers to the distinctiveness of each separate service experience. This derives from a large range of factors, including variability between service deliverers, between customers, from day-to-day, and during times of the day. Therefore, consistency of quality of interaction between service provider and receiver is harder to ensure than in the provision of goods. The inseparability of services refers to their production and consumption simultaneously or nearly so. For example, an interaction between a student and a teacher cannot be specified and manufactured in a factory, then subsequently delivered to be consumed.

These three characteristics, together with the subjectivity of the recipient in appraising the service, the differences in perceptions between recipients, and the fact that a service will be judged on its process and its outcome, suggest that the most appropriate approach to defining service quality is one which is grounded in customer (or service recipient) perceptions. Service quality is therefore determined by the extent to which a given service meets recipients' expectations in terms of both process and outcome.

For Parasuraman *et al.* (ibid, p. 46) there are three factors which will affect these expectations. First, what the customer has heard from others and through advertising; second, personal needs; and third, past experience of the service. From this, they try to identify causes of organisational failure to achieve service quality. In their research they identified four gaps.

- *Gap 1: the consumer expectation/management perception gap*
- *Gap 2: the manager perception/service quality specification gap*
- *Gap 3: the service quality specification/service delivery gap*
- *Gap 4: the service delivery/external communication gap.*

The first three are self explanatory. Gap 4 refers to the gap between expectations engendered when an organisation fails to deliver what it offers, explicitly or by implication. Quality management approaches may differ in terms of the gaps that they address and how they do so. In this model, therefore, we are provided with a framework that helps in their evaluation. It is not sufficient in itself, however, in that it does not address the difference between local government and private sector service deliverers.

Beyond service delivery

Stewart and Clarke's concept of the Public Service Orientation (PSO) proposes an approach to service delivery which recognises this difference. Underpinning the PSO is the concept of service for the public, rather than service to the public.

Service for the public places emphasis on the public for whom the service is provided. Service to the public places emphasis on the service.

(Stewart and Clarke, 1986a, p. 5)

There are seen to be at least seven key differences between private sector and local government services (ibid, p. 10):

- *the customer does not necessarily buy the service;*
- *the customer may have a right to receive the service;*
- *the customer may be compelled to receive the service;*
- *customers may be refused a service because their needs may not meet those laid down;*
- *the conditions of service are not only determined by the resources available but by the political process;*
- *issues about rationing can arise and criteria may have to be laid down not made by decisions subject to the market but subject to the political process;*
- *the customer influences that process as a citizen.*

All this complicates the definition of quality in the service context. From a consumer's perspective, the determinants of, and influences on, expectations have more dimensions than in the private sector. Moreover, those for whom service quality is an issue are not just those who directly receive it, but, in a local authority context, its public. That public has, through the political process and directly, the right to be involved in the determination of service quality. This implies a need for a culture which fosters a far more sophisticated conceptual understanding of quality.

Furthermore, customer expectations in any context are not necessarily permanent. Perceptions of service quality can be increased without changing the service by lowering expectations, or lowered by increasing expectations. In any service organisation expectations will be managed, consciously or otherwise. This may be in terms of the relationship between process and outcome, or between elements within either. How this is done will reflect both the culture and the power of groups within the organisation — its politics. If local government is different, it is because politics in a broader sense should play a part, and the relationship between organisational culture and politics in managing for quality must be explicitly recognised and addressed.

Approaches to quality management

In such a context how applicable are different approaches to quality management? On first examining generic approaches to quality management for insights into the development of culture and quality, and relevance to local government, one finds no little ambiguity. Phrases such as quality control, quality management, quality assurance and total quality management are often used interchangeably. Likewise the terms 'quality culture', 'total quality culture' and 'culture of quality'. Foster and Whittle (1990, p. 3) speak of the 'quality management maze'. Trying to reduce the confusion, they classify QM into four generic categories: quality control (QC), quality assurance (QA), total quality control (TQC) and total quality management (TQM).

In so doing they are aware that elements that some would associate with one particular approach may, for the purpose of categorisation, be aligned with another. The particular focus here will be the distinction between QA and TQM, given that these approaches would appear to be the most widely adopted in relation to quality initiatives in the UK. In so doing we are able to distinguish between, as Walsh puts it, 'quality that derives from systems', (i.e. QA), 'and quality that derives from people and their commitment' (1992, p. 4).

Quality assurance, BS 5750 and the bureaucratic culture

Quality assurance has, Foster and Whittle argue (op. cit, p. 4), 'in Britain become practically synonymous with BS 5750 (British Standard 5750) and SPC (Statistical Process Control), whereby quality management is interpreted as the achievement of a fixed objective, involving the once and for all installation of prescribed procedures'. Overall responsibility for quality rests with a specific department, albeit with individuals having some responsibility for maintenance of systems, procedures, and standards in their own functions.

BS 5750 is a standard, designed to be valid for every organisational setting. As such, there is nothing within it explicitly aimed at addressing the special characteristics of local government in PSO service delivery terms nor in its broader constitutional role. It will help address Parasuraman et al.'s Service Quality Gap 2, the 'management perception/service quality specification gap'. This assumes, however, that every aspect of management perceptions of service quality, even those intangible, heterogeneous, human centred elements are specifiable in the sense QA requires.

QA will assist in bridging Gap 3, the 'service quality specification/ service quality delivery gap'. QA helps to ensure that a service is delivered as specified, and that corrective action is taken where it is not. Again, the question is the adequacy of those specifications. Some (e.g. King 1984, p. 93) have argued that, at the very least, there is a need to specify behavioural requirements when services are delivered. Some organisations do this. Morgan (1986, p. 21) cites a fast food restaurant checklist which specifies, among other things, 'there is a smile. . . . It is a sincere greeting . . . there is eye contact'. However, whether behaviours which match the range and nature of those required in a local government context of, for example, a nursery nurse or social worker can be comprehensively specified (never mind whether they should) still remains open to question.

There is an assumption that Gap 1, the consumer expectation/management perception gap, will be bridged by default; likewise Gap 4. In many cases this essential condition for quality service delivery happens. Management perceptions of consumer expectations are accurate, and external communications appropriate. Those responsible for the implementation of BS 5750 often do appreciate the pre-requisite to continually understand customer needs and build a system accordingly. But the standard itself does not necessarily ensure that this is the case.

It can be claimed that quality assurance is about culture change. For Walsh (1990, p. 398):

> It is about the development of the organisation, its culture and its processes to ensure quality is produced.

Certainly, the installation of BS 5750 will change 'the way we do things round here'; it will lead to changes in behaviour. But there is no mechanism within BS 5750 to diagnose culture, at any level beyond behaviour, before, during, or after the setting up of the system; and, as we have already noted, changes in behaviour do not necessarily mean changes in culture. New behaviour may, however, reflect changing values revolving around the particular image and definition of quality and management that BS 5750 represents. If those values are accepted to have worked over a period of time, they will slip into taken for granted assumptions and beliefs, and change the culture. In that such a change results from a quality management initiative it might mean that a 'quality culture' has been established.

Even if this is the case, there are advantages and disadvantages to that particular culture. Walsh notes, 'there is a danger of quality management becoming a very bureaucratic process focusing on records and control' (1990, p. 399), and stresses the point even more strongly elsewhere (1992, p. 4). Experience confirms this view.

Management theory (see Morgan, 1986, p. 33–38) sees bureaucracy as a mechanistic approach to management, which questionably assumes rationality in individual and organisational behaviour. It can be demotivating to employees who become cogs in a wheel, where the maintenance of the bureaucratic system can become the purpose of the organisation. Bureaucracy is seen as inflexible and inappropriate for a rapidly changing environment where requirements of the organisation are constantly developing. It is also seen as difficult to reconcile with organisations dominated by professionals, or service organisations, where a quality response to needs rests on the discretion of individuals, often not susceptible to specification, measurement and documentation. Moreover, removal of that discretion, besides being difficult, exacerbates bureaucracy's demotivating effect by diminishing individual control over the work process.

On the other hand, some see virtues in bureaucracy (again see Morgan op. cit.) which, one might cynically suggest, BS 5750 has allowed the private sector to rediscover surreptitiously. It enables roles, responsibility and accountability to be clearly defined, work processes to be clearly determined, and promotes the achievement of consistent organisational outputs. In the public sector, this last point is often related to the need to ensure equitable treatment of those receiving a specific service, ensuring the opportunity for unwanted biases and discrimination to be engineered out. Consistency through bureaucracy is also seen as important where it is essential that things do not go wrong and, if they do, that the causes of error can be traced. There are equivalent circumstances in local government, where the result of mistakes can be dire — in Social Services, for example. This would suggest that a QA approach is particularly appropriate. Even here though, Walsh (1992, p. 4) suggests that if QA is adequate (and he suggests it may not be) 'the social service world should establish its own quality assurance procedures and certificating body'.

Total quality management and the PSO

Total quality management (TQM) is, according to Foster and Whittle (1990, p. 4):

> a fundamental shift from what has gone before . . . the systematic analysis, preplanning and blueprinting of operations remains essential but the focus switches from a process driven by external controls through procedure compliance and enhancement to a process of **habitual improvement** where control is embedded within and driven by the culture of the organisation.

They continue (ibid):

> TQM involves a fundamental human and organisational transformation which develops competence across the whole organisation. It requires the underpinning of all activities first and foremost by a 'quality' culture.

It is this explicit focus on culture which can be seen, in terms of Foster and Whittle's archetype as TQM's fundamental distinguishing characteristic. There are four themes which recur throughout definitions of a total quality culture. First, the concept of closeness to the customer, the idea that a clear and thorough understanding of customers requirements ensures the long term continued success of the organisation. Often there is talk about the distinction between those inside and those outside the organisation becoming blurred — 'everyone is a customer'.

Second, quality is defined (in part at least) as meeting customer requirements. Third, there is a holistic conception of quality — it is seen as an issue that pervades the whole organisation, for which everyone has responsibility. People within the organisation should be treated (in the language of TQM) as customers just like those outside it. Fourth, the principle of 'continuous improvement' suggests that the achievement of quality is not a one-off effort or event, but a never-ending search for improvement, requiring organisational culture, systems, processes and structures which enable this to happen.

With respect to achieving quality in a service context, TQM may be seen to be particularly valid. Thus, the definition of quality is based on customer perceptions/requirements. It addresses the critical interdependencies that exist within service organisations and between customer and supplier. It helps overcome the mechanical specification difficulties associated with QA, by rendering them less necessary by engendering a commitment to meeting behavioural requirements through culture.

In having 'closeness to the customer' as a driving force, TQM by definition seeks to address explicitly Parasuraman *et al.*'s Gap 1, the consumer expectation/management perception gap. Indeed, it can be seen to be going further to redefine that gap as relevant not only to managers but everyone in the organisation, all of whom need to be empowered to address it.

The service delivery/external communication gap is closed for the same reason. Similarly, it can be argued that TQM, in its conscious attempt to develop culture, helps organisations to eliminate the manager perception/service quality specification gap (Gap 2) and the service quality specification/service delivery gap (Gap 3). Responsibility for specification of services is no longer a pure management responsibility, but one shared by those delivering the service and thus able to specify it with a meaning which is clear. There is, in any case, an increased organisational closeness between managers and those delivering the service. Finally, as we have already seen, difficulties in specification of services arising from the human-centredness of services, their heterogeneity and inseparability, and from their intangibility are overcome by the creation of a culture which ensures, at a behavioural level, that needs are met.

We have, however, created an ideal archetype. The achievement of this ideal, as in any culture change activity, is fraught with difficulties, many of which are discussed elsewhere in this chapter. We should note here that the empowerment of front-line staff to close the gaps between expectation and delivery by definition upsets the distribution of power within the organisation, and is often a concept to which only lip service is paid. Where authority to specify service quality is devolved, it is often within strict boundaries.

That there are clear similarities between TQM and the PSO as described by Stewart and Clarke is not surprising if Hoggett's view of the roots of 'The New Public Management' is taken into account. Thus:

> the service provided is only of real value if it is of value to those for whom it is provided . . . those for whom services are provided are customers demanding high quality service . . . quality of service demands closeness to the customer.
>
> (Stewart and Clarke, 1985a, p. 2–3)

The concept of an 'orientation' in itself implies a cultural perspective, a set of assumptions about how an organisation positions itself with respect to those outside it. That orientation needs to overcome many of the same issues as TQM, for example intra-organisational barriers (Stewart and Clarke 1986b, p. 5).

Differences occur in three areas identified as distinctive by Stewart and Clarke (1986a, pp. 9–11). First, as we have noted, in the concept of service for the public. Second, in the focus on the recipients of services both as customers and citizens, which requires a higher quality of relationship. Third, in the PSO's differentiation from consumerism, in its being subject to the political process, and its role as part of that process.

The early discussions of the PSO are also distinguished from TQM (as archetypically defined) by the association of the latter with a clearly defined sequence of events which make up a typical TQM implementation programme. That such a programme is not to be found in any detail in early PSO papers is not surprising, given the stage the debate was at (although a Swedish parallel is cited by Stewart and Clarke, 1985b, p. 12). Those papers did, in any case, provide extensive guidance on initiatives that authorities could undertake; and attempts to identify such a process for local government did emerge in the literature and the practice of individual local authorities.

Achieving culture change

In QA we have a systems-led approach to achieving culture change. In TQM, as we have defined it, there is a conscious attempt to manage culture change. Through our discussion of the PSO and the role of local government we have seen that while a TQM approach alone may be of value, it is not necessarily sufficient, and that even the PSO for

---

Table 7.1: Approaches to culture change

A. *PA Consulting Group TQM Implementation Process*
- Diagnosis and preparation
- Management focus and commitment
- Planned improvement
- Review, reinforce and recommence.

B. *An O. D. Approach (Lippitt, Watson and Wesley cited in Warner Burke, op cit, p. 61)*
- Development of need for change
- Establishment of change relationship
- Diagnosis
- Examination of alternatives
- Actual change
- Generalisation and stabilisation of change
- Achieving a terminal relationship.

---

some does not adequately address local government's constitutional role. Consequently, there is a need for a conscious adaptation of TQM processes to meet local authority requirements, and/or the use of other approaches to achieving culture change.

What this adaptation might require, what the alternatives to a pure TQM approach are, and further practical lessons can be drawn from consideration of generic approaches to culture change. In management theory these are typically found within the field of Organisation Development, of which there are many definitions. One is:

> Organisation Development is a planned process of change in an organisation's culture through the utilisation of behavioural science technologies research and theory.
> (Warner Burke op. cit., p. 11)

Table 7.1 shows two change processes. The first is PA Consulting Group's TQM Process which is (implicitly) seen as applicable in most organisations, including local government (Atkinson 1990, p. 21; PA Consulting Group, p. 51). It is chosen as a representative archetype; other consultancies, and other organisations have similar processes. The second is Lippit, Watson and Wesley's Organisation Development Approach, applicable to other issues besides culture. Again, with the field, there are similar processes.

The two processes appear to share a common basis in action research, again a broad field with its own history, but defined here as:

> a data based, problem-solving model that replicates the steps involved in the scientific method of enquiry. Three processes are involved in action research: data collection, feedback of the data to the clients, and action planning based on the data. Action research is

both an approach to problem solving — a model or a paradigm — and a problem solving process — a series of activities or events.

(French and Bell, 1984, p. 107)

Managing the process

When one examines the different stages of the approaches outlined in Table 7.1, the similarities seem even stronger; and whichever process is adopted, there will be common issues. Some have been discussed already, for example the impact of senior managers' behaviour, and resistance to change. Within the action research model the gathering and feedback of data is seen as a means to address the latter. It presents an objective picture of reality, which if collected by an outsider, and/or with methodological rigour, will be less likely to be filtered by cultural biases. That picture will confront previously held assumptions and beliefs, lead to the questioning of their validity, and so, it is suggested, lead to their change.

Often the validity of the data is challenged within the organisation, and there can be controversy about its interpretation. Frequently this is put down to resistance, to an unwillingness to confront reality. This can be true; but it is also the case that the data does have to be seen to be valid, not only in pure methodological terms, but in terms of the issues it purports to represent. Choices do have to be made with respect to the latter – who you ask, what you ask them, how you ask them, all of which will in themselves reflect cultural assumptions. Likewise the interpretation of the data — the significance attached to elements within it and its overall worth.

Throughout, there may be confusion about language, because the field itself is so confused, with different theorists and practitioners using the same words — vision, mission, quality — for different things. Further, when culture is being redefined (in the processes above typically during the 'management focus' or 'examination of alternatives' stages) meanings which once had been agreed become open to question and debate.

All culture change processes take a long time to complete, if indeed it is accepted they can ever be completed. Among the many TQM clichés is the phrase 'TQM is a marathon not a sprint'. John Passmore, in his account of an Organisation Development-based approach to culture change writes:

> After 12 months of the programme slow progress on the implementation of the Action Plan is being made. Some organisations have claimed that change can be a rapid process . . . Welwyn Hatfield's experience is the reverse of this. If participation is sought, progress is slow.
>
> (Passmore, 1990, p. 6)

Expectations of the quality or culture change programme need to be managed, as do the forces motivating those involved in it at every level. Such a programme can be arduous and gruelling. Fear of its failure can cause those leading it to feel threatened and insecure. At the same time, those driving the change need to be sure of their commitment to the process and to the organisation over time. Few contemplate their own departure from the organisation, through choice or otherwise, yet it could happen and should accordingly be planned for.

Participation is seen as essential not least because there is a need to establish 'psychological ownership' of the change initiative throughout the organisation. Failure to do so will, by definition, mean that culture change will not occur. The establishment of quality or organisation development units or professionals who do not spread their responsibilities for developing a new culture, because they are not allowed to, or because they do not have the competence, will have the same effect.

Finally both TQM and OD processes tend to present themselves as iterative; that is, they are not a once-and-for-all effort, but can require repetition (perhaps after time has passed), as can individual elements of within the process.

Differences between OD and TQM approaches

Consideration of the difference between the PA and OD approaches also highlights other practical issues. We commence, however, by noting that it can be argued with justification that processes like PA's are OD approaches, but being more specific in detail are beneficial when clarity of purpose and outcome is required. Having said that, the extent to which the process is specified in TQM implementation also leaves it open to charges of being over-prescriptive.

For example, there will aln.ost invariably be a consideration of Cost of Poor Quality (or COPQ — the notion that poor quality leads to extra, identifiable, costs) within data collection. There will probably be an awareness/commitment building process for managers which looks at TQM in other organisations, making sure they understand the principles and practices involved in service quality; this may also include training in problem-solving methodologies (cause and effect, Pareto analysis). The 'planned improvement' phase is likely to include such training for less senior managers, 'cascaded' from those near the top to first line management, the establishment of (sometimes) cross functional (sometimes) non hierarchical project teams to address the 'vital few' issues, and so on.

An OD approach, it can be argued, begins with no preconceived ideas as to methodologies, actions, or outcomes. Initial diagnostic methods are developed as a consequence of arriving at a shared understanding of the problems which an organisation is facing. The data thus gathered informs the identification, examination and selection of alternative plans of action, and their implementation. Plans also need to include action to embed the change once it is under way. Thus, the way is opened to develop implementation programmes more sensitive to individual authorities' cultural mix. Moreover, rather than being imported lock, stock and barrel from the private sector, this approach allows for the development of a culture change process more sensitive to the unique character of local government as distinct from other service organisations.

However in reality there are limits to the number of methodologies on offer. Consultants and advisers may have their favourites, or know only of a few, which they always present as the most appropriate for any specific circumstance; and within the field as a whole there are some who are more prescriptive than others. Moreover, as we have already noted, the divergence between what are presented here as two archetypes may not be so great in reality. TQM approaches are being adapted to meet individual organisational requirements. The London Borough of Brent (1992, p. 7), for example, in their recruitment material say of 'Total Quality' that it is a 'term we are using as a catch all for our overall programme of change', which addresses organisation, procedures and culture.

Finally, there is one important area covered by OD approaches and not addressed to the same extent in TQM processes. This is the requirement for, and role of, an individual or individuals as a catalyst for culture change — the consultant or change agent. Within the literature, it is recognised that this person may be someone from outside the organisation (the external consultant) or someone from within allocated the role (the internal consultant). 'Establishment of change relationship' and 'achieving a terminal relationship' in the OD process outlined in Table 7.1, refer to the achievement of clarity of understanding and trust between change agent and client at the outset, and the need for both to have established mechanisms which ensure the consultant withdraws having empowered the client to continue as required. There is an emphasis within the OD literature on the need for those in the consultant/change agent role to understand its implications, and the requirements it makes of individuals if it is to be successfully fulfilled — including, in French and Bell's terms (op cit, p. 249), the danger of 'being absorbed by the culture' of the client organisation, and the particular susceptibility of internal consultants to organisational politics.

In concluding this section we should be aware that whichever implementation process we use, each stage will present its own issues and dilemmas in addition to those discussed here. Ultimately, there are limits to what can be learned about how to deal with them, or indeed any other problems in the achievement of culture change, from texts such as this. The source of solutions to problems is in the competence of people dealing with them.

Conclusion

This discussion has been wide ranging. We have considered individual and collective psychological processes with respect to organisational culture; possible determinants of culture in any given local government organisation; the implications of the role and functions of local government for quality and culture; the relevance of quality management archetypes; and culture change processes.

Organisational culture is a complex phenomenon, and any process of planned culture change faces pitfalls. Those discouraged from addressing culture in their own organisations by the issues outlined in this chapter must be aware that whatever happens culture exists. Managers and those with organisational power can choose to try to alter it. They can choose to accept it and to try to perpetuate it through conscious action, or by not doing anything but continuing as before. But they cannot, by definition do nothing about it.

References

Atkinson, C. (1990) 'Mind the quality', *Local Government Chronicle,* 4 May, p. 21.

Bichard, M. (1990) 'The local authority of the 1990s: competent, caring and competitive', *Management Education and Development Special Issue,* Vol. 21, Part 5, Winter pp. 367–72.

Brent LBC, (1992) Recruitment pack for human resources unit.

Foster, M. and Whittle, S. (1990) 'The quality management maze', in *Implementation of TQM — the best of TQM magazine',* pp. 3–8, ISS, London.

French, W. L. and Bell, C. H. (1984) *Organisation development: behavioral science interventions for organisation improvement,* Prentice Hall, New Jersey.

Hoggett, P. (1991) 'A new management in the public sector?', *Policy and Politics,* Vol. 19, No. 4, pp. 243–56.

King, C. A. (1984) 'Service oriented quality control', *Cornell HRA Quarterly,* November, 92–8.

Morgan, G. (1986) *Images of Organisation,* Sage, Beverly Hills.

Parasuraman, A. Zeithaml, V. A. and Berry, L. (1985) 'A conceptual model of service quality and its implications for future research', *Journal of Marketing,* Vol. 49, Fall, pp. 41–50.

PA Consulting Group (undated) *How to take part in the quality revolution: a management guide.*

Passmore, J. (1990) 'Customer care — cultural change at Welwyn Hatfield', *Local Government Studies,* Vol. 16, No. 5, pp. 1–8.

Rhodes, R. A. W. (1987) 'Developing the public service orientation', *Local Government Studies,* Vol. 13, No. 3, May/June, pp. 63–73.

Schein, E. H. (1985) *Organisation culture and leadership — a dynamic view,* Jossey Bass, San Francisco.

Stephenson, T. (1989) 'Ensurers not enablers — the management response to change in Cheshire', *Local Government Policy Making,* Vol. 16, No. 1, June, pp. 3–9.

Stewart, J. and Clarke, M. (1985a) 'Local government and the public service orientation: or does public service provide for the public? *Mimeo,* Local Government Training Board, August.

Stewart, J. and Clarke, M. (1985b) 'The service programme — report on a visit to Sweden, Working Paper 2,' *Mimeo,* Local Government Training Board, October.

Stewart, J. and Clarke, M. (1986a) 'The public service orientation: issues and dilemmas to be faced', *Working Paper 4,* Local Government Training Board, August.

Stewart, J. and Clarke, M. (1986b) 'The public service orientation: developing the approach,' *Working Paper 3,* Local Government Training Board, April.

Walsh, K. (1990) 'Managing quality in the public service', *Management Education and Development Special Issue,* Vol. 21, Part 5, Winter, pp. 394–400.

Walsh, K. (1992) 'Quality contracts and care', *Contracting In or Out?,* Spring, p. 4.

Warner Burke, W. (1987) *Organization development, a normative view,* Addison Wesley, Reading, Massachusetts.

8 The renewal of quality in the political process

John Benington and Matthew Taylor

We would look strangely upon a neighbour who expended consider-able time and energy polishing a car which is likely at any time to be sent to the scrap heap. Yet, the analogy could be applied to the ob-session in local government with improving the quality of local ser-vices at a time when it seems possible that meaningful local govern-ment could soon be scrapped.

For the local government car to be saved from the scrap heap requires work not only on its appearance and fittings but also on its engine. This chapter is based on the assumption that the engine of local government lies in its political values and democratic processes. Our focus is therefore on the relationship of the concept and practice of quality management to political values and to the representative demo-cratic process.

Our chapter begins with a brief summary of our assumptions in rela-tion to local government and democratic theory. We then describe the major elements of the crisis now facing the British system of local government. After the main body of the chapter examining the place of political values in the pursuit of quality and the potential of quality approaches in renewing local representative democracy, we return in our conclusion to these broader themes and their relation to the emergence of quality as the 'key issue for local government in the 90s'.

Democratic theory and local government

Democratic theory describes local government in two ways. Firstly, as an element within a larger national or supranational system of govern-ment. Secondly, as a local democratic system with its own characteris-tics and relationship to its local community (Hill, 1974, p. 25).

In both dimensions, there are significant shifts taking place. Firstly, there have been major changes both in the relationship between central and local government and between these tiers and supranational government in the European Community. Secondly, as we will discuss in more detail below, there has been a fragmentation of local political control away from the formal authority of elected representatives.

These shifts suggest the need for new democratic theories of local government. A central issue for such theories is the status and role of representative democracy within the local distribution of political authority.

This chapter is not the place to discuss democratic theories of local government in detail. However, underlying our case in this chapter are three key-related assumptions: firstly, the institutions of local representative democracy are seen as the necessary centre (but not the exclusive possessor) of local political authority; secondly, the continued role of local representative democracy (among other forms of local political expression) is necessary for the fulfilment of democracy and citizenship in both local communities and the nation state as a whole; thirdly, the role of local government in empowering and politically developing individuals and communities is not an inherent characteristic but a goal whose attainment requires a committed and self-critical approach from local politicians and officers.

This chapter argues that the concept and practice of quality has implications which challenge the capacity for adaptation and renewal within local representative democracy. As such, like all challenges, it offers both a threat and an opportunity.

Local government in crisis

A crisis in local government has been frequently announced over the last decade. Following the 1992 General Election, that crisis can be said to have reached a potentially critical stage.

The attack from central government

The antipathy of successive Conservative governments to a powerful and autonomous system of local government has been demonstrated in a wide variety of measures. These have included; the diminution or removal of local authority influence from services including health, training, further and higher education and economic development; the abolition of metropolitan counties; tight constraints on local capital and revenue spending through a huge array of mechanisms but most particularly capping and the shift of the base of local expenditure from local to national taxation; political and financial encouragement for various institutions and groups such as schools and council house tenants to cut their ties to local government; and suspicion and antipathy to policies which could extend the influence of local government such as a power of general competence, a constitutional guarantee of local government or a voice in Europe.

The 'tightening noose' around local public services

In the post-war period local government spending grew dramatically as relative economic growth combined with the political consensus behind redistributive policies and a growing public sector (although this period can also be seen as one in which central government began to roll back the autonomy of the local authorities). Over the last 15 years local government has faced a tightening noose made up of three strands: limited resources resulting from economic stagnation and political antipathy to public sector expenditure; growing demands such as those arising from an ageing population; and rising real costs resulting from the relatively static productivity of labour intensive services like education and social care.

The fragmentation of local political control

The pattern of post-war local public services could be explained almost exclusively in terms of distribution of authority between central and local governments ruled by elected representatives, with perhaps some reference to the power of professional groups. Over the last decade a fragmentation of the basis of local decision making has taken place. A greater role has been given to appointed bodies with little local accountability ranging from TECs and Urban Development Corporations to health authorities. Considerable powers have been transferred to bodies with their own representative base such as school governing bodies. The necessity of working with voluntary and other statutory agencies means that decision making, particularly in the area of community care, is seen explicitly as a function of negotiation between partners of which the local authority is one, albeit the lead, among many agencies. In some authorities (such as Islington — see chapter 9) attempts have been made to decentralise power to neighbourhood forums and user groups. Finally, there have been a range of policies which in varying degrees increase the powers of individuals and groups of individuals to shape service patterns. These policies range from the right to buy council houses or to vote to join Housing Action Trusts, to the opportunity to have children enrolled at a school of the parents' choice, and to the explicit commitment by many authorities to give community care clients choices over the pattern of care they should receive.

Although the real content of these shifts, particularly those purporting to give more real control to individual clients or citizens, is debatable, it is clear that there has been a significant dilution of local councils' control of public service provision.

Popular dissatisfaction with local public services

The view that there has been an increase in public dissatisfaction with the form and type of local public services has become widely promoted in recent years. There are two sets of causes ascribed to this phenomenon. Firstly, associated with political opinion on the Right, is the view that the problem lies in the characteristics of the public sector such as the tendency for services to become captured by producers and for spending to increase in relation to political and managerial interests rather than the preferences of the local community. Secondly, changes in public attitude have been linked with shifts in the form of private goods and services and the rise of consumerism. As people have been offered and have come to expect diversity, choice and quality in the private sector these expectations have been carried over into criticisms of the form of the services on offer in the public sphere.

Together, these factors suggest a picture of local government facing increasing demands with declining resources, squeezed by hostility from the centre, indifference or criticism from the community and threatened by the emergence of viable alternatives to the traditional model of local democratic decision making. While it would be possible to offer a Panglossian interpretation of these 'challenges' to local government, it is not surprising that some academic and political commentators are now asking whether local government has any future.

While the pursuit of quality is most closely a response to the fourth of our factors — popular dissatisfaction with public services — the claim has been increasingly made that quality is the key which can unlock a door leading to the fundamental renewal of local democracy. The contributions to this book underline the position of quality as the conceptual *sine qua non* of public sector management in the 1990s. In the words of the three local authority associations of England and Wales, 'It [quality] has a role not only in ensuring local government's survival but also in strengthening it. Quality has a role to play in improving local democracy' (AMA, 1992, p. 10).

Quality and the future of local government

We now turn to the place of political values and democratic models in the search for quality in local government.

There can be few words which are more often used and abused in politics than 'democracy'. Politicians occupying diametrically opposed positions on an issue are likely to claim that they are acting in the name of democracy. For example, the Government extolled the virtues of the poll tax as a means of increasing local democratic accountability, while local councillors who advocated non-collection of the tax did so in the name of local democracy and the wishes of the local community.

Yet in spite of the rhetoric, is the representative democratic legitimacy of local government being called into question by the new consensus which has emerged around the idea that 'quality of service to the customer' is the prime purpose and goal for local government?

We can summarise three distinct approaches, each of which either explicitly or implicitly has important things to say about the nature and function of local democracy. We term these approaches respectively, the new right, the new left, and the new managerialism. It is evidence of the ubiquity of term 'quality' that in each of the three cases the specific prescription for quality in local government is almost indistinguishable from the general prescription for the future of local government *per se*.

Quality and the New Right

For new right thinkers, private markets offer the best way of pursuing quality, through competition between producers and choice for customers. A combination of economic positivism and philosophical individualism underlies the new right view that the more the relationship of local authorities to local citizens approximates to that of sellers and buyers, the more likely they will be to provide and receive goods and services of lower cost and higher quality. Reforms such as compulsory competitive tendering (CCT), the creation of purchaser/provider splits in the provision of community care, and the promotion of explicit competition between schools in local education markets, are all designed to replace collective political decision making with individualistic market led outcomes.

The Government's various citizens' charters are generally concerned neither with rights nor with a recognisable concept of citizenship, but with consumer protection. In the words of Graham Mather, a leading new right policy analyst, specifying service standards and creating rights of redress for customers of public services:

> marks a fundamental move away from government as authority, to government as a series of contracts. It breaks with the principle that public services tend to be provided according to the terms of a political and administrative decision-making process, and substitutes economic tests, market derived information, financial incentives and clearly defined general rules.
>
> (Mather, 1991)

Mather's vision of government by contract rather than by ballot, is similar to Nicholas Ridley's picture of local authorities becoming enablers rather than providers (Ridley, 1988). For both Mather and Ridley local authorities stripped of their functions of service delivery and political representation could become lean and efficient businesses, concentrating their time and effort on the process of specifying, letting and reviewing the contracts they had sub-contracted to other (largely private sector) providers. One consequence of the new right model of the enabling authority operating as a commercial business within a contract culture is that councillors would no longer be required to meet frequently. Indeed, both Mather and Ridley suggest local councils could dispatch their business in as little as two meetings per year. Ridley goes on to suggest that this would have the added benefit of making the role of councillor more attractive to the successful and busy people who are discouraged from standing for the council by the prospect of interminable meetings.

Quality and the New Left

The new left is a less precise term than the new right. This is partly because the new left lacks a unifying corpus of distinctive ideas. Unlike, the new right its ideas have not on the whole been crystallized into specific policy programmes.

Three themes tend to recur in new left thought. Firstly, a critique of the 'old left'. This takes many forms but includes an analysis of the failings of centralised statist approaches to economic and social reform, and an assertion of the need for more decentralised solutions to problems of social need and economic restructuring. Secondly, the new left's approach to equality combines policies which recognise the complex nature of social inequality (class, race, gender, age, disability, sexuality), with an acceptance of legitimate and positive differences in people's needs and wants. Thirdly, there is a concern that traditional public services too often demean and disable their recipients, and a search for new kinds of strategies and services which 'empower' people to participate more fully in society as citizens.

It may seem paradoxical to suggest that the new left's approach to quality in local government is ambivalent about the role of local representative democracy. In the mid-1980s it was elected local politicians like Ken Livingstone, leader of the GLC, and David Blunkett, leader of Sheffield City Council, who pioneered the development and testing of many of the new left's ideas for the renewal of local government. However, in practice more emphasis has been given to strengthening the participation of the public, the citizen, and the user of services, than to re-invigorating the processes of democratic representation.

One of the more interesting recent contributions to new left thinking has come from Margaret Hodge, leader of Islington Borough Council and Chair of the Association of London Authorities, in a Fabian Pamphlet entitled 'Quality, Equality, Democracy: Improving Public Services' (Hodge, 1991). It would be wrong to suggest that thinkers like Hodge are antagonistic to representative democracy. However, in her vision of 'empowering people to control their lives' (ibid, p. 3) elected members are given only a limited direct role:

> improving participation in elections is part of this process, but we must also devise ways of decentralising power from politicians and bureaucrats to people as consumers and citizens . . . by opening up our services to public account through democratic policies, we will achieve better quality public services. We will restore faith in their value and move towards equality.
>
> (ibid)

Hodge's prescription for 'quality, equality and democracy' is based on combining representative structures with participatory democracy at neighbourhood level, clearer statements of contractual obligations from service providers, and enhanced powers for individual redress.

Another recent document on quality in public welfare services, from the 'pink think tank', the Institute for Public Policy Research (IPPR), argues for a 'democratic' approach to quality in welfare services, as opposed to the traditional, scientific, managerial, and consumerist models imported from the commercial sector (Coote and Pfeffer, 1991). However, the strategies for a democratic approach to quality focus on making the public more powerful, strengthening public participation, rights for customers and citizens, involving the work force, and changing management and professional cultures. Councillors are not seen as having any central or specific role in improving quality in local public services. Local politicians are not presented as an impediment to the pursuit of quality, but neither are they portrayed as significant in this process.

Quality and the New Managerialism

The 'managerial' perspective is the least explicit but perhaps most pervasive and powerful of the models being adopted for the pursuit of quality in the public sector. The managerial model may encompass aspects of both the new right and new left approach but its central emphasis is on the pursuit of quality through changes in the management of services, rather than through changes in market relationships, as promoted by the new right, or in political processes, as argued by the new left.

Over the past five years or so, the 'search for excellence' and a commitment to the 'public service orientation' have become hall-marks of the progressive local authority chief executive and manager. Many authorities have pioneered new deals between the local authority and its users: to guarantee certain standards of service (e.g. minimum response times to letters, phone calls, complaints, and the reliability of appointments for visits, etc.); to improve the clarity of signposting, the quality of waiting areas, the courtesy of receptionists and front-line staff, the level of information about the authority's services, struc-ture, and finances, the simplicity and user-friendliness of application forms, etc. Many chief executives and managers have personally led this new commitment to quality of service, for example: by developing and publicising statements of the authority's core values, mission and commitment to quality of service to its 'customers'; introducing training in customer care for all levels of local authority staff; by regu-larly 'sampling' services for themselves, by working at the reception desk of the local authority or going out to work with home helps, meals on wheels, refuse collection teams; by establishing a telephone hot line to give members of the public direct access to the top man-agers at certain times of the week; by regularly visiting and encourag-ing the authority's front-line staff, and fieldworkers, in their work directly with the public; by surveys and market research among users of services to monitor their needs, opinions, and their satisfaction with services.

Some authorities do not restrict their attention to direct customer relations issues, but go further to describe the ways in which financial and personnel management structures have been reformed to fit the new management style. Such measures include devolved management, arms' length management boards, decentralised cost centres, service level agreements and performance related pay.

However, a study of a wide range of local authority documents about quality reveals surprisingly little reference to the role of the elected member in the process. The prime focus is on the manager, the fieldworker and the public. There is often little or no mention of the role of elected members as either channel or focus.

Local authority strategies to improve the management, quality and effectiveness of services in these ways are not inherently liable to play down the role of elected members and there are some indications of a re-assertion of the role of politicians and of political values in new approaches to quality management. Particularly significant is an emerging model of 'policy planning'. The policy planning approach is based upon focusing members' and chief officers' attention on the long term values and capabilities of the authority in the context of the major changes and challenges affecting the authority's work. The policy planning approach takes as its starting point the emergence of contractual and decentralised forms of service delivery which remove from members the day-to-day concern with managing and monitoring services. In the local authority of the 90s, fewer decisions may be made, but those that are faced are more important and challenging because they relate to strategy and values rather than operational matters.

The policy planning approach is being pursued in a number of authorities and is soon to be the subject of an Audit Commission review. Unquestionably, the systematic attempt to concentrate the minds of elected representatives on the 'big' issues, to inform their decision making with good data and with frameworks which concentrate members' minds on the key issues offers a major advance on the traditional model of undifferentiated levels of decision making. In the increasingly discredited model of catch-all committee meetings, as much time could be spent discussing the proposed colour for social services minibuses as on the principles underlying an authority's community care strategy. However, policy planning may accentuate one aspect of the representative role at the expense of recognising the unique value which lies precisely in the scope and range of the councillor's role from the strategic centre to the grass roots — an issue to which we return below.

We are not seeking to suggest that all three major schools of thought we have briefly summarised above fail completely to recognise the place of political values and the centrality of democratic processes in local government. Indeed, it is possible to see within each approach a very specific leaning in relation to these issues. The new right's approach is fundamentally a re-assertion of the liberal model of protective democracy (Held, 1987, p. 70). In this model the intervention of government is justified not in terms of any intrinsic value in relation to participative citizenship, liberty, much less equity, but in terms of ensuring the freedom of citizens to pursue their private business or in a specific and limited cases (such as public goods) where intervention can be justified in terms of maximising social good. The managerial approach seeks to compartmentalise the role of politicians and political values in models of management which in the language of quality re-assert the value of rational planning methods based upon technique and expertise. The new left approach emphasises the importance of political values such as egalitarianism but sees these as best achieved through the exercise not of representative democracy but of new channels of participation and direct community decision making.

Quality and political values

Our focus now turns, firstly, to the place of political values in the pursuit of quality and, secondly, to the need to link the pursuit of quality to the strengths and weaknesses of local representative democracy.

There is a much stronger role for politics and politicians in the pursuit of quality in local government when (like the most advanced private sector firms) the pursuit of quality starts upstream with fundamental questions about what is to be produced, why, how, for whom, and with whom, rather than downstream at the point of delivery of services to users.

A growing number of local authorities are producing statements of their core values and mission. Many of these focus on quality of service to the 'customer'. However, these mission statements are often drafted by the officers and merely rubber stamped by councillors. They tend to be very general and rather utopian. These creeds of quality are full of hurrah words, which leave a golden glow. They convey a sense of piety rather than purpose. One genuflects in automatic agreement because no one can disagree with the language of excellence. However, the mission statements from different authorities look surprisingly similar to each other. They do not differ very much from place to place. They are hard to translate into action because they are often not specific in their intentions.

One key difference between the private sector and local government in this respect is that in the latter the mission statement has to be driven by political as well as managerial values. As in the voluntary sector, public authorities must answer Peter Drucker's question, 'What is the bottom line when there is no "bottom line"?' (Drucker, 1990: p. 107). A council's statement of core values has to have resonance not only within the local authority, but also within the local community. To be really effective in regenerating a clear sense of mission and purpose for the council within the local community, it must be rooted in the concrete realities of each particular community. Councillors, and the political parties and party groups on the council, need to be actively involved in discussing what it means to act as the voice of this particular local community in this specific place, at this specific time.

A local authority's mission statements will only provide effective leadership and direction if its values are felt to reflect the various interests of the diverse groups within the local population, and represent the common interests of the local community as a whole. This is one of the distinctive features of local government. It is the only organisation constituted and capable of representing the interests of the whole rather than the separate parts and fractions. As an elected body it has a responsibility to reflect the interests and values not only of the present population but also future generations, not only the young but also elderly people, not only white people but also black and ethnic minorities, not only the employed but also the unemployed, not only the employers but also the trade unions, not only the private sector, but also the voluntary and community sectors.

Nottinghamshire County Council's Directions for the Future, Hertfordshire County Council's Citizen's Charter, Renfrew District Council's Corporate Plan for 1992, Hartlepool Borough Council's Strategic Plan, and North Tyneside Borough Council's City Challenge submission have all been developed in this way, with active involvement from councillors and party groups, and convey a much stronger and more specific sense of purpose and values than many of the more idealised mission and quality statements which emanate from the officer system alone.

However, mission statements by themselves, whatever political involvement and backing they have, are clearly not enough to achieve the overall commitment to quality which seems to have penetrated the whole culture of many successful businesses in the private sector. This requires a high level of investment in communication, organisational development, cultural change, in-service training and continuing education, for both elected members and officers. Local authorities committed to total quality in strategy and management, rather than simply to quality control of service delivery, will want to involve councillors, chief officers, middle managers, fieldworkers, the political parties and groups, and perhaps other public, private, voluntary and community organisations, in a cascading and participative process of debating, developing and adopting the core values which should provide a sense of mission and purpose not only for the local authority, but also for the local community.

In addition to the sense of purpose embodied in statements of values and mission, a local authority also needs a clear sense of direction in a rapidly changing external environment. The many structural changes facing local authorities in the 1990s include:

- *changes in the economic context, as a result of continued industrial restructuring within a more integrated and competitive European market*
- *changes in the social context, as a result of demographic changes and the continuing impact of mass unemployment particularly among the young*
- *changes in the political context, as a result of the continued pressure of Government reform and the wider process of the Europeanisation of government.*

Local authorities searching for a better quality of governance and quality of service have to analyse the local impact of structural changes like these. This involves a commitment by councillors and officers to scan, analyse and interpret changes which might affect the area and its people, in order to develop better maps of the future patterns of need. This might include detailed analysis of census data and health authority projections, in order to establish a sharper profile of the future population of elderly people in the area, by age, gender, ethnic background and geographical location. In addition there needs to be an analysis of key sectors of industry and employment and skills within the local economy, in order to develop a picture of likely trends as well as areas of risk and opportunity.

Mapping of trends within the local economy and local community in this way needs to draw not only on 'hard' statistical data, but also on the 'softer' information and intelligence which is gathered by councillors, fieldworkers, users and pressure groups as they grapple with emerging issues at the grassroots and at the front line. This is often where longer term trends can first be identified. Councillors may also want to complement the data they derive from the above two sources with more fine grain 'market' research and 'consumer' surveys.

Good examples of this kind of politically-led high quality approach to strategy include Luton and Stoke on Trent, where the local councils have been able to give a real sense of direction to their local economy and local community during a period of deep structural change. They have done this by commissioning research studies analysing the strengths and weaknesses of key sectors, technologies and skills within their local economies (focusing mainly but not exclusively on the auto industry in the case of Luton, and potteries in the case of Stoke). These studies and their recommendations were debated widely not only within the local authority, but also in conferences and joint forums with other stakeholders like local employers, trade unions, the Training Agency, the chamber of commerce, regional offices of central government, voluntary organisations, MPs and MEPs, and other interest groups. In both cases this process has led the local council to propose a transitional strategy for the local economy, building organically upon the indigenous strengths of knowledge and skill within local industry and the labour market, and establishing bridges from the present industrial base into new areas of opportunity. For example Stoke on Trent's strategy recognises that the traditional potteries industries are under threat, but that a transition could be made to modern technologies of the future through the area's knowledge of ceramics.

The quality of the local authority's work in these situations is clearly not to be judged in terms of service delivery to individual users, but in terms of the strategic direction which they have given to the community as a whole. Councillors have played a leading role in developing this sense of direction, through their involvement in debating the options and developing the strategy with other agencies and interest groups within the area.

The pursuit of quality through local governance requires not just a sense of purpose and a sense of direction, but also a sense of priorities. Private sector organisations can set their priorities by choosing which markets to operate in, can withdraw from those which are difficult or unprofitable, and can position themselves within market niches where their products and services are of high quality. Public service organisations are not always free to choose their priorities in this way, or to play to their strengths. They are obliged by law and public expectation to operate in some very difficult 'markets' where it is very hard to achieve high quality of service (e.g. provision of care for elderly, mentally, infirm people, or housing the homeless). They have to carry out some duties which are inherently controversial and where it is hard to find a benchmark of quality to satisfy any individual 'customer' (e.g. taking children at risk into care, which may be against the wishes of both the child and the parents). Unlike the private sector, public service organisations often cannot translate increased demand into increased resources for investment in higher quality. Resources are often fixed, so increased demand can lead instead to increased pressure, demoralised staff, rationing, and disappointed expectations by potential users of services.

Finite resources mean that higher quality performance in local government cannot be achieved through incremental growth. It can only be achieved through a very targeted sense of purpose, direction and priorities. High quality local governance requires that the authority's priorities are not set covertly through rationing by disaffected staff and dissuaded users, but overtly through explicit choices. In local government, the process of strategic choice has to start in the political sphere. It is local councillors who must give the lead in setting the authority's strategic priorities, in discussion and negotiation with their party groups, pressure groups, interest groups, and their officer advisers.

Local authorities like Hartlepool, Solihull, North Tyneside, and others are pioneering new approaches to quality of service and of local governance in which councillors are actively involved in developing the strategy and the priorities for the authority, with specific measurable targets to be achieved and monitored by each committee and department each year.

Another of the distinctive features of quality assurance and TQM approaches is that in addition to developing a strategic sense of purpose, direction and priorities, it is recognised that fundamental changes are necessary in the culture of the organisation. These cultural shifts are most often described in terms of the managerial orientation of the authority or in relation to the way in which service users are perceived and treated. Thus, cultural shifts will seek to 'pull down barriers and build bridges' between managers and their departments or will seek to place 'quality care to our customers' at the centre of everything the authority does. But, in local government, organisational culture must also relate to explicit political values and the need to maximise the understanding of these values in the work of officers and members.

Quality and local representative democracy

We turn now, more specifically, to the links and discontinuities between the pursuit of quality and the role of the representative process and its embodiment in elected members.

Part of the case made for new approaches to strategic policy making (such as the Audit Commission's policy planning model) is that new processes are necessary to reflect the shift from direct service provision through vertically integrated bureaucracies into decentralised and/or contracted forms of service delivery. Implicit here is the frequent assertion repeated in literature on 'quality' that by seeking to control everything local authorities are likely to achieve nothing. Councillors should concentrate on the big policy value issues and, by implication, leave the implementation of these policies to managers and deliverers.

The debate about the benefits of the purchase-provider splits and devolved management systems have moved quickly from controversy to consensus as these approaches have come to be less associated with the political agenda of the right and more with generally accepted models of 'loose–tight' organisations and the management philosophy of 'holding on while letting go'. As Sanderson says in chapter 2, this model of greater central control over strategic policy and devolved operational management is based upon three processes: assessing needs and setting aims and targets; organising services so that targets can be achieved; and measuring the degree to which targets are met. Performance review systems provide the bridge between the separated responsibilities of policy formation and service delivery.

Councillors as quality agents.

The critical issues in performance review are who does the reviewing and what criteria they use. The distinction between economy (cost criteria), efficiency (output criteria) and effectiveness (outcome criteria) is well known, but in relation even to the narrowest of these sets of criteria a number of different measures of cost are possible. For example, if costs are measured in terms of labour input, to what extent is the experience of employees (effort, satisfaction, etc.) considered a legitimate measure of input? Performance judgements will clearly vary according to the values and priorities of the observer. For a chief executive or council leader the cost of maintaining surplus places in village schools may be unjustifiable, while to the education department with a commitment to community-based education, or even more to the parent of a child living close by a small school, the additional cost is well worth while. (In passing, it is worth noting that despite radical reform in public sector management, the closure of institutions — whether hospitals in London or schools in Warwickshire — is proving as intractable as ever. In part this can be seen as a reflection of the scope for public mobilisation behind a threatened institution in which many have been treated or taught, but it can also be seen to reflect the enduring need for difficult political decisions to be made in the full knowledge that many 'customers' are going to feel their wishes have been flatly ignored.)

On the face of it, councillors are uniquely suited to a role in performance review. 'Upstream', members are (or should be) involved in setting overall objectives and service targets, while 'downstream' their role in the local ward involves them in observing and responding to the experience of workers and clients at the front line. In addition, the representative role of councillors in relation to their ward and to the authority as a whole gives them an insight into the range of views among the population about the criteria by which services should be judged.

The separation of strategic policy making from operational matters must take place in a way which recognises the range of councillors' concerns. Otherwise, quality management approaches will reinforce an absolute division of councillors into senior policy makers and back bench case workers. This division may appear logical if councillors' roles are reduced to job specifications in which functions are limited to areas of specific skill. A broader view recognises that the range of councillors' duties is a defining feature of their role. Clearly, as any councillor trying to find time both to read important policy documents and conscientiously deal with local case work will testify, this is a question of balance — a balance made more difficult to find by the inadequate and uneven availability of back-up services to councillors (Barron, Crawley and Wood, 1991). But, many councillors would be likely to agree with Denis Healey that:

> The busier a politician is with national or international affairs, the more important is his constituency case work. It is that above all which keeps him in touch with the problems of those he is supposed to represent, and teaches him how legislation at Westminster actually affects real people on the ground — or how powerless he is to help them.
>
> (Healey, 1989; p. 139)

Closer involvement of councillors in performance review also requires a recognition of the diversity of approaches which councillors bring to this role. There are two particularly important contributions. Firstly, review systems must be user-friendly. Aims and targets have to be written in ways which can be easily interpreted and understood by councillors and used as tools in responding to issues raised by constituents. This, of course, is a requirement which is as relevant to empowering the public as to assisting the judgements of members. Secondly, it is important that councillors experience the front line rather than simply hearing about it. Lewisham, for example, has developed links between particular councillors and 'devolved achievement centres' within particular services. As well as encouraging a detailed understanding of the service, members have been encouraged to 'experience the joys and sorrows of providing front-line services (e.g. being out at 6.30 am with a refuse crew. . . '. (AMA,1992; p. 61)

In chapter three of this book, Lucy Gaster outlines some of the key factors in a successful merging of the processes of devolution and the aims of quality. One aim is that those who are at the front line of service delivery in decentralised systems have real devolved power. Another is the value of an 'holistic' approach to the customer which focuses on their needs by breaking down boundaries separating contracts or departments. Councillors' decision-making authority and the wide range of their concerns makes their role potentially consistent with local strategies linking devolution and decentralisation to the pursuit of quality.

Local representative democracy: a suitable case for the quality treatment?

By emphasising the importance of political values in progressive approaches to quality, and recognising the need to build on rather than narrow the width of the councillor's role, we move closer to an approach to quality which reflects (and even celebrates) the democratic basis of local government. Is it possible that in addition to bringing councillors into the pursuit of quality we can also bring some of the insights of modern quality management into the representative role? Our answer to this question is 'Yes', qualified by a recognition of the difficult issues raised.

The processes of representative democracy could hardly fit less well some of the central tenets of quality management. Modern management practice in both the private and public sectors emphasises the importance of replacing a model of quality control in which quality is checked and problems rectified at the end of the process by a quality assurance or TQM process which aims to get it 'right first time'. An electoral process in which councillors stand for election or re-election only every three or four years appears to be a clear example of such an old fashioned 'end of pipe' approach to quality control.

The electoral process performs equally poorly in relation to other principles in the pursuit of quality. Although constituents have the collective ability to elect whoever they prefer to office, for many individuals, especially for those who do not support the sitting councillor in a 'safe' seat, the electoral process is hardly empowering. Even more glaring is the weakness of the electoral process in relation to the emphasis on choice as a criterion of quality. Even in those council seats where there is a conceivable chance of the incumbent councillor being successfully challenged, the effective choice is still restricted to at best three candidates and three sets of policies. In both the private and public sector the range of relevant choices given to the customer is seen as a crucial benchmark of quality. If the process of casting vote is compared to, say, buying a car, the voter if faced with a choice between two or possibly three models each of which comes as a fixed package with no scope for further specification in relation to the features of the model chosen. Casting a vote is a very different process to that involved in buying a car, but the growing interest in local electoral reform (Stewart, 1989, p. 251), can be linked to the desire of voters to have real choices and to feel their decision matters.

A final quality factor found in variable supply in the electoral process is information. Access to reliable information is portrayed in many accounts as a crucial aspect in expanding customer choice and increasing service responsiveness. The Government's Citizen's Charter reforms include the developing of quantitative performance indicators for local authorities. Notwithstanding the narrow criteria of these indicators, they are a blunt tool for local communities to assess the effectiveness of their own representatives. Our own immediate experience as a former councillor and an ex-local authority chief officer suggest that the dynamics of the electoral system and the limited resources of political parties leads to a highly variable distribution of information about the activities of elected representatives. In marginal wards, parties will tend to shower electors with information, propaganda and opportunities to make contact with their councillors and candidates. Obversely, in safe seats electors are unlikely to receive any information apart from a token election address.

These limitations of the electoral process in a society in which many are increasingly orientated to expectations of quality, choice, information and of empowerment raises a number of issues. Clearly, many would find in our argument a case for electoral reform. However, in this context, our point is simply that there is a tension between the traditions and political imperatives of the electoral system and the experience of electors. At the least, this tension requires a concerted attempt to improve those aspects of the electoral and representative process which are amenable to change.

Yet, the local democratic system, and in particular the representative process, is noticeably missing from the focus of quality reforms. There has been surprisingly little recent research into aspects of the councillor's role, but that which has taken place, most notably the recent work of Barron, Crawley and Wood (1991) has emphasised the deeply inadequate level of support given to assist councillors in carrying out their duties. Whether the issue be specific forms of enhancing the councillor's work like secretarial support, councillor friendly information systems, training in time management or case work skills, or more generally the development and implementation of systems to enable councillors to achieve quality in their work, good practice stands out against a background of apparent indifference.

Why is it that councillors, whose role potentially embodies many of the principles underlying the pursuit of quality are so disregarded in the literature and practice of quality management in local government?

One set of answers lies in the phrase 'quality management'. The strength of democracy (underlined by parliamentary electorates in cases stretching from John Wilkes to Bobby Sands) is that people elect whoever they want to power including candidates with idiosyncratic and unconventional views and approaches to their role. The diversity of councillors' approach has indeed been praised as one of the strengths of local democracy (ibid, pp. 185–86). The view that councillors' duties should be placed within a more explicit framework of expectations and standards appears to legitimate, firstly, a reversal of the power relationship between councillor and officers so that the latter define the task of the former and, secondly, a de-politicisation of electoral choice whereby electors are encouraged to vote not on the basis of political values and programmes but the professional and technical abilities of the councillor according to a series of 'objective' criteria.

Indeed, the attempt to provide a structured framework to enhance the quality of councillor's work can be seen to revive concern over the quality of democratic representatives. This concern can be traced back to J. S. Mill's fear of the potential tyranny of the uneducated mass over the enlightened minority. The issue of councillor quality was a factor leading to the emphasis in the Redcliffe-Maud Commission on the need for bigger councils and, implicitly fewer, more selectively chosen, councillors. It has recently been revived in Ridley's assertion that one advantage of having an enabling authority which meets once a year to agree contracts is that it would then attract busy and successful people (particularly from business) to stand for election. Such criticism of the quality of councillors is, of course, elitist in that is is based on a single hierarchy of values and characteristics, and fundamentally anti-democratic in that it implies people cannot be trusted to choose their own representatives.

However, there is a world of difference between seeking to enforce a single pattern of representation and offering resources for, and models of, effective working to those councillors who choose to avail themselves of them. Also, an element of all models for maximising councillors' effectiveness should be that they are adaptable to a range of different political and personal priorities. With the exception of the declining number of independent councillors, members have different roles and responsibilities in relation to their council, their Party and their constituents. The danger with councils as corporate entities seeking to over prescribe the way in which councillors carry out their role is that the sovereignty of the local electorate and the democratic process is undermined. Similarly, it can be argued that an authority confuses its role with that of the Party if it steps too far in directing councillors.

A recurrent claim by candidates seeking to remove incumbent councillors in elections is not only that they offer better policies but that they will provide a better service to the locality in terms of services like newsletters, surgeries or general accessibility. If sitting councillors have their performance enhanced, resourced and monitored through the authority such councillors may have their ability to beat off challengers unfairly enhanced. A way around this objection and one which would see quality in the political process in broader terms than the proficiency of councillors would be a system of local public resourcing of political parties. As well as simple financial assistance such an approach could, for example, include training on effectiveness to prospective candidates for office as well as sitting councillors.

Besides the many practical issues raised, the proposal that local political parties receive financial assistance and other forms of resourcing from local authorities may appear, in the light of prevailing attitudes to the role of local government, highly unrealistic. However, such a system exists in Swedish local authorities (Barron, Crawley and Wood, 1991, p. 195). Also, the principle lying behind this proposal is already partly embodied in the largely successful system in many authorities of research assistants for Party groups. Finally, the idea of local council support for the political process in the community, whether through the funding of parties or other means, offers an important link between the pursuit of quality and the essential need to re-invigorate local governance. It is this broader issue of the future of local government and governance to which we turn in our conclusion.

Conclusion

We suggest above that the magnitude of the crisis facing local government is such that pursuing service quality as a means of defending the
system could be likened to polishing a car on its way to the scrap heap.
We have sought to show in this chapter that attention needs to be spent
on the democratic engine of local government. In examining the faults
of the engine it is also possible to develop and expand our ambitions
for improving the quality of the local government vehicle as a whole.

As the threat to democratic local government has grown and as local
authorities have been encouraged or compelled to hive off an ever
greater range of direct service provision responsibilities, attention has
begun to return to what could be termed the 'essence' of local government: what, if anything exists if the services have been taken away or
devolved?

The concept of 'local governance' offers one way of responding to
this quest. The attention paid to this concept and the degree to which it
requires development, is emphasised by its choice as the title for a
major ESRC research initiative whose primary aim is:

> to analyse the transformation of the structure of government beyond
> Westminster and Whitehall from a system of local government into a
> system of local governance involving complex sets of organisations
> drawn from the public, private and voluntary sectors.
>
> (ESCR, 1992, p. 1)

This shift in academic emphasis from the in-house structures of
local government to the processes of local governance can be linked
not only to the changing context and pressures facing local government
but also to a normative case for local government. This case seeks to
re-assert the activity of government (or governance), rather than simply
the provision of services, as the essential function of local government.

A number of accounts (Stewart, 1989; ACC, 1991) have correlated
the decline in the vitality of local government with the growth in the
responsibilities vested in it by central government. This process, particularly during the post-war period, is seen to have led to the locality
becoming the implementation arm for central policy. If a growth of
direct service provision was linked to a loss of local autonomy, is it
possible in the current context to suggest a more positive scenario than
the new right vision of the virtual withering away of local government?
Indeed, can the idea of the enabling authority be extended into notions
of community government (Stewart, ibid) or of local authorities as the
hub of a 'local public political community' (Gyford, 1991).

Such aspirations underline the need to examine the mutual relevance of concepts of quality and of local governance. For, the funda-

mental changes affecting local government are not only restricted to the pluralisation of forms of service delivery, but also to major shifts in the locus of local decision making. As Gerry Stoker put it in his account of 'local government for a post-Fordist society':

> the institutional fragmentation of local government . . . brings with it a parallel fragmentation of the mechanisms of political representation and control.
>
> (Stoker, 1989; p. 165)

The pursuit of quality through the contract culture, devolution, maximising customer choice is both cause and effect of this political fragmentation. In terms of the broader crisis facing local government outlined above, the various applications of the concept of quality have a relevance which goes beyond the attempt to increase public satisfaction with services. The pursuit of quality is not only an important theme in the fragmentation of political control. Central government policies which have reduced local autonomy, including CCT and the break-up of local education authorities have been, in part, justified through reference to quality considerations. In ideological terms there is even a link between the rhetoric of quality and the funding of local government. Faced with meeting quality targets in a period of severe public spending restraint, government ministers are increasingly heard to stress that the *Citizen's Charter* is not about increasing funds to public services but about ensuring more quality orientated ways of using current resources.

Whilst the Government's use of the language of quality to justify further limits to local authority autonomy may appear opportunist, even those who view quality as a way of renewing local government have tended to focus on the planning and provision of services rather than the governmental function.

A commitment to achieving the highest quality of local governance, which imbues every part of the work of the council, every stage of the process of representation of community needs, and the planning, managing and delivering of services, requires a new vision of the kinds of relationship which could be established between councillors, the controlling party, pressure groups and interest groups, chief officers, middle managers, fieldworkers, the trade unions, users of services and the wider public.

The process needs to begin with a commitment by the local authority to move both beyond its traditional role as primarily a machine for the efficient delivery of standardised services, and also beyond the Government's model of the local authority as a clearing house for contracted out services. A council committed to local governance and to local democracy (rather than merely to administration or procurement of services) searches for improvements in quality not only in service delivery, but also in the political process. This includes:

- *representing the diverse, changing and sometimes conflicting needs of its local community*
- *empowering and giving a stronger and clearer voice to the various groups and classes of people within its population*
- *negotiating on their behalf with other agencies (e.g. the health, transport, police, water and other authorities, central government, private and commercial firms, the European Commission, etc.) to achieve the best possible range and mix of policies and services to meet those needs*
- *mobilising coalitions of organisations and interest groups from the public, private, voluntary and community sectors to work for the achievement of the best possible quality of life for the local community.*

The search for excellence through and in this more pro-active political process requires councillors to be actively involved (alongside officers, the political parties, trade unions, users and other stakeholders) in all the various processes of strategic policy making, mobilisation and implementation of programmes, and monitoring of impacts and outcomes.

It seems clear that the representative democratic role for local government can no longer be taken for granted. As we have shown, this role has a low profile in many current prescriptions for quality in local government. Those who share our view of the enduring necessity and value of local representative democracy face, we believe, three ambitious tasks. Firstly, we must ensure that explicit political values are seen to underpin the drive for quality. Secondly, we must revitalise the experience and enhance the value of local democratic representation. In this the concepts and techniques developed in the pursuit of quality have much to offer. Thirdly, we need a better model of the role of local democratic government in modern society — a model which is not only academically rigorous but also provides the basis for political mobilisation within local government and their communities.

References

ACC (1991) *The Constitutional Role of Local Government,* Association of County Councils, London.

AMA (1992) *Signposts to Quality,* Association of Metropolitan Authorities, London.

Barron, J., Crawley, G. and Wood, T. (1991) *Councillors in Crisis,* Macmillan, London.

Coote, A. and Pfeffer, N. (1991) *Is Quality Good for You?*, Institute of Public Policy Research, London.

Drucker, P. F. (1990) Managing the Non-Profit Organisation, Harper Collins, London.

ESRC (1992) *Local Governance Initiative*, Economic and Social Research Council, Swindon.

Gyford, J. (1991) *Citizens, Consumers and Councils*, Macmillan, London.

Healey, D. (1989) *The Time of My Life*, Penguin, London.

Held, D. (1987) *Models of Democracy*, Polity, Cambridge.

Hill, D. (1974) *Democratic Theory and Local Government*, George Allen and Unwin, London.

Hodge, M. (1991) *Quality, Equality and Democracy*, Fabian Society, London.

Mather, G. (1991) Serving You Rights, *Marxism Today*, May 1991.

Ridley, N. (1988) *The Local Right: Enabling not Providing*, Centre for Policy Studies, London.

Stewart, J. (1989) Local authorities as community government, in Stewart, J. and Stoker, G. (eds.) *The Future of Local Government*, Macmillan, London.

Stoker, G. (1989) Local government for a post-Fordist Society, in Stewart, J. and Stoker, G. (eds.) *The Future of Local Government*, Macmillan, London.

9 Local experience of managing quality

Wendy Thomson

Introduction

In most local authorities, managers carry out their activities with little regard to books or articles on management theory. So, although this book is concerned with quality of service in local government, the practice which I describe in this chapter should not be expected to follow neatly from the ideas outlined in earlier contributions.

Some management texts give the impression that change is merely a matter of management applying the correct thinking or strength of will. Shortcomings are put down to managers' lack of individual ability, bureaucratic defensiveness or inertia. Sometimes managers themselves give the impression that they could do anything if only they were left alone — without the interference of politicians, government, or reality. Alternatively, many public service managers feel there is little they can do, faced with staffing and financial problems, misunderstood by public and politicians alike.

Of course none of these simple views of managerial performance is accurate. Managers are neither totally powerful nor powerless. Nor will they become effective by seeking to remove themselves from external influences to function autonomously. The capacity of managers to implement anything effectively depends upon their relationship to a range of democratic relations in the public sector, and in turn to the economy and social life. So, although we take management here as the starting point for implementing quality, this does not imply that things really get done in local government through top-down chains of command. A range of other forces — elected members, residents, individuals and groups of consumers, wider social movements — are relevant to improving the quality of public services. Management alone cannot achieve change.

The experience described in this chapter may be more useful if this perspective on the role of management is kept in mind. Locally, authorities across the country are trying out ways of improving service quality. Their achievements are the result of a combination of local factors and capacities, of which management is one but not the whole part. In this sense, it does not contain a set of prescriptions for what will work everywhere.

First, I consider what is meant by quality of service in the national and local context, and the argument that is resonating through local town halls and management teams. My greatest attention is given to the methods that are being used to strengthen principles of public service in local authorities and enhance quality, such as involving consumers, surveys and polling, empowerment which balances citizenship with consumerism, the notion of rights versus care, and complaints policies and practice. Consumer contracts are a more recent innovation that is generating experience and an emerging process which is described in some detail.

In contrast to these local practices stands the national league table of performance indicators — the Citizen's Charter approach to local government services. Quality audit addresses some of the shortcomings of traditional financial audit, and the advantages of different organisational arrangements are outlined briefly. Finally, I ask if this interest in quality is likely to be sustained during the next few years facing local government.

What is quality?

Those studying the 'quality' phenomenon may be frustrated in their search for a crisp and coherent definition of what quality means. A number of definitions are provided in this book indicating a variety of perspectives. In terms of local management practice, in my experience definitions of this kind are not the main point of reference. For local authority services, the matter of quality has arisen predominantly as a political concern to make services relevant and popular with local people.

In this context, quality is a way of communicating a commitment to improved public services. It recognises that public services are coming through a highly unpopular period. The emphasis on quality is a movement against cheapness, against the value that accountants count — the domination of the economy and efficiency aspects of the Audit Commission three 'E's. Essentially quality services are those which meet people's needs, as they vote and pay for them to be met, and as they are assessed through popular experience and attitudes.

A handful of authorities may have adopted a particular quality guru or model. But regimes such as TQM, British Standards, or Peters and Waterman's 'pursuit of excellence' are more commonly a source of away day discussions than an integrated part of managers' practice. Most are trying out a variety of approaches, and all are operating in a dynamic political context which managers need to understand realistically. In the contemporary local community and authority, neither public nor individual interests can be ignored. Where public interest is the main aim sought through the policy function, objectives set for services are often contradictory and not widely communicated or understood by the majority of the public, and sometimes the workforce. Where the individual is the focus of responsive service delivery, there will be as many perceptions of quality as there are consumers and their relationships as tenants, pupils, clients, etc.

Detailed local strategies to improve quality of service need to address both these democratic levels — with the community agreeing the widest possible consensus about the purpose and extent of public intervention/services, with service users agreeing what is most important to them about how services are delivered, and then ensuring that it is provided. The purpose and processes on which quality of service will really be assessed will be locally determined by residents and service users.

The national scene

In October 1989, Labour published its policy document — *Quality Street*. It reflected some of the practices which were being developed in a number of Labour authorities such as York, Leicestershire, Rochdale, Harlow, Lewisham, Islington. *Quality Street* made the link between quality of service and such issues as decentralisation, equal opportunities, consumer participation, development and training, and performance monitoring. New ideas began to take on a distinctive local authority character, such as consumer care, service contracts, complaints service, service sampling, quality audits and circles. Shortly afterwards, the Audit Commission established its Quality Exchange, countering criticism made of its bias towards cost reductions. Prior to the 1992 General Election, the Government's Citizen's Charter was launched, and then re-launched.

I will describe some local experience of improving quality of service through *Quality Street* practices. For most managers the process has not involved a master plan, starting with one idea and working through the rest. Rather, it has been a question of introducing pilots and gaining from experience, extending support and confidence from one service to another. With the benefit of this experience, it may be possible to see how the process of improving the quality of local services could be managed in the future.

Local conditions

Much of this experience is drawn from the London Borough of Islington. Wherever quality is being implemented there will be particular conditions that will need to be understood to make quality a success. Islington works with conditions created as a result of a decade-long commitment to making services more relevant and popular to local people. This commitment was approached through three main programmes: first, the decentralisation of services to 24 neighbourhood offices; second, democratising public services through neighbourhood forums and user groups; and third, promoting equality of opportunity in employment and service.

In Islington, equal opportunity and decentralisation are seen as key policies for involving people in changing the way that services are organised and respond. By decentralising housing, social and environmental services to 24 neighbourhood offices, Islington has an extensive capacity to communicate directly with its residents and consumers. This is a real asset. It involves ensuring that residents have a say through Neighbourhood Forums in how services are determined and how their performance is assessed. These forums are formally constituted and create the opportunity in every neighbourhood for local residents, voluntary organisations, and other services to take a role in shaping the future of their community and its services.

Creating an equal opportunity for everyone to work for and receive services from the Council involves another dramatic change in the way that services are organised and consumers are understood. Most simply, it means no longer assuming that all consumers are the same. With that single insight, service standards no longer can be equated with a single minimum standard. We have learned that making only one service available, in the same form or place, will result in discrimination against some individuals and groups in favour of others. In the 1980s Islington, with many other authorities, came to recognise that equity and difference are inextricably linked. That difference does not have to imply better or worse. Making that link between equity and quality of service requires a great deal of knowledge about the residents we serve, their needs, and experience of local services.

Decentralising services and equality of opportunity open up organisations to local people's views and preferences. This knowledge and experience makes quality of service a process that can be successfully undertaken only in partnership with local residents, consumers, and communities. In Islington these policies involve ways of working and a commitment to public services on which quality of service is built. Other authorities in other parts of the country will have other histories and strengths on which a quality culture can be fostered. That local context is a crucial understanding to winning the argument for quality. The argument has to be conducted in the local language and culture, but I will highlight some general issues.

Arguments for quality

An important aspect of managing quality is persuading people inside and outside the organisation that there is something that they can do about the quality of local services. We will consider a few of the questions most managers are likely to face.

Haven't we always been managing for quality?

Most managers feel, understandably, that they *have* been working for quality public services. At the same time, many feel that they could do more were it not for politicians, spending cuts or outdated professional obstacles. Managing for quality is a practice which must direct these political, financial, and professional forces for quality services. Managers' interaction with the public, consumers, and politicians will be central to making this change. Enlisting outside interest in the future of quality public services will require leadership which involves more than assurances that we are doing the best we can.

Can local managers really make any difference?

With the imposition of Compulsory Competitive Tendering, the Housing Revenue Account, Local Management of Education, capping of revenue expenditure, central control of capital borrowing and receipts, and so on, many managers may feel that there is very little they can do. The result of these and other changes has been to create one of the most highly centralised political systems in Europe where many Council leaders see themselves as little more than administrators of centrally determined local services.

It cannot be assumed that this trend will continue inevitably. Politically, it may become less and less desirable for any government to attempt to control everything from the centre. The political risks involved can be observed elsewhere. Does government really want to be responsible for the learning of every child in the country, or for making a litter-free environment in every nook and cranny of the nation? For whatever caveats government may make about opted-out institutions and markets, the evidence is that the public holds it responsible for the actions of the institutions which it funds, whether grant aided schools, housing action trusts, hospital trusts, or training and enterprise councils.

However, if the Government really controlled everything, then every local authority in the country would look the same and carry out the same activities to the same standard and level. This is demonstrably not the case. Though diminishing, the capacity for local difference continues to exist.

How can we worry about quality when there are constant cuts?

Cutting spending is a management-intensive activity. It often involves reducing staff, reorganising functions, dealing with political and public pressures. Managers may feel it leaves little time, and certainly no money, to do anything about quality.

Yet without regard for service quality, cuts and the restructuring they involve can become an end in themselves. Achieving a reduction of 10 per cent in spending takes over as the primary managerial objective. What is being delivered for the remaining 90 per cent can be overlooked. Sometimes, means become confused with the ends in this way. If spending has to be reduced, it should be done with quality in mind. What quality of service can we provide with x level of resource? It is important to make an explicit political choice over range and level of service.

Often cuts are made in a totally pragmatic way: not replacing staff where vacancies happen to fall: withdrawing funds where resistance is likely to be least; not developing new services where needs or demands call for them; avoiding difficult choices by leaving management to juggle priorities within cash limits. Expediency is the guiding principle.

Public services in the 1990s could approach priorities differently. People have a right to know what services they are voting and paying for and the standards they can expect. They are less likely to settle for the paternalistic fudge. Managers too are less likely to take on this responsibility, for when the service is not there, or the quality has deteriorated, it is their management and the public service as a whole that is brought into disrepute.

Isn't this quality just public relations hype?

In some cases the quality image is more apparent than the reality. The market in management fashion is a growing business. Much is primarily about selling consultancies and training, some are keen on spreading the idea that private is always best, others assume a world of free, marketing choices, and organisations devoid of politics or local context. Yet these factors are crucial in analysing a management approach which will work. People will seek evidence of real changes against the claims that are made for implementing them.

In the next few pages I will point out the actual political and managerial changes that need to precede any public communications about quality of service. Publicity cannot convince people that they are receiving a different or better quality service, when their experience tells them they are not. If there is a gap it should become clear, and that in itself often creates the pressure from public and politicians which managers need to put things right. Without that outside link, internal policies and practice cannot be counted upon to respond to public needs and preferences. Without the internal procedures and systems, public relations can only affect the attitudes of people who have no real experience on which to build. Sooner, rather than later, they talk to someone who has and the public relations strategy is over.

Consumers and quality

Consumer research

The public service has a unique opportunity, really a duty, to become acquainted with its residents and service users. Service managers do know, by and large, where users live, where their children go to school, the parks, leisure and other amenities nearby. With a relatively modest investment, managers can find out more about the needs, expectations and views of residents to provide the basis on which services for the present and future can be shaped.

A range of population-based official statistics exist which, though depleted over the last decade, continue to be published on a local or regional basis: the Census, unemployment, local earnings surveys, public health and disability, social and economic trends. The local authority produces a vast range of data which it collects for statutory returns: CIPFA, one-off Audit Commission surveys, Department of Health returns for social services, Department of Environment returns for housing, manpower (sic) watch, budgets and other financial information, Department of Social Security for housing and Poll Tax benefits. In most authorities these are processed routinely or not at all. Though rarely in a form useful for management purposes, they can be pooled and, with relatively modest investment, made useful (see chapter 6).

Internal management information often tends to focus to a considerable degree on controlling inputs — financial, personnel and plant. Sometimes this extends to outputs — number of places, beds, units, swims, etc. Those concerned for efficiency calculate ratios of inputs to outputs and monitor variations in unit costs and productivity. Less is usually known about the extent to which the service is used, and by whom, but this can be achieved for many services. If this information can be tied to targets drawn from local policy objectives and circumstances, the manager is in a good position to know about the services he/she is managing.

To assess the quality of a service we need to find out what residents and users think about it. This can be achieved by a range of methods, from the expensive household survey with a large sample, involving a mix of socioeconomic facts and attitudes from households and individuals, to a quick exit poll for the first hundred people leaving a local service outlet. Some authorities have used consumer mapping techniques. Surveys can be replicated regularly to test whether attitudes or opinions have changed over time or in response to particular publicity campaigns, service improvements or policy changes.

For example, Islington conducts exit polls of residents leaving the neighbourhood office. These provide a snapshot description of who is using the office and their views of the service they received. The practice should be built into the management process, rather than standing back in more traditional research approaches. The neighbourhood forum of local residents discuss the poll results, and agree with the neighbourhood management what action is needed to make improvements. Crawley Council's Recreation Department asks that people fill in a 'View Point' card whenever they use Crawley's leisure centres, theatre, golf course or catering facilities. People can ask for personal replies, if they wish. Information from the cards is reported to members and used to improve services.

This information is not intended to replace political decisions made by elected members. The role for public service managers which I am advocating, needs to provide both politicians and themselves with population-based information on which strategy for the whole population can be drawn. Surveys and polling information, as well as internal management information and official statistics, are important additions to the information which members obtain from their surgeries, casework, ward and other community meetings.

Consumer care?

The idea of consumer care is being promoted to bring a consumer orientation to public services. Traditional ideas of bureaucratic administration tend to deal with people as objects to be processed which fit uniformly into rational procedures. In this model administrative world the public are treated as if they are a nuisance — people get in the way of well-ordered, efficiently-administered services, they can be an inconvenience to good working conditions for employees and management alike. Similarly, public bureaucracies often become preoccupied with their role in protecting the public, and in case they cause harm or offence, people are instructed in the rules of safety and society.

When organisations adapt to personal needs and preferences, procedures become means not ends. A simple way of changing the ends/means relationship in public bureaucracies is to establish a guiding principle — put the consumer first. This perspective, it is argued, will transform the whole way that services are organised and employees relate to the public.

Bureaucracies also have a tendency to seek order by removing themselves from the pressure of people and the messy demands which they make. This tendency is reinforced by a growing specialisation and division of labour among professional groups, which has the effect of distancing personal services from the public and relating to people in specialist components. The order and apparent control which such distancing creates comes at the cost of limiting the interaction between the organisation and its clientele. Opportunities to learn from, and respond to, the public are lost, and in fact the order and distance disables the organisation from dealing with and effectively achieving the changes it seeks.

To combat this tendency for the bureaucracy to withdraw into itself, we are encouraged to 'get close to the customer'. Look out for negative messages — how many signs in public facilities indicate things that the public are not allowed to do, rather than what they are entitled to do or have? 'Do not run'; 'No entry after dark'; 'Closed on Wednesdays'; 'No entry'; 'Children not permitted'; 'Trespassers will be prosecuted'. Is the language oriented to the public, or does it assume an insider perspective and impose it on the public? A common example is the way in which entitlements are communicated — 'priorities' implies that the institution's priorities are everyone's. 'Emergencies' relays the institution's understanding of an emergency. Are benefits posed in careful legal language to protect the institution from legal challenge rather than inform people about their rights? Do reception services seem to be staffed by people who are the lowest paid and least trained? And do they always seem to have many other tasks to carry out, of which helping the public is the lowest priority?

As organisations come to recognise the uncaring nature of some of their public contact, the part played by central and support services comes to the forefront. A pleasant service depends on the computer working, finance processing cash received and issuing payments accurately and on time, the publicity unit advising staff about a new programme before they read about it in the local press. Then the personnel dimension argues that staff have to be treated well if they are going to treat other people well. From this view stems much of the consumer care work which talks about valuing people and all the changes associated with human resource initiatives.

However, there are limits on the extent to which these ideas can be applied usefully to organisations, particularly real public service organisations. These have purposes beyond making people feel good and the firm profitable. The main message to take away from consumer care is that it is not essential for public services to make people feel bad. This counterfactual may in practice be a significant move forward.

Citizens and consumers

Simply adopting consumer care slogans conceived in private sector services will not work in local authorities. Residents relate to the council as citizens and consumers. This brings a number of important features to consumer care which managers need to recognise. Otherwise the credibility gap with the public will undermine the best intentions, as the reaction to British Rail's and the London Underground's passenger charters attest.

Firstly, the authority has responsibilities to the people in its area as a whole. Its powers are established in law and exercised through local policy-making and implementation. This means it cannot always respond to consumers. There will be differences between particular consumer's interests and those of the population as a whole. The job of the public service is to find the best way of reconciling those differences between user and representative views and interests.

This important distinction between private and public services means that consumers come to use local authority services in a variety of ways. Some are consumers, some are denied the opportunity to become consumers, and others become consumers whether they like it or not. For example, consumers using services like pools or leisure centres have a fair degree of choice. Although the services are often subsidised, no one has to use them, and if they are 'full' there are market alternatives for those who can afford them. Those who cannot may experience a lesser quality of life, but generally this is not seen to warrant public action.

However, many public services are in short supply. They are allocated to individuals and groups agreed as priorities in accordance with public policy. Applying policy in this way will mean that many residents are denied the right to consume. Here again, the contrast with commercial firms is marked, for the authority is rarely in a position, financially or legally, to increase its level of service to meet demand. Politics would be entirely different were this to be the case.

A third differentiation flows from the fact that not all consumers have a choice about being involved with public services. Some of the services which authorities provide aim to protect the public interest, such as regulatory health, environment, building and trading standards. Certain services exist to protect the interests of people considered in need of protection such as children, or people in emotional distress.

The many relationships which public services have with their citizens and consumers make consumer care different but no less important than in the private sector. The job of treating people fairly and courteously is more of a challenge when consumers are not just able to buy what they can afford and go elsewhere if they are not satisfied. Many of our consumers have nowhere else to go and increasingly have no intention of leaving until they have received what they want.

Many local authority services have growing experience of violence against staff which indicates people's frustration and anger. A consumer in one local office was so determined to have his problem dealt with that he superglued himself to the reception desk! If we are to avoid increasingly conflictual relationships with the public, we need to find ways of enabling people to exercise rights, without expecting always to get what they want. Even with increased consumer choice, a simple commercial model is not applicable to consumer care relationships in public services. Such services have a greater responsibility to ensure that their consumers feel satisfied with how they have been dealt with, even if they cannot always consume what they would like.

Consumer rights

An appropriate approach to consumer care in the public sector brings together for the individual both the public purpose and process. Citizens as consumers could bring a set of rights and expectations to their dealings with public services. Authorities such as Harlow are committed to the consumer's rights:

- *to information about services and enable informed choices*
- *to clear communication, in writing and verbally, in plain language, taking account of diverse language and communication needs*
- *to equal treatment, without discrimination on the grounds of race, gender, disability, or sexuality*
- *to complain and receive a swift response to put things right*

- *to be heard when decisions are taken which affect you and to be fully and quickly informed of the outcome*
- *to expect that the effort has been made to guarantee the environmental and personal safety of the goods and services received*
- *to make signing and interpretation services available*
- *to be dealt with honestly by politicians and service providers, even when that means explaining the limited extent to which help is available and what other options are open*
- *to ensure that all staff understand their role in serving the public, including support services.*

Other authorities have focused on particular consumers and the rights which they can expect from particular services. For example, Worcester City Council's Tenant's Charter spells out 10 key rights for tenants, which include rights such as: to quiet enjoyment, to succession, to consultation, to repair, and to buy. Southwark Council's charter of rights for the elderly guarantees all residents of its residential homes 15 basic rights, such as to personal privacy, to looking after your own medication, to access to elected councillors and MPs, to participation in decisions about daily living arrangements within the home.

Complaints

The Ombudsman, the Commissioner for Local Administration in England, is charged with responsibility for independently investigating individual complaints alleging maladministration. Although this central service has received increasing numbers of complaints over the last three years (increasing by 44, 24 and 28 per cent respectively), the 9,169 cases received in 1990/91 must nevertheless be considered as a relatively low number (Commission for Local Government Administration, 1991). The majority of Ombudsman complaints are in housing (44 per cent) and planning (28 per cent).

Where authorities wish to learn from, and respond to, complaints rather than rely solely on people using the Ombudsman, they are establishing complaints policies and staff. This experience suggests that the success of a complaints service will depend on:

- *publicising the complaints policy, who to contact, and what to expect*
- *the public's perception of its relative independence*
- *delivering responses within specified time limits*

- *explaining what went wrong*
- *providing appropriate forms of redress.*

The National Consumer Council (1991) has circulated guidance for housing services on how to run a good complaints and appeals service. A survey which they conducted showed that only a handful of complaints had been dealt with to tenants' satisfaction.

Independence and putting things right

The public's confidence in the independence of an authority's complaints service can be encouraged both structurally and in practice. In terms of structure, it is possible to appoint an agency or individual outside the authority's line management arrangements to investigate complaints. The local Consumer Council, advice agencies, solicitors or newspaper might be appointed to carry out this function. Making the service operate in this way strengthens its perceived independence.

On the other hand, independent agents are not in an easy position to ensure that the bureaucracy reveals its secrets to their investigation. Partial information and delay are common bureaucratic obstacles. Similarly, if an independent investigation finds fault and recommends restitution, external agencies rely on the line management to carry out its recommendations. The national Ombudsman has experienced both these problems — authorities delaying and failing to carry out recommendations arising from investigations.

Alternatively, a complaints service will be located within the local authority, with an option for cases on application or appeal to be heard by members. This option should overcome problems with delays and executing action arising from investigations, but the public may be more likely to doubt the impartiality and thoroughness with which their complaints have been investigated. There may be a temptation among managers to suppress complaints, in order to make their service appear to have good performance particularly in the current competitive environment. They should be aware, however, that a really dissatisfied consumer is more powerful than a good public relations image.

Structures in themselves do not settle the question of public confidence nor effectiveness. These will be settled in practice, as people gain and relay their experience of the service. If they feel that the service approaches complainants on an adversarial basis, they may be more inclined to make use of formal judicial procedures. If the matter becomes narrowed to a fine point of technical maladministration, then the Ombudsman will seem a more suitable option. A complaints service should aim to provide more than that — a genuine interest in finding out what happened, explaining it clearly, apologising where called for, and making good wherever possible.

A good complaints policy

A complaints policy presents the council from the public's viewpoint, bringing together for the individual the local as well as the statutory complaints policies which have been introduced in education, community care, the Children Act, and environmental protection. This is not easy, for the grand departments of state do not think of pupils, parents, clients and litter haters as the same people. Publicity and procedures need to reconcile these different rights and entitlements into a simple, easy-to-use service.

The policy will generally guarantee time limits for acknowledging and responding to complaints, and give access to a last resort service located outside of the council or in the Chief Executive's office. The policy should be publicised in every council location through a leaflet and tear-off slip, with a named person who is responsible. Interpretation, signing and audio/tape facilities should be available. More than a set of procedures, no matter how rigorous, the policy encourages staff to take a positive attitude to receiving the views of residents and users of services, including any complaints they might have.

Once a service has been operational for a while, monitoring reports should be produced which describe the complaints received by the authority, by service point and outcome. Complaints have a role in identifying areas where performance is below par or where policy needs to be reviewed for change. The advantage of a central complaints service is the ability to address interdepartmental problems that contribute to poor service and lead to complaints. A common problem which is the subject of many complaints is the delay to housing benefit which wrongly results in the issue of eviction notices. In many authorities this individual problem can involve three or more departments — finance, legal, housing and/or benefits. It is wasteful for the authority and causes unnecessary worry for tenants. In such a case, a central complaints service makes sense for management, public, and consumer.

Consumer contracts

Residents need to know exactly what they can expect from a particular service and what they can do if something goes wrong. General statements of good intent do not work. It is best to focus on a particular service, and be specific about its purpose, standards and forms of redress. For the authority to provide a service, as publicised, residents and users may have to do their part: following safety rules for swimming pools; using the refuse bins issued; or disposing of needles or pharmaceuticals safely. The idea of a contract implies an agreement — a two way partnership that involves both rights and responsibilities for the local authority and the public.

In local authorities such as York, Lewisham, Merton, Harlow, North Tyneside, Oxford and Islington, contracts have been implemented in such services as refuse collection, swimming pools, environmental services, meals-on-wheels, home school contracts, community care, housing repairs, and planning applications. In each service the process of preparing and implementing contracts has common stages and elements. The outcome is always different.

Process of implementing contracts

The more people are directly involved in the process of implementing and assessing local service contracts, the more effective they will be in practice. This is an important distinction between much of the work on service contracts being done by local authorities and that attempted in the Government's Citizen's Charter. Unless there is close contact from conception through to implementation and review, a contract will not be sufficiently powerful to overcome the yawning gap in credibility between users and public services. A contract only works when both parties enter into it, if not freely, at least actively and with some expectation that it has a chance of really happening.

The first step is selecting a service. The main concern is that the service is working well. It has to be capable of meeting the standards set out in the contract, or providing the redress promised, otherwise the contract as a currency will become discredited and worthless. Secondly, the capacity to deliver determines a range of detailed practical considerations related to capacity to deliver such as whether or not to use pilots, how extensive a range of services to encompass, how gradually to extend contracts across appropriate services. Where the capability of the service warrants it, some authorities allow residents to select the service which is their priority, through polls and surveys. This approach offers another advantage: residents involved in selecting the service to be subject to contract, can form a reference group for other stages of the process where outside involvement is crucial, such as setting standards and monitoring results.

The contract is a process not just a publicity product. The written contract only represents the end result of a process by which the authority agrees with its residents and users what the service will be and how it will be delivered. There are six basic steps:

- *consulting residents and users*
- *consulting employees*

- *setting the contract with standards, access for complainants, and rights to redress*
- *managing the change in quality*
- *communicating the contract*
- *evaluating and publicising the result.*

Consulting residents and service users

Standards are more likely to matter to the people who use services if they are directly involved in determining them. Too often standards are considered as a management or professional purview, confined to the rarefield techniques of the British Standards Institute or a professional certifying body. Taking consumers seriously means rejecting the idea that there is one universally correct way of providing a service, and one universally accepted view of what constitutes a good quality service. Users' views on service standards are based on their experience and aspirations. This is not an unfortunate inadequacy of consumer thinking, this is, in fact, their indispensable value. Finding the means of managing the frontiers between public services and the public is a primary management task in this sector. Meaningful public consultation is one of these means.

Residents can be consulted in a variety of ways. The role of consumer research and polling was discussed earlier. Existing groups, such as tenants' associations, neighbourhood committees, community organisations, amenity associations, market stallholders, black and minority ethnic organisations, women's groups, merchants' associations — can all be useful. Each can generate views from their particular and considerable experience of how a service is working. Of course, such groups are not themselves representative of the community as a whole, or even of the particular section of the community whose interests they claim to express. Nevertheless, they can provide a useful view which is no less valid for its partiality.

Managers may need to make additional effort to consult users whose needs may not be currently met from existing services. It may be useful to organise an ad hoc group where none exists, for example a special discussion among residents in social care homes, or gym or pool users.

Serious consultation is focused on practical options, rather than open-ended questions about preferences or satisfaction. The operational principle is how these views can improve the service. Where small numbers of consumers are involved, such as child protection or residential care, the consultation can develop precise agreement about what the ground rules for the service will be.

Consulting the workforce

The workforce has a wealth of knowledge about how the service is operating at the front line and how it could be improved. The way in which they are involved will differ depending on authorities' industrial relations culture. Managers need to talk to staff — communicating the authority's policy about quality of service, the purpose of the local service contract, and what is expected from staff to make the contract work. Front-line staff may themselves be involved in consulting users, though residents may sometimes feel freer to voice their opinions where they are not faced with those directly providing services to them. As with service users, the basis of consultation needs to be clear. If the purpose is to achieve change in the short term, this needs to be clear and suggestions then need to be implementable practically and within the authority's agreed policies and resources.

Quality circles may be a useful device, provided that middle management is able to lead discussion with front-line staff and follow through with changes which demonstrate a result. Service sampling by senior management and central support staff may be effective in helping them get in touch with what services are like. These activities can identify the detailed organisational problems which can block the delivery of quality services. It can also identify training needs, opportunities for increasing intrinsic job satisfaction and employee development.

Managers will want to keep trade unions informed of proposals on service contracts. If implementing the contract requires changes in working practices or conditions, these will need to be negotiated through locally-agreed procedures. Local service contracts, like other quality initiatives, may bring into focus the effectiveness of these agreements in bringing about change and resolving conflict within a timeframe that is consistent with publicly responsive services.

Setting the service contract

The contract includes three key elements:

- *Standards:* specify what residents have a right to expect from the service. The standards will be different for each service and will be informed by local preferences and priorities determined through consultation. Some authorities have included a 'help us to help you' section in their publicity, which sets out residents' role in making the service work and the community safer or cleaner. This message encourages people to recognise the social side of public services, emphasising the common interests that individual users share.

- *Enquiries or complaints:* where to contact for more information or help if the service is not provided as promised. Often this is publicised as a 'hot line' which, as the name implies, requires a prompt response to complaints and enquiries. The type of service covered by the contract will determine the hours during which the line should be open, and this needs to be written on the contract as well. The Directors' name and number can be included if that gives residents confidence in a second route if they are not happy with the hot line response.
- *Right to redress:* the purpose is to give people a feeling that there is something that they can do when the service fails to live up to their expectations. Some people already make use of the legal system quite extensively in the battle of the individual citizen against the state. They are a small minority. Most people need other, more accessible, means.

Redress can take a variety of forms, depending on the service which is being covered by the contract. The first step which is popular with residents is the authority listening to their complaint, responding quickly and, where warranted, offering an apology. In many cases, particularly universal services, there is no alternative to a local government service. What people want is for the service to work — refuse collected, the pavement swept, the streets lit. The contract promises to put things right within a time limit, using the hot line and a rapid response system.

Where services like swimming pools are closed when they should be open, or fall below health and safety standards, users can be offered a voucher for a free swim at another pool. Where housing repairs are not carried out within the time limits or to an agreed standard, people can be offered the right to use alternative builders, vetted and recommended by the council. Financial compensation is a recourse which is being guaranteed in authorities such as Lewisham. This idea is similar to the award by the Ombudsman for cases of maladministration. When cash compensation is being offered, the contract should make clear how claims will be vetted and systems established for verifying claims.

Managing the changes in quality

Once residents have been consulted and the contract agreed, management must ensure that the service can be delivered consistently to the standards specified and guaranteed. That means organising every aspect of the service, putting the right management and information systems in place, training staff in the skills, communicating the right public service values, making sure that everyone involved knows what they have to do and feels confident in doing it. With service contracts, specifications are being communicated in plain language directly to the public. In these circumstances it is not enough to get the paperwork right. The service has to be working right, in practice every day, for every service user.

You may find that the service is not what it should be. Policies and procedures agreed at management meetings are not always widely communicated and do not always result in changes in practice on the ground. Even where detailed specifications have been set out and agreed through competitive tenders and contracts, there can be significant variations in how things operate in reality. In some public services, a culture has become accepted that allows for two management worlds: one that exists 'in theory' — in policy and procedural advice and in response to member enquiries; and another that exists 'in practice', where services delivered depend on whether staff are sick or on leave, cash limits tightened, staff vacancies frozen, or whether the transport fleet is fully mobile. The challenge in contracts is that the service has to be working as guaranteed, not sometimes or when possible, but always.

Publicising the contract

People must know their rights if they are to exercise them. This requires an ongoing and imaginative publicity strategy. The basic contract is often communicated through a leaflet, with posters, press stories and other council publicity making reference to it as often as appropriate. The use of coherent design and a publicity image can be useful in getting the message across.

As with the service itself, publicity needs to be sensitive to its diverse audience. Many residents' first language will not be English; some cannot read English or any written language; some will have visual or hearing impairments; some will not have permanent homes to receive leaflets or local papers: all their needs should be catered for. Budgets are not limitless, so managers need to find out a great deal about the most effective means of communicating information about contracts. Information must be made known and accessible across the authority as well as to information and reception staff in contact with the public.

Like everything to do with quality and service contracts, the publicity has to be right — accurate information, communicated clearly, distributed to the right people at the right time.

Evaluating and publishing the results

Strengthening the accountability and, in turn, the quality of the service, is done through building public evaluation and feedback into the contract. The basis upon which the results of the contract are to be assessed has to be decided. Results might extend beyond the performance of the service and the views of users, to how well the contract itself operated.

The hot line and complaints service require systems for recording feedback from the public and elected members. Staff have ideas and information to be taken into account. More formal evaluations are sometimes done, with managers from another service bringing together different members, users and staff perspectives.

Publishing statistical results is another option. This will be considered more widely later, but in general it is important to give the whole picture, not only the picture that could be statistically represented, not only the numbers, but what lies behind them.

The process of agreeing and implementing consumer contracts, then, provides a focus on one service for every aspect of improving quality. Its main advantage is the active role it offers residents and consumers, and its specificity. On the other hand, it is important to be realistic about the number and range of consumer contracts any resident would want. The principle must be 'user sensible', for example, with community care services older people may rely on many services. The contract should encompass simply the whole package.

Measuring quality — a national league table?

Although we know when we experience quality, it is far more difficult to speak of measuring quality. Yet the 1992 Local Government Act gives the Audit Commission the power to identify performance indicators for all local government services and to publish them in a national league table. Precisely how this will work is not clear, but the Audit Commission states that their approach will ensure uniformity, standards, comparisons across the country, and objectivity in their measurement (Audit Commission undated paper). Each service will be measured in terms of amount provided, level of use, quality, value for money, and cost.

Local authorities are concerned that a national league table will be another in a series of centralising devices which undermine the credibility and accountability of local services. As you will have noticed, central/local relations have not been coloured by a rosy glow of trust and collaboration in recent years. In these circumstances the Audit Commission's ability to remain independent of government influence may be subject to question, as that of the BBC and other institutions. The highly politicised environment around local authority spending and services such as education, housing and even litter, make the Audit Commission's new role unenviable.

In order to protect itself, as well as local government, from any undue pressure, the Audit Commission could clarify the basis on which it would exercise its power to publish selectively national performance information. One safeguard would be to make an *explicit agreement* with local authorities, and the public. An agreement could cover issues such as:

- *a public right to access background data and its sources, methodological and technical notes and working papers* used in preparing any publication;
- *a right to know the basis upon which the treatment, analysis, and publication of information*, would be, and has been, undertaken;
- *a simultaneous right to reply* by a local authority concerned, and *allocation of equivalent resources for that reply to be published and communicated* as those deployed by the Audit Commission.

National standards

National standards are a key issue in the concern for national performance measurement. It is not logically possible to specify *how* standards should be measured without someone, determining *what* these standards should be. The standards would have to be uniform in order to allow comparison across authorities, across the county. No such standards have been agreed. It is not the role of the Audit Commission to set standards, but a national league table will leave someone with the job. To do it effectively requires political and public legitimacy. Without this there is a risk that the numerical average may become a national standard, without any debate about its adequacy to fulfil the function of a standard agreed though legitimate processes.

Although there is certainly support for local performance measures, democratically agreed and published locally, little support exists for centrally-determined performance measures publicised nationally (AMA, 1992). CIPFA statistics and the Audit Commission profiles (drawn from CIPFA data) are problematic sources on which to build a single measure of local government performance. The statistics count what can be counted rather than what may really count for people. They tell you how many swims have been paid for, or library books borrowed during the last year. But they do not tell you what portion of which local residents are using these services, how often or whether this profile lines up with local priorities for targeting.

The limitations of CIPFA data in terms of validity and reliability are also well documented. As the data are largely unused for practical management purposes, returns tend to be poor in some parts of the country, and family, regional or national analysis is then based on a handful of authorities claiming to be representative. Categories of data collection are not consistent or reliable, particularly in relation to 'administration' and central services. As local authorities increasingly try out new ways of organising local services, the pre-fixed categories of national data do not encompass the local reality. These are some of the reasons why the data do not provide a legitimate basis for comparative analysis, even in their own terms.

Comparative quantitative statistics cannot adequately address quality of service, if the user's view point is taken seriously. I have pointed out the relationship between equal opportunity and services which are shaped to respond to the diversity of local authority users and their needs and preferences. CIPFA statistics do not always reflect the public's point of view, as a recent paper by Brian Gosschalk so aptly demonstrates (Gosschalk, 1992). The Quality Exchange contains no significant departure from traditional quantitative analysis. Many of its indicators, by their nature, emphasise an old-fashioned drive to maximise throughput of standard service units. But the real potential for quality services which we have been considering, lies in a move away from the mass production of cheap standard goods.

Nor is it clear what the approach will be for determining centrally 'how effectively each service meets the needs of its consumers' (Audit Commission, op cit, p. 2) across all social groups in all localities across the nation. This requires analysis based on a relationship between policy objectives, service standards, and consumers. It can only be done for local government services locally — where policy and service standards are democratically determined and consumers have a real local experience of these services and policies in practice. People living in local authorities up and down the country will not be able to see their experience of local services reflected in the large national numbers. People want to know about their services, which they know and use, and how they can be improved. One uniform service could prove to have a discriminatory effect.

Another fear is that the league table might be used to form an alternative basis for the allocation of the Revenue Support Grant. Though this would be a major departure, it would be consistent with the competitive principles upon which programmes such as the Housing Improvement Programme and the City Challenge (for inner city funding) are now based. A national table of service indicators based on uniform service headings will create increasing pressure for authorities to align the structure of their decision-making and service delivery with the national structure contained in the league table. This is not conducive to improving local government performance, and certainly undermines local democracy, innovation, and responsiveness.

Indicators should measure performance against objectives. This is fundamental and it is not at all clear this will be done nationally for services. But within local authorities, this is crucial. It provides a way for the organisation to learn how far individual services in particular locations are achieving objectives set, and how this achievement compares over time. Indicators should also ensure that what is measured to indicate performance is what the consumer feels should count.

If government wishes to have some form of national comparator then it might make sense to devise ways of measuring:

- *the extent to which services are delivered in line with locally agreed policies and identified needs, and the extent to which this can be demonstrated*
- *how performance is judged by consumers, and the extent to which this can be demonstrated.*

Instead the Audit Commission is proposing to establish one perspective of what constitutes performance measurement. Quantitative measures need not, in themselves, have an inhibiting effect on quality, but this could well be the result.

A different kind of audit: for quality

If audit is to assist in improving service quality, in terms which citizens and consumers understand, then a radical new approach is required. The audit method should contain a capacity to both investigate and act, rather than rely solely on the traditional 'objective investigation'. It needs to make explicit whose *problem* the audit is organised to address, rather than assume a single perspective and purpose. The effectiveness of the audit should be assessed in terms of how *useful* it would be in contributing to desired change, rather than the absolute correctness of its conclusions. It needs to make explicit *whose* evaluation of that usefulness counts, rather than assuming the auditor is always right. Otherwise the audit makes a mockery of a consumer-orientation.

An audit of the kind I am describing recognises that there will be different views of service performance, depending on your position in and outside the authority. None of these views are wrong, but all are partial. To obtain a fuller picture means looking at the problem from a range of perspectives. An important part of public management is attempting to develop as wide a consensus as possible about the aims and effectiveness of public services. Residents and service users as well as elected representatives, provide an important reference point in that process. In the current balance of relationships between members, managers, providers and service users, the consumer perspective is a priority.

The Quality Audits being undertaken in authorities such as York, Leicester and Islington contain some of these characteristics. This approach tends to involve a series of professionals and sectors, rather than relying on public or private sector accountants alone. In addition to the traditional concerns of financial and establishment control, unit costs and productivity, a quality audit obtains the views of service users and residents. For example, when we audited the careers service in Islington, the audit team included educationalists, management services, a research, policy adviser and accountant; and the views of secondary school pupils and outside agencies such as the Training and Enterprise Council were analysed. In addition to codes of professional practice, the local context and local policy framework form an explicit point of reference. Performance is assessed in terms of explicit quality standards, which have been negotiated with public involvement. Issues of equality are as important as probity, as this form of audit seeks to ensure that services are not directly or indirectly discriminatory.

This kind of audit process makes a positive contribution to improving users' experience of the quality of the service. It overcomes many of the criticisms made of more traditional processes familiar in the public sector. It combines standing back with a capacity to intervene. And it constructs a dialogue between audit teams, users and managers/providers.

A specialist quality unit?

This is a question that local authorities tend to ask whenever they are faced with a new project or idea. As with most questions of structure, there is no one correct answer for all localities at all times. The main requirement is for managers and members to consider the options, and to be clear about the objective being sought for one strategy rather than another. It can then be monitored and evaluated, and there may come a time when it is appropriate to change the structure to deal more effectively with another stage of the change.

There are a number of arguments in favour of a new specialist quality unit. First, it is a new initiative and the authority may wish to signal to the bureaucracy, in the way it knows best, that something new is happening. Second, it concentrates new knowledge and experience in one unit which can then disperse it across the authority. Third, it dedicates resources to one purpose, ensuring that quality is somebody's priority (whilst everyone's concern).

On the other hand, there are arguments against a specialist unit: the initiative may be new but it is being implemented in the same old local government way of 'adding on bits'; it isolates knowledge and experience in one unit which can then become involved with itself, while the rest of the authority ignores it; it makes quality the preserve of the 'unit' and no one else has anything to do with it.

A third option, a 'middle way' between setting up a new unit or totally integrating quality everywhere, is to transform the sections that have traditionally had a quality-related remit, and harness resources to work together to find new ways of working. A number of different functions could be integrated: Internal Audit has a value for money function; Management Service's organisational review function; the Policy Unit's policy or performance review function; the Research Unit's 'finding out' function which is increasingly directed to perform-ance evaluation and consumer research; the training and staff develop-ment function; registration and inspection work with a statutory remit for standards of service; and trading standards work in consumer advice and standards enforcement.

In some authorities, where members are in a hurry or the quality culture is starting from a tiny toe-hold in the bureaucracy, a small new unit may be good value. If the political or bureaucratic obstacles can be won over, the 'third way' offers potential for changing exist-ing quality and inspection resources to a new way of working. Where there is broad-based support among top management and workforce, and the detailed quality systems are in place to manage and monitor quality, then it is probably most effective to embed quality manage-ment into mainstream planning, budgeting, and monitoring practice.

Whatever the internal organisational arrangements, they will not be successful in turning around public services working in isolation, any more than management can. Their effectiveness will be enhanced by forging links with outside organisations. Groups such as those provid-ing independent information and advice, legal aid, and advocacy often know a great deal about where residents experience problems with local authority services. Similarly, people turn to the local press and media with their stories about 'the Council'. Other public agencies are sometimes more reluctant to communicate frankly about shortcomings in service, but this traditional professional courtesy may be changed. The role of elected members in representing their constituents is a much underused force for quality, which could be drawn upon (see chapter eight).

Conclusion: quality now and forever?

There is more than the normal level of cynicism among public service managers and staff about 'quality'. Anything which receives the public relations focus which the Citizen's Charter has may inevitably produce this sentiment, given the contempt in which the public sector has been held over the past decade. Wry commentaries can already be heard about the meagre contingency guarantees being offered by the public services so many love to hate. What chance do British Rail's Passenger Charter, or Guy's Hospital Trust's Patient's Charter have in eliciting public credibility as deficits soar, services are cut, and staffing is reduced. The gap in legitimacy and credibility is too wide in many areas to be bridged by one press release supported by a full colour glossy.

For the reasons to do with local democracy — its slowness as well as its capacity to involve people, I argue that quality of service in local government has some potential even where national initiatives falter. The real question is whether the reality of the public service will live long enough to catch up with the hype surrounding the Citizen's Charter. The next few years will witness how quickly the peculiarly English experiment of compulsory competition and privatisation matures to a more balanced approach, one where contracting is one of a range of management arrangements rather than an orthodoxy. If the extremism of privatisation does not stifle the growth of a modern public service in Britain, there may be an opportunity to develop further the potential of a renewed public interest and accountability. Local government can play an important part in such a future.

References

AMA (1992) *Leagues Apart?*, Proceedings of a seminar on Performance Indicators, February, 1992, Association of Metropolitan Authorities, London.

Audit Commission (undated) *The Citizen's Charter – Local Authority Performance Indicators*, Audit Commission, London.

Commission for Local Government Administration (1991) *Local Ombudsman, Annual Report 1990/91*, HMSO, London.

Coote, A. (ed.) (1992) *The Welfare of Citizens*, Institute for Public Policy Research/Oram Rivers Press, London.

Gosschalk, B. (1992) 'The role of survey research' in AMA *Leagues Apart?*, Proceedings of a Seminar on Performance Indicators, February 1992, Association of Metropolitan Authorities, London.

HMSO (1991) *The Citizen's Charter – Raising the Standard*, Cm 1599, HMSO, London.

Labour Party (1989) *Quality Street*, The Labour Party, London.

Labour Party (1990) *Learning from Mistakes*, The Labour Party Local Government Section, London.

Labour Party (1991a) *Guaranteed Delivery: Customer Contracts in Practice*, The Labour Party, London.

Labour Party (1991b) *Best Practice News*, The Labour Party, London.

Labour Party (1992) *Consulting with users of service*, The Labour Party, London.

Local Government Information Unit (1991) *Going for Quality: Results of a Survey of Quality in Local Services*, LGIU, London.

National Consumer Council (1991) *Consumer concerns 1991*, HMSO, London.

Pfeffer, N. and Coote, A. (1991) *Is Quality Good for You?*, Social Policy Paper No. 5, Institute for Public Policy Research, London.

Index